LIVING OVER THE STORE

Urban buildings that combine commercial and residential uses have been found throughout history in cities all over the world. These are the shophouses of China and Japan, corner stores with apartments above in American small towns, merchants' houses in northern Europe, apartment buildings with shops at their ground floors in cities in Europe and America, English terraced houses where the front room has been converted or extended into a shop. Although these buildings make up much of the built fabric of cities, no comprehensive book on them has been written, until now.

Providing a historical and cross-cultural account of these buildings, the book describes how twentieth-century cities developed to exclude such buildings, and offers a series of contemporary initiatives that are intended to bring back this archetype of the mixed-use building. An important feature of this kind of building is its flexibility to different family circumstances and economic change. The book describes how this adaptability is useful to people who are part of the "new economy" of self-employed "knowledge-worker" entrepreneurs as well as to people who are at the lower end of the economic ladder, who find economic benefit in being able to combine business and family life.

Architectural history and analysis, economic understandings of the city, and contemporary architectural and urban practice are combined here to provide a comprehensive look at the architecture, function and meaning of one of the most common buildings of historic and contemporary cities. It will be of interest to practicing architects and planners, architectural scholars, and students and others with particular interests in urban vernacular architecture, sustainable urbanism, and how our buildings and cities can best support the everyday lives of the people who inhabit them.

Howard Davis is Professor of Architecture at the University of Oregon. His work is concerned with the social and cultural frameworks of architecture, the process of building, and the relationships between building typology, urban morphology and grassroots economic development. His book *The Culture of Building* was named Best Publication in Architecture and Urban Studies by the Association of American Publishers in 2000.

LIVING OVER THE STORE

Architecture and Local Urban Life

Howard Davis

LONDON AND NEW YORK

First published 2012
by Routledge
2 Park Square, Milton Park, Abingdon, Oxon OX14 4RN

Simultaneously published in the USA and Canada
by Routledge
711 Third Avenue, New York, NY 10017

Routledge is an imprint of the Taylor & Francis Group, an informa business

British Library Cataloguing in Publication Data
A catalogue record for this book is available from the British Library

Library of Congress Cataloging in Publication Data
Davis, Howard, 1948–
Living over the store: architecture and local urban life / Howard Davis.
p. cm.
Includes bibliographical references and index.
1. Shophouses. 2. City and town life. I. Title. II. Title: Architecture and local urban life.
NA4177.D38 2012
728'.314—dc22 2011016350

ISBN: 978-0-415-78316-3 (hbk)
ISBN: 978-0-415-78317-0 (pbk)
ISBN: 978-0-203-60959-0 (ebk)

Typeset in Corbel
by Florence Production Ltd, Stoodleigh, Devon

Printed and bound in Great Britain by the MPG Books Group

CONTENTS

PREFACE

This book has its origin on the streets of Manhattan where, during a walk in the summer of 2001, I realized that I was surrounded by buildings that had fascinated me for most of my life, but that I had never really stopped to think about. In New York, and in my travels, I was always attracted to the straightforward complexity of the historic "mixed-use" building, and saw in it the richness of the city and of urban life. This kind of building was not getting the attention and research it deserved but was passed over, in practice and scholarship, in favor of the building with a singular and less-mundane purpose.

Several things about these buildings always appealed to me. First was their spatial complexity, and the way different functions were deftly fitted into each other. Second was often a beautiful resolution of their façades. And there was often a four-squareness and ordinariness about the buildings, which appealed to that part of me that also liked subway cars and thinking about the people with brown shopping bags who rode in them, many of whom were going home to apartments located over stores.

But above all, perhaps, these buildings are purposeful. The story I have tried to write in this book is one that describes the shop/house as embedded in the social and economic life of the urban district, that recognizes its continuities across different cultures and historic periods, and that sees it not only as a historical curiosity but as a kind of building that has relevance for the future. As global urbanization continues, as there is an increasing need to (re-)discover sustainable forms of city life, and as the restructuring of economies continues, there is a growing need for urban and architectural forms that can flexibly accommodate innovation and enterprise at the grassroots.

So although this book includes historical descriptions of buildings in different cultures, and accounts of their transformation over time and geography, this is also a work of advocacy. One of my intentions is simply to understand a phenomenon that is one of the most ubiquitous in cities – that fact alone gives the study justification. But at the same time, as people continue to search for more connected ways of living in cities, the historical and cross-cultural evidence may provide one foundation for maintaining and reinterpreting these kinds of buildings.

* * *

Two years before she died, I was able to thank Jane Jacobs for her contributions to our urban future. The ideas in this book owe a lot to her work, and particularly to her common-sense way of observing the city – no less vital now than it was when she wrote *The Death and Life of Great American Cities*. Conversations with different people helped me develop these ideas. Matt Brown and I have talked extensively about the relationships between building types, urban morphology and local economic life, and are continuing this research. Tom

Hubka has been a passionate and knowledgeable guide to American working-class housing, and more generally to the importance of including the most humble buildings in our view. John Rowell, Greg Brokaw and the staff of their firm have helped me understand the issues in contemporary mixed-use projects. And my friend and mentor Christopher Alexander helped me see the shop/house as an economic/social phenomenon at least as much as an architectural one.

People in different places helped by providing knowledge about local buildings, and opening up opportunities to study them first hand. These included: in Ahmedabad, Azhar Tyabji; in Amsterdam, Paul Rosenberg; in Bangkok, Tom Kerr, Khanin Hutanuwatr, Kamonat Chaturaphat, Khun Prasert; in Guangzhou, Patrick Luk, Jessica He, Stanley Lo, Beisi Jia; in Kathmandu, Nick Seemann; in Kyoto, Yumi Aoki Nelson, Ron Lovinger, Daisuke Yoshimura, Ryoichi Kinoshita, Akira Mizobuchi; in Luang Prabang, Naoto Sekiguchi and Xayaphone Vongvilay; in Lübeck, Esther Hagenlocher, Michael Scheftel and Annegret Muhlencamp; in Paris, Jean Castex; in Seattle, Jerry Finrow; in Valparaiso, Paz Undurraga and Michi Bier; in Vancouver, Ron Kellett, Harold Kalke, Trish French, Tom Stanizskis; in York, Ann Petherick. Also thanks to Vin Buonanno, Erin Cunningham, Frances Holliss, and Jim Tice.

I am grateful to several organizations for providing forums to talk about the topic, and to hear and discuss related work: the Vernacular Architecture Forum, the International Seminar on Urban Form, the International Association for the Study of Traditional Environments, and the European Association for Urban History. David Lung invited me to Hong Kong to speak at a UNESCO-sponsored conference on Asian shophouses in 2007, and Matt Brown and I presented a paper at a conference in Cardiff on contemporary Chinese cities in 2007.

Several units of the University of Oregon provided funds and research leaves: the Office of Research and Sponsored Programs, the School of Architecture and Allied Arts, and the Department of Architecture. I am grateful to Dean Frances Bronet and Department Head Christine Theodoropoulos for their support. I had dedicated research and graphics help from University of Oregon students Lucas Gray, Wyatt Hammer, Allison Hirzel, Kaarin Knudson, Will Krzymowski, Sean Landry, Peter Makrauer, Steven Miller, Andrea Solk, Nick Venezia, Tuan Vu and Sam Yerke. Christine Sundt kindly advised me on copyright issues. Kaarin Knudson edited the manuscript with discernment and literary skill.

My friends and colleagues Don Corner and Jenny Young have helped this book not only through conversations about its content but also through their confidence and support over almost forty years. Recently, with Stephen Duff, we conducted fieldwork in Rome that helped sharpen some of the discussion in Chapter 2. I am grateful to my teaching colleagues Brook Muller and Peter Keyes with whose collaboration I was able to convey some of this material to students and put it in the contexts of broader understandings of how buildings fit in the world.

Hundreds of millions of people in the world live in the buildings described in this book. As these buildings are essential to the physical structure of the city, so their inhabitants are essential to urban social and economic life. This book is written in the hope and expectation that architecture, building and planning will increasingly recognize the importance to our common future of the daily life that is harbored by the ordinary urban building.

Eugene, Oregon
April 2011

INT.01 Liverpool, 1927.
Courtesy Liverpool Record Office, Liverpool Libraries, and with thanks to Esther Hagenlocher.

INTRODUCTION

A quintessential urban building

[Space] is at once a precondition and a result of social superstructures.[1]
(Henri Lefebvre)

[1] Lefebvre, *Production of Space*, 85.

This book is about one of the most common urban buildings: the shop/house, consisting of dwellings and work/retail space in one structure, usually with the workspace at the ground level and the dwellings above.

The building is found in cities, towns and villages, throughout history and across the world. It is the spatial manifestation in one structure of two common economic conditions of the city: it puts commerce on the street, and it lets people live where they work. The prevalence of the building across cultures comes as a result of the commonality of these fundamental economic and architectural relationships.

These buildings include *insulae* of ancient Rome; the small buildings on American main streets with stores below and apartments above; American houses to which a room has been added to serve as a store or workshop; New York apartment buildings with stores on their ground floors; London terraced houses with ground-floor shops or with shop extensions toward the street; shophouses in Japan, China and southeast Asia; seventeenth-century canal houses in Amsterdam; and many others including colonial versions of these forms. Many of these buildings have been the subject of individual investigations, or described in architectural studies of particular cities. This book looks at them together, as a cross-cultural phenomenon.

Collectively, these buildings are not definable as a singular architectural type – a building configuration clearly defined in function or geometry. But they do exhibit common ideas. They are located in places where densities allow for commercial activity. They put commercial activity on the ground level, prioritize it over domestic functions, and ensure the privacy of family life relative to the public realm. They support the diversity of urban neighborhoods. And they exhibit flexibility of use over time.

Shop/houses incorporate a variety of living situations. They include buildings in which the family that works in the shop also lives in the building, and other buildings in which the dwellings are independent of the shops.

The building in which the family that runs the shop lives upstairs, or in the back, is typical of Asian shophouses even today, and was once more typical of buildings in Western cities. It houses a way of life with little distinction between "work" and "family," often with strong, personal connections between the

INT.02 (above left) Luang Prabang, Laos.
Photograph by author.

INT.03 (above right) Vancouver, British Columbia.
Stephen Duff.

INT.04 Paris.
Photograph by author.

INT.05 (facing, top left) Valparaiso, Chile.
Photograph by author.

INT.06 (facing, bottom) Enkhuisen, Netherlands, painted by Cornelis Springer in the nineteenth century.
Rijksmuseum, Amsterdam.

INT.07 (facing, top right) The block of Hudson Street, New York City, where Jane Jacobs wrote *The Death and Life of Great American Cities*, first published in 1961.
Photographed in April 2009 by author.

PECO'S
CRISTAL

W 11 ST
TAVE

business and its customers. Such integration of social and economic life has largely disappeared from view in post-industrial Western cities – but may represent a critical ingredient in the emergence of a new, humane economics.

The building with commercial functions at its ground floor and separate families living upstairs is typical of many Western cities, such as New York and Paris, and is becoming more widespread in Asian cities as districts of family shophouses disappear. It brings together people of different professions, economic levels and ages. The adjacent street is a place of shopkeepers, of people who work for them, of people who live in the apartments above, and of people who are coming to do business in the shop. Even though the building houses families whose members work elsewhere, along with employees of shops who live elsewhere, the street may bring them all together. Upper Broadway in New York and the Boulevard St. Germain in Paris are examples of such streets.

But these two kinds of building are aspects of a single phenomenon, and the boundary between them is unclear. Hybrids, which have existed at least since ancient Rome, include both conditions: a shopkeeper's dwelling connected to the shop, and also independent apartments. New York has apartment houses in which shops and doctors' offices are directly connected to apartments. Bangkok and Hong Kong have shophouses that were subdivided to allow independent families to live above the dwelling/shop combination. These building types are not "pure." There is a continuum of relationships between the traditional, family shop/house and the building with independent apartments and shops. The continuum exists because people use their buildings in flexible ways – ranging from their own use of a shop, to the rental of a shop, to the rental of dwelling space – to maximize economic opportunity. This results in myriad architectural relationships between the dwelling and shop or workplace.

Because of this functional and cultural diversity, the phenomenon is not easily nameable, and I am not using a single architectural descriptor for it. In this book, I use several terms: *shop/house* (with a slash between the two words to distinguish it from the Asian shophouse[2]) to refer to the overall phenomenon; *shophouse* (without the slash) to refer to the smaller Asian building; *family shop/house* to refer to the small building in which the same family lives and works; *commercial/residential building* to refer to the building with independent shops and apartments; and occasionally *mixed-use building* or *live/work building*.[3] Yet, this varied terminology, encompassing buildings of different sizes, different economic situations and a wide variety of specific types, circles around a single set of ideas.

Such hybridity represents a departure from two main approaches to building types.

One approach is that of Nikolaus Pevsner in *A History of Building Types*, [4] which depends on a taxonomy based on function, in which the world of buildings is divided into houses, markets, town halls, factories, theaters, schools, and so forth. This emphasizes buildings that are "pure" in their function, since understanding the essentials of the type does not depend on understanding how other functions may also be included. Talbot Hamlin's *Forms and Functions of Twentieth-Century Architecture* [5] has a similar classification system. Indeed, both of these works are particularly consistent with modernist architectural ideals in the way they separate functionally defined buildings from each other.

2 Scholars of the Asian shophouse are very precise in using the term "shophouse" to refer to the party-wall building in Chinese commercial cities and east and southeast Asia in which families live and work. David Lung pointed this out to me and brought me in contact with these scholars at a conference in Hong Kong in 2007.

3 The phrase "live/work" is a common one and has been the subject of research and practice in both the U.S. and the U.K.

4 Pevsner, *History of Building Types*.

5 Hamlin, *Forms and Functions*.

The second approach, based originally on the work of eighteenth-century French theorists such as J.N.L. Durand and A.C. Quatremère de Quincy[6], is more formal, in which function plays a secondary role. It stresses the meaning of configuration itself, and looks to formal types: courtyards, pavilions, processions, allées, centralized plans, linear plans. These spatial types have human meaning, reinforced by architectural form. Certainly, this approach accepts the idea that actual buildings are often composed of combinations and transformations of formal types. But there is again a stress on the "pure" examples, and hybrids and transformations remain on the fringe.

Shop/houses have not been studied as a singular architectural idea because they deal with a phenomenon that is hard to categorize and easy to ignore. In most books about New York apartment houses, retail space may get a short mention, if mentioned at all. In works about commercial buildings, there may be only a mention of apartments, if they exist. Indeed, mixed-use buildings are so much a part of everyday urban experience that they are on the edge of our conscious experience. In a busy city we pass dozens of such buildings every day. We tend not to notice them, in favor of the unusual and the monumental. In this respect, they are like many vernacular buildings, doing their part to make up the world's 2 billion buildings, but relatively neglected in architectural history and theory. This is the unnoticed fabric of cities, the slowly changing ground against which cities grow.

Vernacular architecture scholarship has emphasized the specifics of individual cultural forms and the uniqueness of building types. Most scholarship has been place specific, in which locally based researchers have made extensive observations, and carried out documentary research of buildings in that place. Except for a few theorists such as Amos Rapoport and Christopher Alexander, the idea that there might be characteristics of buildings shared across different cultures has not been a significant part of discourse. Indeed, the idea of common forces that act on buildings, leading to similar results, is often looked at with skepticism. More general or universal ideas are usually present more by inference than by specific assertion, if they are present at all.

The shop/house is a kind of building in which universal and culturally specific attributes are both present, and in this book I emphasize the universals. The shop/house type in a particular place results from two kinds of influence: those that are culturally determined (for example, the façade of a shophouse in Kyoto), and those that arise from economic or social factors that tend to be shared across cultures (for example, giving over almost the entire frontage to a retail shopfront). The aim of this book is to explore the common features and to try to understand the common forces that helped to shape them, within the individual frameworks of particular cultures and places.

Contemporary cities

Shop/houses have not only escaped scholarship, but the theoretical emphasis on the pure form or singular function has shaped contemporary practice. Since the beginning of the twentieth century, zoning laws, building codes and lending policies have favored buildings with a single function, resulting in urban monocultures. Such policies have made it difficult for people to live their lives in an integrated way, if they should want to live and work in the same place – which many people want to do. Pre-modern understandings of "mixed-use buildings" were largely implicit, all to be forgotten as twentieth-century practice came to favor explicit knowledge and unambiguous classifications.[7]

[6] Durand, *Précis des Leçons*; Lavin, *Quatremère de Quincy*.
[7] Davis, *Culture of Building*, 201.

The architecture of everyday life does not depend on formal categories, but exists within them and even in spite of them, in modes of continuous transformation. According to Michel de Certeau, what actually happens in daily life has been more and more obscured by the intellectual and formal structures that have emerged in the last 300 years.[8]

In Western cities today, the two activities housed by this most ordinary building – dwelling and commerce, or dwelling and work – are almost mutually exclusive. Henri Lefebvre wrote about the suppression of "habiting," as an active and multifunctional process, by "habitat," as the container for "a handful of basic acts: eating, sleeping and reproducing." Repressed were:

> . . . the diversity of ways of living, urban types, patterns, cultural models, and values associated with the modalities and modulations of everyday life. Habitat was imposed from above as the application of a homogeneous global and quantitative space, a requirement that "lived experience" allow itself to be enclosed in boxes, cages, or "dwelling machines."[9]

The urban transformation that accelerated during the eighteenth and nineteenth centuries included the steady growth of the size of retail operations, the decline of the apprenticeship system and the development of clear distinctions between management and labor, along with the class-conscious desire of merchants and business people to live away from their businesses and the people they employed. This fundamental change in attitudes toward urban life was eventually manifested in the divided, fragmented city.

Social divisions abetted by particular features of urban form accompany the growing gap between rich and poor in the United States. Zoning and development practices have separated the residential areas of different economic classes from each other and have separated retail establishments of different market levels and types from each other. All this has been further exacerbated by low density and the prevalence of larger and fewer stores and workplaces, which increases distances even more.

Similar arguments appear in writings about contemporary cities in the developing world. There are some who see slums – and the informal economic activity that takes place in them – as objectionable in themselves. But others see slums and informal settlements as essential mechanisms for urban economic growth.[10] In an op-ed article about the 2008 Oscar-winning film *Slumdog Millionaire*, the characterization of Mumbai's slums as a place of human despair is protested:

> Dharavi's messy appearance is nothing but an expression of intense social and economic pressures at work. Most homes double as work spaces: when morning comes, mattresses are folded, and tens of thousands of units form a decentralized production network rivaling the most ruthless of Chinese sweatshops in efficiency. Mixed-use habitats have often shaped urban histories. Look at large parts of Tokyo. Its low-rise, high-density mixed-use cityscape and intricate street network have emerged through a similar Dharaviesque logic. The only difference is that people's involvement in local development in Tokyo was seen as legitimate.[11]

The distinction between cities in the "developed" and "developing" worlds is artificial: people in both have similar motivations with respect to their families and economic lives. Understanding places like Mumbai may help shed light on

[8] See Certeau, *The Practice of Everyday Life*, 69, and throughout.
[9] Lefebvre, *Urban Revolution*, 81. I am grateful to Christopher Alexander for directing me to this book.
[10] Correa, *Housing and Urbanization*, 130–131; Oliver, *Dwellings*, 216–221.
[11] Echanove and Srivastava, "Taking the Slum Out of 'Slumdog'."

questions of the structure and workings of mixed-use urban districts in Milwaukee or Miami as well.

The shop/house is therefore not only of historical interest, and this book is a work of advocacy as well as of history. People continue to recognize the value of living and working in the same place. Contemporary initiatives are seeking to reverse problems such as the predominance of the automobile, sprawl and high energy consumption, the separation of uses and social groups enforced by zoning regulations, and the disappearance of the street as a place for informal, face-to-face meeting. Other initiatives are recognizing the importance of the physical environment in promoting social and economic equity, and governments in developing countries are beginning to understand the crucial role of informal settlements to the economic health of the city. "New urbanism" projects employ time-tested features including buildings that incorporate dwellings and commercial space. In many cities, new shop/houses are being built. These are new versions of the old type, with the essentials that define the shop/house building, but incorporating parking, contemporary standards for light and air, and following modern building codes.

Diversity and connectivity

This book is partly an extension of Jane Jacobs' argument about the importance of urban diversity. Her observations for *The Death and Life of Great American Cities* were made in Greenwich Village in the late 1950s, a place that then had, and still has, a rich texture of urban life, including numerous buildings in which families lived over their own shops.[12] The book is also related to Christopher Alexander's ideas of a city in which the ordinary elements of daily life should be taken seriously in design and policy, presented most clearly in *A Pattern Language*.[13]

The analyses of Jane Jacobs and Christopher Alexander are sometimes described as nostalgic visions of a lost world. The integration of physical, social and economic attributes in the mid-twentieth-century American city is vividly described by Michael Johns, writing about St. Nick's parish in Chicago:

> The life of St. Nick's centered on Sixty-third Street, a retail strip that was especially dense and lively toward either end of the neighborhood. The street had a Walgreen's and a Kresge's, which were chain stores, but also a bank, a movie theater, a men's store, a shoe store, a candy store, a sporting-goods store, and a grocery store, all independently owned by local businessmen. Shoppers walked to these commercial clusters. Women wheeled shopping carts in the mornings, kids made late afternoon runs for fresh dinner bread, and couples and entire families took strolls on Monday and Thursday evenings, the weekday shopping nights.[14]

But is this a lost world? Although Jacobs' work was published a half-century ago, and Alexander's over thirty years ago, their ideas have held up remarkably well. They both saw fundamental structural/morphological ideas in the traditional city, and contemporary theory is saying similar things, sometimes clad in different intellectual clothing. There is a growing understanding that architectural and urban practice must be more explicit in recognizing the city as a complex and dynamic system, rather than as a disembodied entity that may be reduced to fragmented zones, functions and professional institutions.

12 Jacobs, *Death and Life*.
13 Alexander et al., *Pattern Language*.
14 Johns, *Moment of Grace*, 49.

15 Ellin, *Integral Urbanism*, 9–15.

The contemporary city is a place of change, contestation and experimentation, and the earth has now passed the point at which half the global population is urban. Cities are faced with the need to combat sprawl and adopt sustainable principles of transportation and land use; with the need for social equity; with the need to accommodate shifting cultural groups; with the need to reorder their structure of land use as industrial economies give way to post-industrial ones; with the need to maintain cultural memory even as they grow and self-transform.

In all of this the shop/house, in its many different guises, is a critical building. Indeed, far from being a mere artifact of the past, it is central to current initiatives intended to revitalize cities. By putting functions together in the same building and the same street, the shop/house helps to support diversity of neighborhood life. By putting dwelling and work into the same unit, the shop/house gives economic support to a family that wants to start a business with minimum resources – and this is as true for the "new economy" of web designers and one-person consultant firms as it is for a low-income family wanting to start a hair salon or repair business. By helping to support the small-business opportunities of low-income people, in turn, the shop/house may continue to provide recent immigrants with a means of entering the formal economy. By using land intensively, the shop/house supports increased urban density and the city's ability to maintain viable public transportation.

These issues are larger than those that are often discussed as "new urbanism," which has been criticized for too often being concerned with the caricature rather than the deep structure of active city life. That deep structure has to be concerned with rich and poor alike, with production as well as consumption, with the life inside buildings as much as what buildings look like from the outside. The shop/house cannot by itself cure all the ills of the city – but it is significant that a single kind of building, that has been relatively unstudied to date, can be implicated in a number of different approaches to questions of urban form.

In contemporary theory and work there is recognition of the importance of mixed use, of flexibility of use, of thick or ambiguous boundaries and of spatial connectivities. The biological idea of the ecotone – a place of overlap between two ecological systems – is analogous to function at a building's edge, where a business overlaps with potential customers, or activities on a neighborhood shopping street, where a residential block may overlap with the neighborhood or city as a whole. Nan Ellin writes about principles of hybridity, connectivity and porosity, critical to what she calls "integral urbanism."[15]

Much of this is consistent with Jacobs' and Alexander's ideas of functional overlaps and spatial proximities and mixtures. Some of these ideas, like spatial ambiguity including building/site connectivity, were present in modernist architecture, at the building scale. But functional ambiguities and overlaps were deliberately absent from modernist city planning. The reintroduction of these everyday ideas into architectural and urban thought will result both in the continued validation of Jacobs' and Alexander's work and in the development of new forms. While new forms may not be like those of the past, they will likely incorporate similar principles of spatial and functional organization.

Hybridity

The theme of hybridity is therefore central to this book, in four different ways.

There are, first, hybrid relationships between types, throughout history and across geography. This is not a new idea, but it is particularly important here, as the common economic forces that shape shop/houses act on them similarly in different places.

Second, the building and its urban context represent a single, hybrid unit – so much so that the words "building" and "context" lose their fixed meanings with respect to one another. The shop/house exists in a matrix of other shop/houses and in a particular urban condition or location, and functions only as part of the larger whole of its urban district.

Third, flexibility of different kinds is essential to the shop/house's success – and even for a building to be a shop/house in the first place. Buildings and rooms change their use over the course of a day or week, in a regular cycle; they change their use over the course of their lifetime as families change and grow; and they change their physical form as well.

And finally, there are different approaches to implementation in the contemporary building culture, ranging from developers to the grassroots, from large projects to small, from incentives to regulation. Some of the most effective approaches are hybrid approaches – allowing for zones in which there are multiple rather than single uses, seeing the value of both developers and grassroots entrepreneurs. Here again is the need to overcome and transcend traditional categories, this time in the realm of processes that build the city.

Within this attitude to buildings, fluidity and hybridity are normal. Instead of describing a "special" condition, they represent what people do and see to be reasonable, when they are unfettered by rigid institutional constraints. And it is of course human use – and the unpredictable contingencies of family life, economic activity and life in the city – that bring the idea of architectural hybridity down to earth and express its true purpose.

* * *

The everyday experience of cities is made up of a continuous sequence of moments, a rich and layered series of impressions, social interactions and economic exchanges. These moments include many different places, people and buildings. They include walks along busy streets and vacant lots, leafy all-residential neighborhoods and noisy markets, warehouse districts and cemeteries, districts dominated by students and others by wealthy families, news-stands and bus stops and sidewalk grates. They include houses and gardens, curbs and trees, factories and schools, symphony halls and funeral parlors, firehouses and synagogues, gas stations and bus terminals. They also include the monuments and public spaces – town halls, libraries, museums, transit terminals, playgrounds, great streets and squares – that together represent and facilitate the collective, public side of urban life.

None of these things is more important than the other. But among hundreds of elements of urban form, the shop/house is a significant contributor to urban life, one that strongly helps the city realize its social and economic imperatives. This building rejects the pure functional categories of modernism, which severed and fragmented the traditional city. It incorporates two of the most essential urban functions: dwelling and work. It promotes a diverse street and neighborhood life. Through the diversity of functions apparent on the façade, the building *expresses* all of these things, and by extension, the diversity that is the city itself. This kind of building cannot make up a city – the city requires hundreds of kinds of buildings and objects, working in coordination with each other. But there is something about the simple shop/house, in all its multiplicity and ambiguity, that comprises the layered depth of the city itself.

Part I

THE SHOP/HOUSE AS A GLOBAL PHENOMENON

Part I: THE SHOP/HOUSE AS A GLOBAL PHENOMENON

The shop/house is probably as old as commerce and cities themselves. Because the basic economic conditions of living and working in the same place are so fundamental, it is likely that commercial/residential buildings did not have a common origin, but instead arose independently in different places – and historic evidence confirms the early existence of the shop/house in numerous cultures.

At the same time, shop/house types – like most vernacular buildings – are partly the result of cultural migrations, and represent an amalgam of local practice and non-local ideas. They are part of a continuously dynamic process of cultural diffusion and adjustment, and bring together different influences – the overall plan type from one source, details of the plan from another source, construction details from another, ornamental motifs from yet another. New York buildings were influenced by the Dutch and the English. Jakarta buildings were influenced by the Dutch and the Chinese. The Chinese influenced buildings not only in the East Indies, but all over southeast Asia, and in America. There is a web of influences, and these influences may affect different attributes of buildings in different ways, leading to recombinations and typological complexity.[1]

Although shop/houses exist in most cities of the world,[2] important trading cities are particularly important in their evolution because of the way these cities helped to hybridize different cultures. Trading cities of south China such as Guangzhou (formerly Canton), of the Chinese diaspora such as Bangkok and Singapore, of the Hanseatic League such as Lübeck, of the Dutch empire such as Amsterdam and Batavia (now Jakarta), of the Mediterranean trade such as Venice, of England and America such as New York, were all places in which new types developed and evolved out of combinations of imported and local practice. The colonial enterprise that brought new populations to the Americas, Africa and Asia was fueled partly by active commerce, supported by resilient building types.

Many individual shop/house types were originally variations of dwelling houses. Until the proliferation of new building types in the Industrial Revolution – railroad sheds, large factories, department stores – many functions that today occupy unique buildings were accommodated in houses. Specialized buildings existed – churches of course, town halls, barns, theaters – but apart from those buildings most daily life happened in houses or in variations of them.

In fact, the word *house* did not necessarily imply "dwelling" and in many documents of the eighteenth century and before, the word had to be qualified: dwelling house, counting house, etc. We still sometimes do that, with the term "school house." Moreover, the word "house" has a broader meaning than just a physical building. Publishing companies and fine-art auction businesses are "houses;" the House of Windsor is a family; the White House makes public announcements.

Many of the buildings described in the following four chapters evolved out of dwelling-house types. The ease with which a business could be accommodated in a house before the Industrial Revolution had to do as much with the small size of businesses as with the fact that houses were designed in ways that were not as functionally determined as houses are today. The distinction between family life and the life of the shop was not a firm one.

[1] The study of vernacular architecture is, to a large extent, an examination of the question of cultural diffusion, and the literature contains hundreds of works that deal with the question. Two seminal works, the first by a cultural geographer and the other by an art historian/sociologist are Kniffen, "Folk Housing," and King, *The Bungalow*.

[2] Cities of North Africa and the Middle East, during times of Islamic influence, represent something of an exception. In many of these cities there was a strict separation between commercial districts and residential districts, with little commerce inside the gates of residential neighborhoods that housed permanent residents of the city.

This ambiguity means that the combination of shop and dwelling in the same building is sometimes visible in the building's architecture, and sometimes not. It is possible to look at the ruins of some houses in ancient Pompeii and make a clear inference that a certain room was a shop. It is not possible to do so by looking at most houses built in seventeenth-century Amsterdam. Nevertheless, this combination existed in both places and in many others, where before the nineteenth century the shop represented an adaptation of rooms of the dwelling house for sales or manufacture.

The historical close relationship between the shop/house and the dwelling house has emerged because of spatial/organizational attributes that have allowed for an easy transformation of functions back and forth between different uses. This often occurs because the ground-floor front room of the house can be connected to rooms behind it, or can be bypassed so that the house can be accessed without going through this room. Change of use may happen on a daily basis, as it does in the Japanese *machiya*, where bedding is put away every morning and brought out again at night, or gradually over time, as in the American row house where the front room may be converted into a shop, or as the result of an architectural transformation, as with London houses on commercial streets where the front is extended toward the street for a shop.

This fluid attitude toward building use is essential to the lives of people who inhabit shop/houses, for whom the building's flexibility allows them to develop businesses in their houses with a minimum of financial investment, and to expand and contract the space devoted to the business as necessary. It is also important to larger buildings, in which dwellings and business spaces may be occupied by different people, but where the building owner may optimize rent by not restricting use.

From one point of view, the shop/house is a product of urban morphological conditions that result in the two functions of dwelling and commerce each being optimized for the same location. As will be described in more detail in Chapter 6, it is the attempt to maximize the financial return on a particular piece of land that leads to mixed use. Since commerce and industry often take place at or near the street – for visibility and ease of moving goods and supplies – this leaves upper floors or areas away from the street available for other functions, typically dwellings.

Location is also affected by the particular non-dwelling function that is included in the house. Functions such as retail that may require pedestrian traffic will put shop/houses on busy streets that are at the edge of otherwise residential districts that may "collect" pedestrians from smaller, quieter streets.[3] Shop/houses that include workshops may be on back streets, indicating the lower social status of the artisan as well as a lesser need for visibility. And wholesale houses may have been on streets leading to and from places of trans-shipment, such as docks – as they were in Lübeck, and originally along the canals of Amsterdam.

Chapters 1–4 deal with shop/houses of Asia, of southern and northern Europe, and of England and North America. These chapters are not intended as a catalog or comprehensive description of shop/house types, but instead as an attempt to explain the variety of types, their origins and their commonalities. Those descriptions will in turn provide part of the basis for Part II, which will describe the common features of the design and location of shop/houses.

[3] In the West, this locational attribute – and the functional zoning that ultimately emerged – became more important, beginning in the eighteenth century, when the marketing and display of goods and the development of shop windows through which goods could be displayed, emerged along with large-scale industrial production.

1.01 Shophouses in Guangzhou, China.
Photograph by author.

1

SHOPHOUSES OF ASIA

Nguan Tong, his wife, and their two daughters live in a store. That is, except for the kitchen and their bedrooms upstairs, every inch of the house is devoted to the storage of incoming merchandise. Their store stands in the center of a row of wooden houses; in every one, a family shares space with a business of one kind or another. The front of each store is open to the street, so that during the day all the neighborhood opens onto the busy life of Sampaeng Lane and is absorbed by it. Then, there is little sense of the separateness of families one feels in the evenings, when the great wooden doors are pulled shut all along the row and across the street too.[1]

(Botan, *Letters from Thailand*)

[1] Botan, *Letters from Thailand*, 17.
[2] Xu, *Chinese City*, 69–70.
[3] A famous scroll painting, *Qingming Shanghe Tu*, painted during the Northern Song Dynasty (960–1127), is often cited as evidence of the existence of shophouses in the medieval Chinese city.
[4] Xu, *Chinese City*, 76.
[5] Xu, *Chinese City*, 75.

From the West, the shophouse is often seen as something uniquely Asian, representative of enterprising families with close personal ties. The Asian shophouse not only sheds light on the mixed-use phenomenon in general, and on Asian cultures, but also embodies human and economic relationships that existed in the West until – and in some cases beyond – the Industrial Revolution.

The Asian shophouse is not represented by a single type. The Chinese shophouse is different in different places in China and throughout the Chinese diaspora, and the Japanese *machiya* developed differently according to its location and the kind of business being housed. In colonial situations in China and southeast Asia, indigenous forms hybridized with European styles and were influenced by European-style regulations.

Shophouses have been present in China for at least a thousand years. Although ancient Chinese cities had strong distinctions between commercial and residential districts, these distinctions lessened by the time of the Southern Song Dynasty (1128–1279), allowing for a mixed distribution of functions throughout the city.[2] Shops and houses became intermingled.[3] In Suzhou, a center for silk weaving, districts were specifically allocated for business and for the textile industry, which was based on individual family shops.[4] The business district was crowded with two-story shophouses, "with quarters that were cramped because of high land values, the normal desire of businessmen to keep nonessential overheads low and the frugality of soujourners out to save as much as possible of their income."[5] This describes the essential economic motivation of the family shophouse.

In south China, the typical pre-twentieth-century urban shophouse is a party-wall building, with a length several times its width, in which the family lives above or behind the shop. It typically has a roof of one or more gables parallel to the street, sometimes with courtyard(s) located immediately behind the front wall or further into the site. Before the Westernization that came following the establishment of the Republic in 1912, these buildings might have had open arcades in front, made by an extension of the roof, forming an outdoor living and work space. The stair to any loft space would likely have been deep inside the building, so that one would have to pass through the shop – which might also have served as the main "living room" of the family – to reach the private quarters in the back or above.

This narrow, urban building is a typological transformation of the rural courtyard house (*siheyuan*, with rooms at the gate; or *sanheyuan*, with no rooms at the gate). The house is organized symmetrically around an axis that passes through a central courtyard and leads to an ancestral hall or shrine. In smaller urban houses the courtyard may have evolved into a recessed space at the front, or into a tall space inside the house, and the ancestral hall replaced with a small shrine on the main axis. And work still took place in the "courtyard" or front room. A strict separation of men and women meant that work carried out by women, such as silk weaving, happened in private quarters removed from public view. But selling and business affairs happened in the public space of the courtyard, on the principal axis.

In addition, principal house types in China vary between the north and the south. In the colder north, where sun angles are lower, larger courtyards allow the walls of the house and the courtyard floor to be warmed by the sun. In the hotter south, courtyards are smaller, sometimes disappearing altogether in favor of vertical spaces that link the ground floor with a ventilation opening in the roof. In these cases, the "courtyard" helps cool the house in summer rather than warm it in winter.[6]

[6] Knapp, *Chinese Houses*, 17.

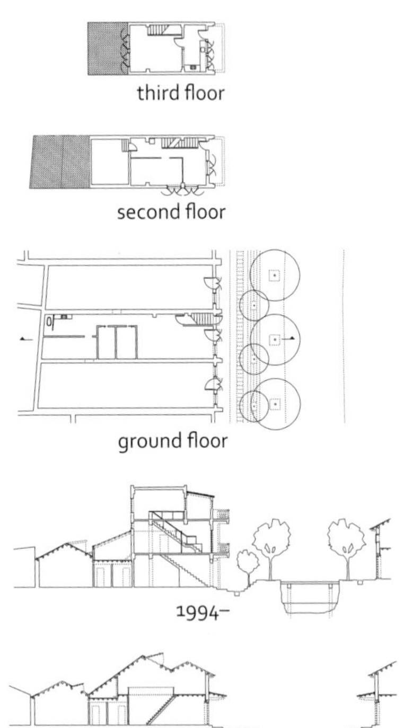

1.02 (left) The ground-floor plan shows three adjacent houses in Guangzhou that were built as one unit in the late ninteenth century. The central house, for which the upper floors and sections are shown, belonged to the family head. It had the ancestral shrine and, originally, an opening in the roof.
Diagrams by Matthew M. Brown.

1.03 (right) Guangzhou, China, showing row of shophouses built in the late nineteenth century and recently converted into shophouses housing antique sellers.
Photograph by Matthew M. Brown.

In commercial cities of China, houses underwent fundamental transformations all through the twentieth century. Beginning with the end of the Qing Dynasty in 1911, and continuing through the years of the Republic, the formation of the Communist state in 1949 and the economic reforms beginning in 1978, political and economic change altered how and where people worked, and the role of the family in economic life.

A group of three adjacent party-wall houses in the Liwan (Xi Guan) district of Guangzhou, formerly Canton, were transformed as a result of these economic changes (Figs 1.02 and 1.03). The houses are now owned by three descendants of a man who built them together, for his three sons, during the late Qing Dynasty. When they were built, the central house was designated for the eldest son. In this house, the ground floor was open to the roof as the loft level consisted only of a balcony surrounding a tall open space. The houses were linked through their party walls by doorways that have since been bricked in; the vertical space in the middle house has also been eliminated and a full floor built in place of the opening.

The family business – the manufacture and sale of chestnut powder – took place in an arcade outside and in the main hall of the house. Storage and some sleeping was in a loft above the hall. Women lived and slept in small rooms in the back of the main hall, where an ancestral shrine was also accessible by a ladder from the ground floor.

This linked group of houses contained, in modified form, the elements of the traditional courtyard house. The principal axis in the central house led to the ancestral shrine. The doors in the party walls linked the three buildings into one – a transformation of the three-bay courtyard house. The great-grandfather gave his oldest son the most honored position, with the tall space, in the center. The affairs of the business took place under the outside arcade and in the most public space of the building – which was also the space in which the ancestral shrine is centered. This group of houses represented a transitional form, between the traditional courtyard house and the urban shophouse. Today, the original order is not easily visible, but the buildings have reverted to a shophouse function after decades of residential-only use during the Communist era.

The Chinese shophouse and foreign trade

The Chinese shophouse took on a wide variety of forms, partly as a result of trade at the treaty ports such as Shanghai and Canton, and partly by trade by members of the Chinese diaspora in southeast Asia and other places outside China. In Shanghai, the establishment of the city as a treaty port in 1843 led to the designation of certain land for foreign traders and agents. Although Chinese people were forbidden by law from establishing themselves in this territory, the foreign merchants who leased land employed Chinese contractors to build houses. As in Guangzhou, houses were variations of the traditional *sanheyuan* house and often included commercial activity.[7]

Outside China, Chinese businessmen established firms at port cities in southeast Asia and further afield, and sent the profits from those businesses back to families who remained in China. The buildings they built were hybrids, melding Chinese forms, indigenous forms, and European styles that were also being brought to those cities by people from colonial powers.

7 Liang, "Where the Courtyard Meets the Street," 482–503.

In Malaya, shophouses built by Chinese immigrants were, in their earliest forms, simple party-wall structures that had no front walls and in which people slept either in the back of the shop or in a loft under the roof.[8] In towns and cities, subsequent versions of the type were more permanent, with masonry party walls and eventually incorporating European organizational ideas and motifs on their façades (Plate 10).

Malay shophouses were flexible in their plan arrangements, so that for example they could be subdivided into many cubicles for different families. In these cases the position of the stairs in front and sometimes in the back, accessed through a side passage, allowed different tenants to access their rooms without going through the space of the owner or principal tenant. The shop was always open to the street; the kitchen was often behind the shop; and living and sleeping quarters were behind the shop and/or upstairs.

In Batavia (the Dutch name for what is now Jakarta), Dutch traders built near the canals (Plate 10), as in Amsterdam. Houses had stoops to lift them up above the ground, as they also did in Holland and later in New York, and roof and gable details derived from Dutch buildings. But they also made concessions to the hot and humid local climate, sometimes with a projecting eave to give shade.[9] And at the same time, the Chinese built in ways that combined the traditional Chinese shophouse with European stylistic details.[10]

Shophouses were also built in cities such as Penang, Hanoi, Hoi An and many others where Europeans established trading outposts, attracting Chinese entrepreneurs. Some of these cities, Penang in particular, still retain large districts of shophouses, now the subject of conservation efforts. But perhaps

1.04 Shophouses in Singapore.
Photograph by author.

[8] Kohl, *Chinese Architecture*, 178.
[9] Abeyasekere, *Jakarta: A History*, 17–18.
[10] Abeyasekere, *Jakarta: A History*, 25.

the best known of the southeast Asia shophouse types was developed in Singapore, where Chinese immigrants who positioned themselves to take advantage of British trade built houses that were hybrids of English terraced houses and buildings in southern China's coastal trading cities (Fig. 1.04 and Plate 11). In 1823, Sir Stamford Raffles, who was Britain's administrator of Singapore after Britain acquired rights to the territory from the Dutch, instituted strict building regulations that defined what we now know as the "Singapore shophouse" and that provided a model for shophouses throughout southeast Asia. Raffles was apparently influenced partly by Dutch buildings in Batavia where he lived between 1811 and 1815.[11]

The regulations required brick construction (up until that point many shophouses were built of wood), uniform fronts, and an arcade, linked to other buildings: "All houses constructed of brick or tiles have a uniform type of front each having a verandah of a certain depth, open to all sides as a continuous and open passage on each side of the street."[12] The "certain depth" turned out to be the "five-foot way" – the covered arcade that is characteristic of Singapore shophouses, providing protection against tropical sun and rain. Building width was controlled by available timber that spanned from party wall to party wall, and by the economic pressure to have as many shophouses as possible on commercial streets. This made shophouses narrow and long, and light wells were introduced along their length. Later, alleys were designed in the back of the buildings so that night soil could be carried away without taking it through the house. Subsequent versions of the shophouse maintained this essential organization, while they also got wider and taller, and their façades reflected current styles.[13] The buildings continued to be built well into the twentieth century, as Chinese immigrants who built shophouses displaced Malays who were already there.[14]

Bangkok

The Thai shophouse as it exists today represents an evolution from a hybrid of the European party-wall building introduced into Thailand during the nineteenth century and the traditional Thai wooden dwelling, that itself was adapted to commercial use even before European influence. The building is also, in its form but particularly in its use, representative of a particular attribute of some traditional Thai vernacular architecture – ambiguous boundaries between adjacent spaces.

Traditional southeast Asian houses are very open, and often have lightweight wooden partitions with spaces between the boards that allow spatial separation and good air circulation at the same time. They also rely on changes of level instead of walls to make functional separations within large spaces. As in many parts of southeast Asia, the main dwelling rooms of houses may be partly raised above the ground. The space below the house is used for animals or agricultural storage. This arrangement allows the dwelling to be kept clean, and for circulating air in the shaded space to help cool the house. In villages, shops are located in those spaces (or in the front of houses when houses are located directly on the ground).[15] There may be a smooth gradient between "storage under the house" and beginning to sell things that are stored there, particularly when there is an agricultural surplus – so some traditional two-story wooden houses are similar to shophouses (Fig. 1.05 and Plate 4).[16]

With a diversity of origins including the vernacular, the introduction of the shophouse into Thailand and other countries of southeast Asia needs to be

[11] Lim, "Shophouse 'Rafflesia'," 51–52.
[12] Lim, "Shophouse 'Rafflesia'," 49.
[13] Lee, "Singapore Shophouse," 115–134.
[14] Edwards, *Singapore House*, 93.
[15] Chaichongrak et al., *Thai House*, 46.
[16] Panin, "Thai-Mon Vernacular Houses," 36.

1.05 Shophouse in Siem Reap, Cambodia.
Photograph by author.

seen in a nuanced way.[17] Certainly there was commerce before the arrival of the Chinese in the nineteenth century, and much of it operated out of houses. In many of these houses, the shop was below and the dwelling was upstairs or in the back. There were also shophouse types that included courtyards, until the introduction of ordinances that transformed shophouses into buildings that were more like imported terraced houses.[18] So although the European version of the shophouse that was adopted by Chinese immigrant-merchants is often seen as an imported type, its morphology was consistent with what was already present in southeast Asia. Innovations in style and construction, and regulations concerning width and arcades, happened along with the continuity of indigenous types.[19]

One aspect of the traditional Thai use of space strongly lends itself to the openness of the shophouse to the street (Fig. 1.06). In traditional wooden dwellings, a spatial ambiguity blurs the distinction between inside and outside, and between public, semi-public and private territory. Level changes within houses are similar: spatial differences happen under the same ceiling. This characteristic is extended to the shophouse, where the sidewalk is a mixture of public space, business space and dwelling space, in varying relationships to each other. This ambiguity is not inconsistent with the "five-foot way" in shophouse legislation, where the area on the sidewalk was privately owned but for public use.

Early Bangkok shophouses were wooden (Fig. 1.07) but beginning with King Rama V (1853–1910), buildings had brick party walls, brick walls in front and rear, and wooden beams. Singapore shophouses influenced Rama V when he visited Singapore in 1871. He later sponsored the construction of 458 shophouses in Bangkok, spurring the construction of more European-influenced shophouses.[20] They are party-wall buildings, built as identical units in a row, and two, three or four stories tall. The basic unit is one room wide (but they are occasionally combined into double-bay buildings) and three rooms deep, with the center room in the older buildings having been transformed from an open court into a roofed space.

17 Tjoa-Bonatz, "Ordering of Housing," 124.
18 Tjoa-Bonatz, "Ordering of Housing," 131–136.
19 See for example Lim, "Shophouse 'Rafflesia'," 47. Ignoring possible indigenous or other Asian influences, Lim's abstract begins: "It has been assumed that the pre-war shophouses in the Malaysian region, consisting of a narrow frontage and a plan of considerable depth, had its origins in China. However, this view does not take into account the distinctive regular façade and 'five-footways' [sic]. It was in fact Sir Stamford Raffles who was the 'architect' of this prototype. Hence, it is hereby termed the 'Shophouse Rafflesia.'" But early in the article itself, Lim acknowledges the probable influence of shophouses in China as well as Dutch precedents in Batavia (later Jakarta).
20 Lim, "Shophouse 'Rafflesia'," 62.

1.06 Bangkok street.
Photograph by author.

1.07 One of the last remaining wooden shophouses in Bangkok.
Photograph by author in 2003.

The front, ground-floor room is the shop, and has an opening to the street that is the full width of the building, blurring the boundary between inside and outside. The family kitchen is often behind the shop on the ground floor, in a room that may also include storage. The stair is accessed from the space in between the shop and the kitchen, and the foot of the stair faces toward one of the side walls, or toward the back, helping to preserve the privacy of the upstairs quarters.

Variations are often occasioned by the way older houses were transformed over time. In some cases the kitchen was originally a separate room behind the courtyard, with a sloped roof/ceiling. The stair leading to room(s) over the shop was in the courtyard and open to the elements. In these cases, expansion of the house could have been done in one of two ways: by taking down the kitchen and building a new wing, or by keeping the kitchen in place and building new rooms over the courtyard. In many cases, the original kitchen had a shed roof that sloped toward the courtyard, allowing for a clerestory window in the back that permitted ventilation after the courtyard was roofed. In addition, if the courtyard was turned into a room, the stair was moved to make that room more efficient. The second floor, added over the courtyard, was not necessarily at the same level as the second-floor room that was over the shop, and houses may contain complex stair arrangements that resolve these levels. Plans of two contemporary Bangkok shophouses are illustrated in Chapter 7 (Fig. 7.09).[21]

The contemporary Bangkok shophouse shares organizational features with those earlier ones. Modern shophouses are higher and wider, and have reinforced concrete frames and slabs, and infill walls of brick. While in older houses the opening in the front could be closed with moveable wooden shutters, contemporary buildings may have large plate-glass windows and/or rolling metal shutters. But with these transformations, the party-wall organization, the ambiguity of use of space inside the building and the openness of the façade remain.

The Japanese *machiya*

The traditional Kyoto *machiya* (*machi*=town; *ya*=house) is typically a long, relatively narrow party-wall building, no more than two stories tall, with its short dimension parallel to the street. It has a spatial organization similar to the row or terraced house, with the wide part consisting of a series of raised *tatami* rooms and courtyards, and the narrow part a passage through the length of the building, alongside the rooms (Fig. 1.08).

Because of the way traditional Japanese buildings embody ambiguity in their spatial adjacencies and flexibility of use over time, *machiya* are particularly effective examples of buildings that incorporate varying relationships between commercial and domestic uses.

There were multiple urban and rural origins for the *machiya*. Very early Kyoto *machiya* may have originated during the Kamakura period (1185–1333) when there was a devolution of power from the imperial government to aristocratic families, who in turn patronized communities of craftsmen and merchants. Before this time, common people were not allowed to have shops in their houses, but now commercial activity began to spread. Some early *machiya* may have been transitional forms, in which workshops and associated dwellings appeared in the walls surrounding large villas.[22]

[21] For a description of this transformation process, see Ongsavangchai and Funo, "Spatial Organization," 1–8.
[22] Lofgren, *Machiya*, 59–63.

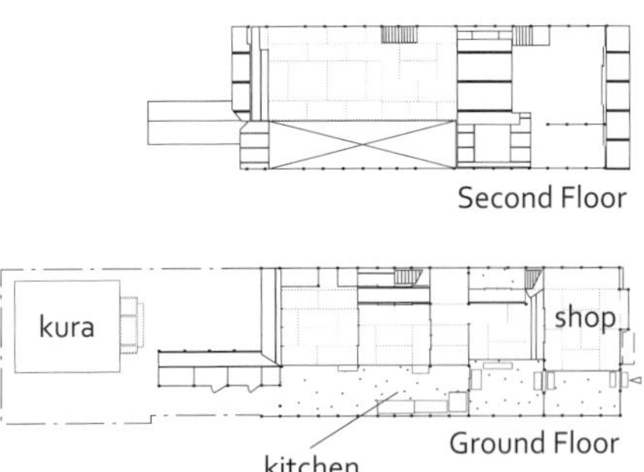

1.08 **(top) Plan of typical *machiya*.**
Drawing by Will Krzymowski.

Moreover, the *minka* (rural farmhouse) typically had features similar to those of the *machiya*, suggesting a cultural link between rural and urban building practice. Like the *machiya*, entry into the *minka* was into a space with an earthen floor, with productive and service functions, including the kitchen. This space often led all the way through the house, allowing work and kitchen functions to proceed without disturbing life in the living/sleeping rooms, which were raised up on wooden floors. Kawashima describes the plan of even the largest *minka* as the typological evolution of a simple two- or three-unit prototype that has an earthen entrance passage on one side and room on the other (Figs. 1.09 and 1.10). In this evolution, the most formal room, specifically designated for sleeping, is away from the earthen entrance passage. [23]

[23] Kawashima, *Minka*, 64–70.

Its origin in the *minka* may help explain why the *machiya* demonstrates two central ideas of Japanese houses: the fluidity of space and the strong relationship between indoors and outdoors, or between the man-made world and the natural world. Although the passage runs through the entire house from front to back, and is adjacent to even the most private spaces of the house, it can be regarded as a continuation of nature. It traditionally had an earthen floor; it was the place for the kitchen fire; and it was understood as a space into which visitors and tradesmen could easily enter, perhaps without being greeted by the householder. The sequence of gardens along the length of house provide each room with a connection to the outdoors so that there is never more than one room in between the interior and a garden. Although

1.09 **(bottom left) Traditional *minka* (farmhouses) in Japan.**
Drawing by Will Krzymowski.

1.10 **(bottom right) View of traditional *minka* in Takayama.**
Photograph by author.

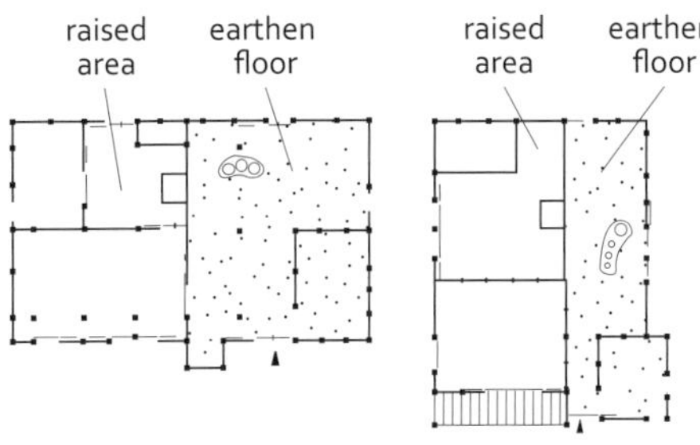

1.11 The side passage in a Kyoto *machiya*.
Photograph by author.

physical spaces are clearly distinguished from each other, and social protocols strongly control their use, different uses and indoor and outdoor spaces are so strongly adjacent that they are almost physically intertwined. Takeshi Nakagawa writes that "Space in Japanese architecture is made up of transitory units. Each unit serves, in essence, as a bridge between the foreground and the deeper interior, and space consists of series of such units, like the links of a chain. It is endlessly fluid . . ."[24]

The earthen- or stone-floored passage through the *machiya* contains the entrance (*genkan*) at its street end, access to the various, raised *tatami* rooms, and the kitchen – traditionally with a masonry stove and a well – which is deeper into the house. It also allowed goods to be brought to any room of the house, when the house was used for manufacture or trade (Fig. 1.11). Although the passage is under the roof, street shoes may be worn anywhere in the passage, to be removed before stepping up onto the wooden or tatami floor. The second story rooms do not cover the passage, which therefore may be a

[24] Nakagawa, *Japanese House*, 1.

tall space open to the roof, overlooked by windows from second-story rooms, and with the ability to bring smoke up from the kitchen.

The *machiya* has a low-pitched, gable roof, with its ridge parallel to the street. If there is a second-floor room facing the street, it will often be very low on the street side, with windows behind an ornamental masonry opening. This was not always the case. At the beginning of the Edo period (starting in 1601), two-story shophouses were commonly built (Plate 15). But a 1723 law restricted building heights to one and a half stories, so common people could not look down on the samurai. This rule was circumvented in some cases by continuing the slope of the roof upward, as it went back from the front façade, allowing for taller rooms in the middle of the house.[25]

There are typically one or two interior courtyards, and in the back of the house, the *kura*, or storehouse, a separate masonry or heavily plastered building, was used to store valuables of the family or business and provide protection in case of fire.

Although the house was internalized and private, its street wall could be open if the front room were used as a shop, with wooden screens that slid away or that could be removed. This allowed goods to be displayed and passers-by to easily see into the first room of the house. Alternatively, if the front wall were closed, shop customers would enter the *genkan*, and step up to the shop – or sit on the edge of the raised floor – to be served. In this case, a *nori* curtain or screen divided the *genkan* from the rear part of the passage.

Sliding *fusuma* screens between rooms allowed rooms to be used flexibly so that, for example, the relationship between the front room or shop and the second room (often used as a reception room for household guests) could easily change. During the day, when the shop was open, the *fusuma* screen could be closed to preserve the privacy of family life; but at night it could be open to allow a connection between the shop space – transformed into living space – and the rest of the domestic quarters. The *fusuma* screen was more solid, with wood instead of paper, in a room that got heavier daily use, and more delicate in rooms that were treated more gently.[26]

The simple spatial order of the *machiya* belies a subtle social organization. In traditional Japanese houses, rooms have multiple functions, and can be used for sleeping as well as eating, studying or entertaining guests. But there is still a hierarchy in the house. Generally, privacy is greater with increasing distance from the front entrance. Domestic visitors and commercial visitors all enter into the *genkan* from which the first *tatami* room, adjacent to the street, may be accessed (Fig. 1.12). If the house includes a shop, it is here. The visitor who is more intimate with the family may proceed into the next segment of the passage, from which s/he can step up to the second *tatami* room, a room in which visitors are received, and from which the third *tatami* room – a formal guest room where the visitor is entertained, the *zashiki* – may be accessed. This room contained three important ceremonial alcoves – the *tokonoma*, the Buddhist altar, and the family altar.

The second *tatami* room, the *daidoko*, is in between the shop and the *zashiki*, serves both of these rooms and is the room through which food is brought from the kitchen. It is an intermediate position, into which guests may first enter from the passage, and from which it is possible to see the goings-on throughout the house.[27]

25 Lofgren, *Machiya*, 106.
26 Lofgren, *Machiya*, 173.
27 Lofgren, *Machiya*, 217.

1.12 View toward street in typical *machiya* in Imai-cho, Japan.
Photograph by author.

The privacy gradient also affects the position and design of the stair. The stair may come up from the shop, if the second-floor room is being used for shop storage, or from a room behind the shop, if the second-floor room is being used for domestic purposes. The foot of the stair, in either case, is often located on the side of the *tatami* room away from the passage, deeper into the house, to help preserve the privacy of the upstairs rooms. The stair may be behind a sliding door or disguised as a chest of drawers, providing extra storage space but also giving even less emphasis to the private upstairs space than its position deep inside the house implied. The side of the room away from the *genkan* could also have been the location of the office, simply marked by a low railing.[28] Wider *machiya* had their office, for money transactions and record-keeping, on the side of the passage away from the linear sequence of *tatami* rooms, near the main entrance.

Within the basic layout, there were many variations and modes of use. Larger houses belonging to wealthier people had two rows of *tatami* rooms rather than one, and there were different possible locations of shop, office, workshop or manufacturing facility (Fig. 1.13 and Plate 17).

Shops selling rice, or shops making tofu, where there was boiling water, had an earthen floor, accessed by customers directly through an opening from the street. In these cases the raised floor was adjacent or behind. Shops for fan makers, calligraphers and other functions without such heavy use, had *tatami* floors, and admitted customers from the *genkan*. In all cases the comfort of the customer and setting up the building to fit the transaction were paramount.[29]

[28] Lofgren, *Machiya*, 197.
[29] Lofgren, *Machiya*, 197.

1.13 Living over the fishing in Ine-cho, Japan.
Photograph by author.

The shop was also built with a subtle marker of its function – the wooden screen on front – with different styles of woodwork for different kinds of shops. Nakagawa cites the following:[30]

- komehagoshi (for rice shop) – a rough grid with an unfinished surface;
- sakayagoshi (for liquor shop) – a rough grid with a stained surface;
- sumiyagoshi (for charcoal shop) – a grid with a solid backing of thick, unfinished wood panels;
- kigoshi (for timber shop) – a grid of split logs;
- sasamegoshi (for haberdasheries and teahouses) – a lattice in which the vertical bars have beveled edges or in which thin bars are set close together.

Machiya housed manufacturing operations, often located in the rear, with access through the passage allowing the privacy of the *tatami* rooms to be preserved. This was the case, for example, with *sake*-making operations that can still be seen in the town of Imai-cho, near Kyoto. In Tsuchiura, near Tokyo, Mr. Ryutara Terauchi's parents ran a rickshaw business from their house, and on the earthen floor inside the door there were "rows of rickshaws."[31] And workers often lived upstairs, as a plasterer and woodcutter who were employed by the family did in a general store in Tsuchiura.[32]

In Kyoto, one variation is centered in the Nishijin district, which traditionally housed thousands of silk-weaver families, each of which worked and lived in its own shophouse. The Japanese textile industry was traditionally based on small individual shops that were under the patronage of larger firms.

30 Nakagawa, *Japanese House*, 57.
31 Saga, *Memories of Silk and Straw*, 58.
32 Saga, *Memories of Silk and Straw*, 109.

1.14 Old shophouses in modern Kyoto.
Photograph by author.

These firms financed the construction of the *machiya*, in exchange for an understanding that the shop and its weavers would be available to provide woven goods to the firm.[33] In these shops, children who grew up working at the loom often took over the business as adults,[34] and the household also included apprentices who lived in the house.[35] In the Nishijin house, the third room back from the street was sometimes a two-story space containing the looms. The additional height this required was obtained by keeping the floor lower than that of the rest of the house,[36] or by continuing the roof pitch from a lower level in the front to a higher level over the room with the looms.[37]

The shop is a strong part of the imbricated and fluid system of the *machiya*. In retail situations the shop is the front room – but this room may share an ambiguous zone with the street or with the first part of the indoor passage. With the use of *fusuma* screens, the shop may be either separated from or connected to the room immediately behind it. Depending on the kind of trade that takes place in the shop, it may take on a living or sleeping function when the shop is closed. This was the case of shops selling dry goods, such as cloth – it was typical for samples to be brought out by assistants, and not kept on display in the shop – allowing for a quick transformation at night.[38]And if the shop were to go out of business, it could easily be converted into a room that has only residential functions.

[33] Hareven, *Silk Weavers of Kyoto*, 13.
[34] Hareven, *Silk Weavers of Kyoto*, 51–52, and throughout.
[35] Hareven, *Silk Weavers of Kyoto*, 56.
[36] Hareven, *Silk Weavers of Kyoto*, 176. Hareven describes a shophouse in which the looms are sunk in ditches in the earthen floor to give them more room vertically, and so that the earthen floor will provide more humidity that is necessary for the silk.
[37] Lofgren, *Machiya*, 199.
[38] Saga, *Memories of Silk and Straw*, 102–103.

In contemporary Kyoto, many traditional, wooden *machiya* have been destroyed to make way for the new development of multi-story commercial and residential buildings (Fig. 1.14). In some cases these new buildings were built by the same family who owned the original wooden *machiya*; they saw it as outmoded, drafty and difficult to maintain. The new buildings may house the family business along with separate apartments for different children of the family. But many *machiya* also remain. In some cases, modern façades have been built onto buildings that retain their wooden structure and much of their older internal organization. In others, buildings have been modified internally and functionally specific rooms introduced. Elements of the sophistication and subtlety of the traditional buildings are often hidden behind the modern façades (Plate 16).

The Newari house in the Kathmandu valley of Nepal

Finally, although a very different type in Nepal is not closely related to Chinese or Japanese traditions, it shows how a single shophouse type can be unaltered between city and country, taking on different productive or commercial functions in each place (Figs. 1.15 and 1.16). The Newaris form the predominant cultural group of the Kathmandu Valley, and their principal house type makes up most of the historic core of its cities and villages. Hindus first settled in the Kathmandu Valley in the twelfth century, but their planning principles combined with some building traditions that were local and others that came from Buddhist Tibet to the north. The valley was a meeting ground between Hinduism and Buddhism, and most people's religious practice incorporates at least elements of both.[39]

Systems of organization of towns and buildings are based on the mandala. The towns are ideally organized in a square, with four gates, and the buildings are ideally organized around square courtyards, each side of which is composed of a building wing with a longitudinal wall in the middle. Smaller houses are segments of the whole, and individual houses are often grouped around courtyard-like spaces called *bahals* that have small religious structures in the center.

In city and village alike, houses are four stories tall, and their functional organization varies little. The top floor, under the roof, is given to two functions: the kitchen and the prayer room. The two floors in the middle are for living rooms and bedrooms, often with a main living room on the floor just below the kitchen.

The ground floor takes on different functions depending on the family's occupation. It may be a workshop or storage; in urban situations it may be a shop; in villages it is for animals or the storage of agricultural implements.[40] Families living in cities often still own and work agricultural land outside the city, so even city houses have agricultural uses at their ground floor.

When the ground floor is a shop, the outer brick wall is replaced by a row of columns spanned by a deep wooden lintel to open the selling space to the street. In this case, the building traditionally has shutters that can be moved out of the way and hooked to the ceiling, to allow for the opening to the street to be as large as possible.[41] Or, a workshop may remain behind the door, relatively hidden from the street.

39 See for example Slusser, *Nepal Mandala*, 4–7.

40 Auer, Kolver and Gutschow, "Domestic Architecture of Nepal," 66.

41 Gutschow, Kolver and Shresthacarya, *Newar Towns and Buildings*, 233.

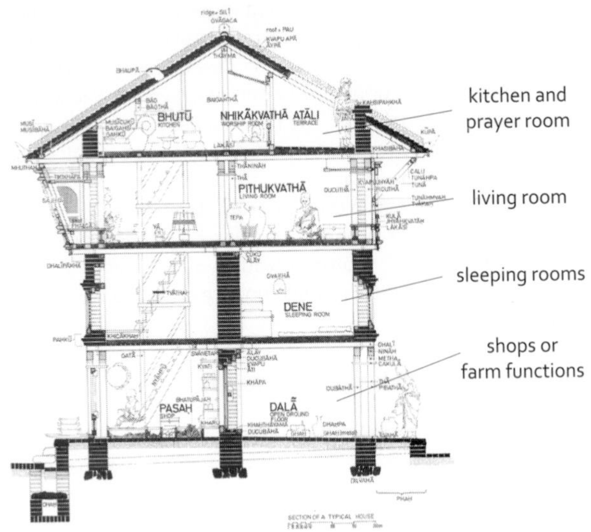

1.15 Section of typical Newar house.
Courtesy of Niels Gutschow.

1.16 Newar house with shop.
Photograph by author.

This is a unique house type. It is only peripherally connected with China, through the diffusion of some stylistic and construction ideas through Tibet. The Hindu central courtyard configuration is strongly connected to a theology that emerged in south Asia. The aspects of the building that make it a shop/house are not particularly south Asian. But in its function, and particularly in the flexibility of its ground floor, it shares features with shop/houses in many other places.

2.01 Street scene in ancient Pompeii.
From Falke, *Greece and Rome*, opposite 232.

2

THE SHOP IN THE PALAZZO

Rome, southern Europe and beyond

We find ourselves in a paved alley, some seven feet wide where it is widest, full of people, and resonant with cries of itinerant salesmen – a shriek in their beginning, and dying away into a kind of brazen ringing, all the worse for its confinement between the high houses of the passage along which we have to make our way. Overhead an inextricable confusion of rugged shutters, and iron balconies and chimney flues pushed out on brackets to save room, and arched windows with projecting sills of Istrian stone, and gleams of green leaves here and there where a fig-tree branch escapes over a lower wall from some inner cortile, leading the eye up to the narrow stream of blue sky high over all. On each side, a row of shops, as densely set as may be, occupying, in fact, intervals between the square stone shafts, about eight feet high, which carry the first floors: intervals of which one is narrow and serves as a door; the other is, in the more respectable shops, wainscotted to the height of the counter and glazed above, but in those of the poorer tradesmen left open to the ground, and the wares laid on benches and tables in the open air, the light in all cases entering at the front only, and fading away in a few feet from the threshold into a gloom which the eye from without cannot penetrate, but which is generally broken by a ray or two from a feeble lamp at the back of the shop, suspended before a print of the Virgin.[1]

(John Ruskin, *The Stones of Venice*)

The shop/houses Ruskin saw in the nineteenth century were uniquely Venetian in their organization and construction, but connected to the long tradition of domestic architecture on the Italian peninsula and around the Mediterranean. Although the present site of Venice was settled only in the eighth century, the original settlers came from the mainland, where the traditions of ancient Rome themselves had antecedents in the courtyard houses of Greece and the civilizations before it.[2]

The courtyard/atrium house is the most commonly known house type of ancient Roman cities, and many such houses incorporated shops. In Pompeii, houses with shops or businesses were owned by people in all income groups, with shops most prevalent in the lowest income group and bakeries and fulleries more prevalent among middle-income groups. Of a total of 122 houses investigated in one study of Pompeii's economy, over half incorporated shops and only one third had no sign of economic activity at all.[3]

The presence of the shop side-by-side with the door to the residence suggests a social structure in which there was no stigma associated with the inter-mingling of classes. Although entrance to the house itself through the *fauces* (entrance passage) was controlled, it was perfectly acceptable for a wealthy man to live in a house that was flanked by shops occupied by people of a lower class. Indeed, important streets were both prestigious places for residences and lucrative places for business.[4] Classes and occupations were intensely mixed, and the house was very much part of the public world.

[1] Ruskin, *Stones of Venice*, 2, 65–66.
[2] Boethius says that there is "not a scrap of evidence" to suggest that Roman architecture was influenced by indigenous Iron Age huts rather than the buildings that came from the East – i.e., Greece. Boethius, *Golden House of Nero*, 7.
[3] Wallace-Hadrill, *Houses and Society*, 137.
[4] Wallace-Hadrill, *Houses and Society*, 130–131.

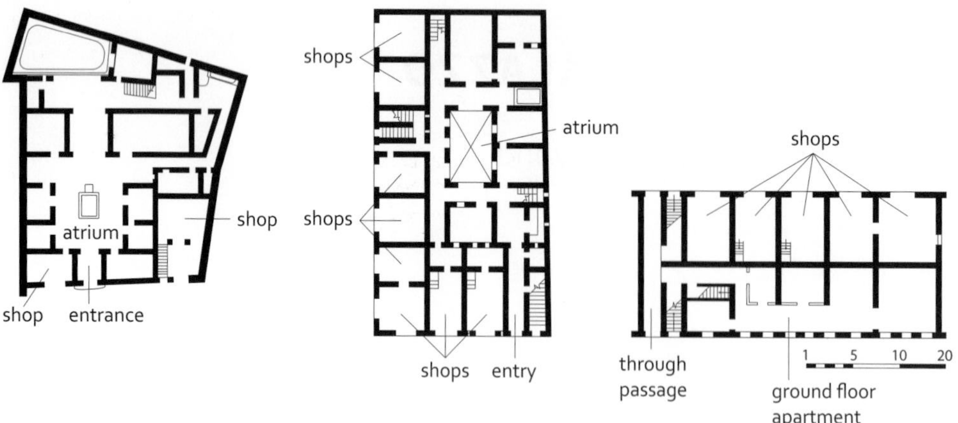

2.02 (above left) House of the Surgeon, Pompeii.
Drawings by Will Krzymowski.

2.03 (above, centre and right) Two buildings in Ostia Antica. At left, house with atrium and multiple stairs. At right, House of the Painted Ceiling.
Drawings by Will Krzymowski.

The Roman city was understood differently from today's zoned cities, and mixed use did not come about only as a result of high density. Although class distinctions existed, they were manifested more in the architecture of the house than in the overall structure of the city. Small and large houses had non-residential uses attached to them and people of different classes came together in the same streets. This was the case in Ostia, with multi-story apartment buildings, as well as in Pompeii, with lower buildings.[5]

The House of the Surgeon in Pompeii is a typical Roman house (Fig. 2.02), symmetrically organized with rooms around an atrium and an entrance on the axis. The principal part of the house is completely internal, with only the single entrance from the street, with rooms surrounding the atrium, and internal stairs leading up from a place beyond the atrium. The house has two kinds of shops: shops without an internal stair, and one corner shop with an internal stair that might have led to an apartment upstairs.

This building incorporates three independent kinds of accommodation: the main part of the house, including upper floors accessed from internal stairs; a ground-floor shop without stairs; and a ground-floor shop with an adjacent stair that could have been accessed independently. The same features can be seen in Roman buildings built a millennium and a half later.

Some of the same principles applied to higher buildings in places of greater density. As a vibrant commercial city, Ostia Antica, the port of Rome, had a high population density and an active street life. As with many commercial cities, the mobile population – of dockworkers and warehouse workers, traders and businessmen, business owners from Rome, sailors – resulted in a need for buildings that could accommodate this variety. The intense economic activity prompted the need to use land intensively, leading to building speculation, increased building height and a variety of arrangements of rental and occupancy.

The building fabric was characterized by buildings known as *insulae* ("islands"). Separated from each other by narrow alleys, *insulae* were buildings four or five stories high with rental apartments above and shops below, where the shops may have had mezzanines directly connected to them by internal stairs, and where some of the buildings were organized around atria.[6] Some

[5] Wallace-Hadrill, *Houses and Society*, 118–142.
[6] Robertson, *Greek and Roman Architecture*, 307–308.

of the apartments above had independent stairs leading down to the street (Fig. 2.03, left).

The multi-story, mixed-use buildings found in Ostia and Rome are likely not imports but local inventions, emerging out of the high population density of these cities. They are not found in ancient Greece or in colonial cities of the Roman Empire. In those places, when higher buildings are found, the buildings do not necessarily have shops at their base, and fit into an urban configuration in which commerce and dwelling were in different zones – a configuration also found in later Islamic cities.[7]

In the densest parts of Ostia, there were many *insulae* without atria in which upper-story rooms faced outward (Fig. 2.03, right). In the House of the Painted Ceiling, the evidence of the stairs suggests that the upper floors were quite complex. The through passage on the left leads to an entrance to a ground-floor apartment that is on the east side of the building. To the right of the passage are two stairs, one from each street. It is conjectured that those stairs led to apartments on the *third* floor (i.e., two floors above the ground floor), that the stairs inside two of the shops led to a mezzanine on the second floor, and that the stair internal to the ground-floor apartment also led to a mezzanine level of that apartment.

Shop/houses in far-flung cities of the Roman Empire were not necessarily as high as those in Ostia. In Roman towns in Britain, typical buildings were on long, narrow strips, perpendicular to the street, and often had a shop or workshop in the front and living quarters above.[8] This type characterized medieval and post-medieval buildings as well, and formed the basis of local urban form in England and northern Europe. The *spatial unit* of the shop connected to the dwelling by a stair in the two-story row house was similar to that in the single-shop-plus-connected-mezzanine of the Roman or Ostian *insula* (Fig. 2.04).

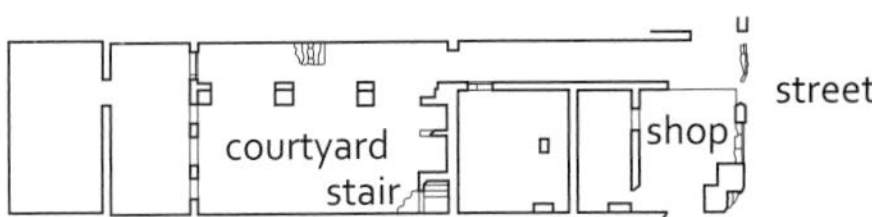

2.04 Single "row-house" unit found in large buildings. The room at the right is likely a taberna or shop, and entry to the upper floors of the house is gained through the passage and courtyard. The stair is at the lower right of the courtyard.
Drawing by Will Krzymowski.

This unit may be a transitional form in Ostia and Rome. In some *insulae*, where ownership was divided among different people, it is likely that a vertical volume, including both a single shop and the corresponding floors of the building above, was a typical unit of ownership. There is evidence of this unit having party walls, effectively turning it into a building of its own[9] – with a strong relationship, therefore, to the houses of Roman Britain, to the narrow merchants' houses of northern Europe, as well as to the houses of Rome and Florence that persisted through medieval times.

7 Boethius, *Golden House of Nero*, 140–146.
8 Aston and Bond, *Landscape of Towns*, 47.
9 Boethius, *Golden House of Nero*, 162–165.

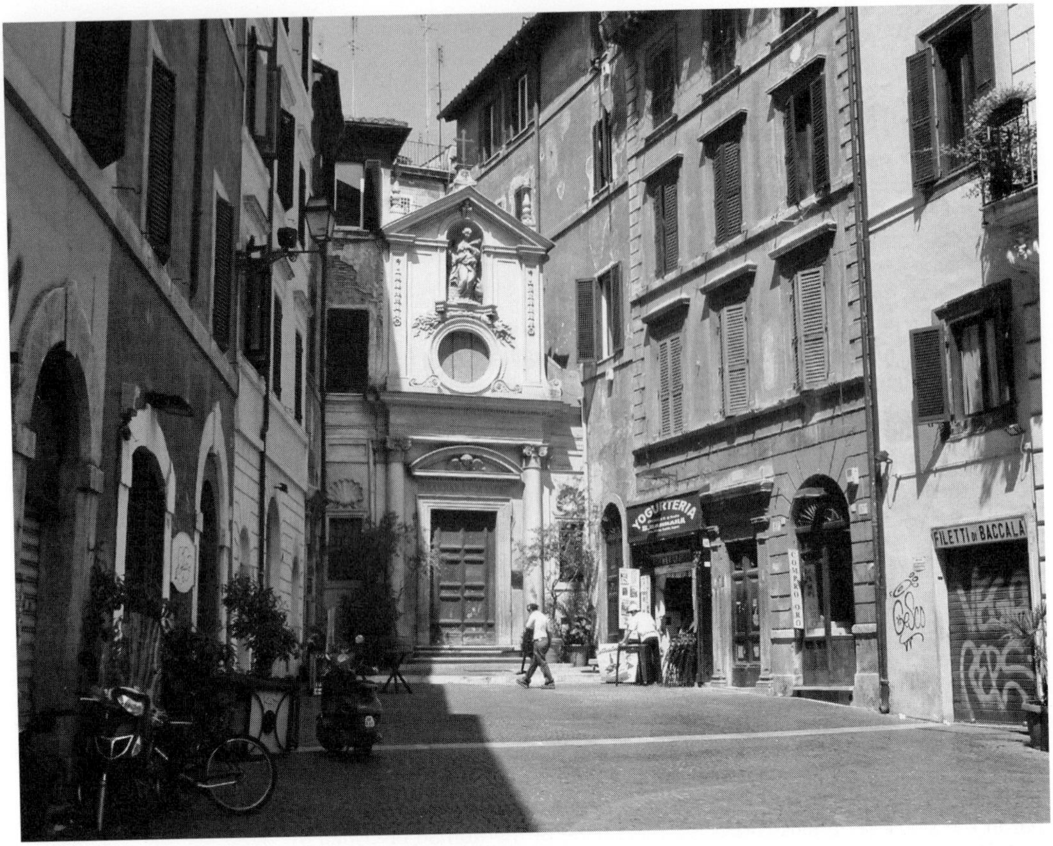
YOGURTERIA
FILETTI di BACCALA

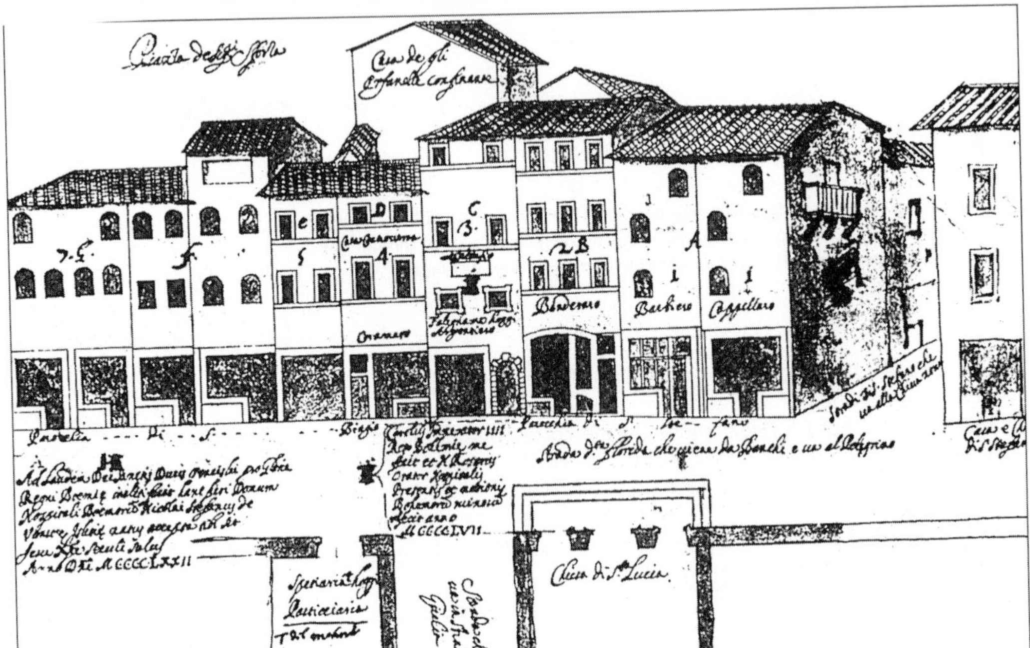

Italian descendants of ancient vernacular forms

Buildings with shop and dwelling, or shop-mezzanine-rental apartments continued to be built into modern times (Figs. 2.05, 2.06 and Plate 21). Three cities – Rome, Florence and Venice – have buildings that are locally specific, yet related through their common origins. The buildings of Rome and Florence are similar to each other. Venetian buildings are more different because of the city's unusual geography, but even these vividly demonstrate the balance between locally specific features and common typological principles. In all three cities, a large number of vernacular buildings and palazzi that are at least several centuries old remain, with clear connections to buildings of ancient Rome.

2.05 (facing, top) Shop/houses in piazzetta off the Via dei Giubbonari in Rome.
Photograph by author.

2.06 (facing, bottom) Roman shop/houses in the eighteenth century.
From Bascià et al., *La Casa Romana*. Courtesy of Alinea Editrice.

2.07 (left) Roman shop/houses in the eighteenth century, with different stair arrangements and shop designs.
From Bascià et al., *La Casa Romana*. Courtesy of Alinea Editrice.

2.08 (below) The Jewish ghetto in Rome in the nineteenth century.
Watercolor by Ettore Roesler Franz. Roma, Museo di Roma, Archivio Fotografico Comunale.

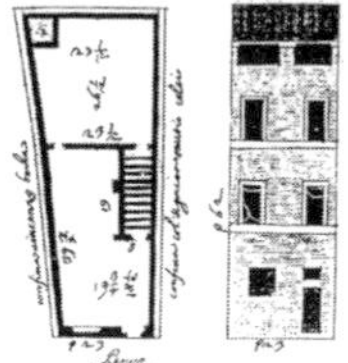
stair inside front room/shop

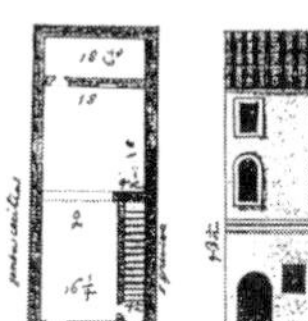
stair near street

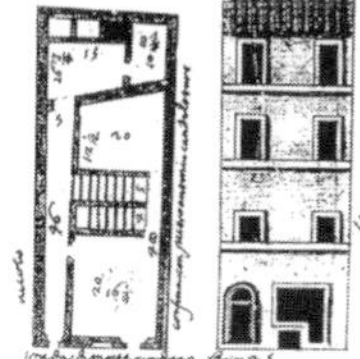
passage bypasses shop

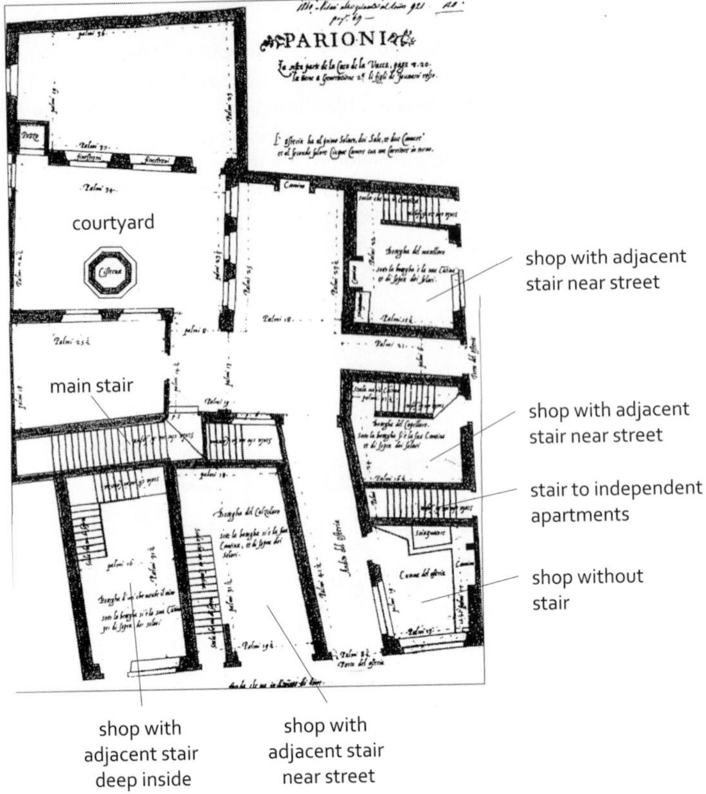

2.09 Building near the Campo de' Fiori. From Bascià et al., *La Casa Romana*. Courtesy of Alinea Editrice.

In Rome, a corner building on the Campo de' Fiori (Fig. 2.09) incorporates, in one structure, the wide variety of conditions and types – ranging from larger *palazzi* with *cortili* to simple one-bay-wide houses – that can still be seen in Rome. The building is organized around a *cortile* and has shops, facing the two streets, that were likely producing additional income for the building's owner. The *cortile* and adjacent stair, leading to a dwelling that begins on the *piano nobile*, is directly accessible from a passage leading from the street. On the streets are two shops with stairs, one deep into the shop and one just inside the door, and two shops with adjacent stairs, but accessible from the street and not from the shop. And there is a corner shop that does not have a stair. This building brings together a variety of typological ideas that are usually found in separate structures, ranging from large *palazzi* with ground-floor shops to buildings that are so narrow that they include only a minimal courtyard or no courtyard at all (Fig. 2.07).

The *palazzo*, often the home of a socially prominent family or important institution, could easily accommodate shops on its ground floor. The Cancelleria (the Papal Chancellery) has shops at its ground floor, facing the Via del Pellegrino, that were built into the building at the time of its construction, and that are still in place today. Numerous other *palazzi* also included shops. Near the Cancelleria, in the Via de Giubbonari, is the back of the Casa Grande, a *palazzo* built in a number of stages by the Barberini family. Shops were maintained on the ground floor of this building during several phases of

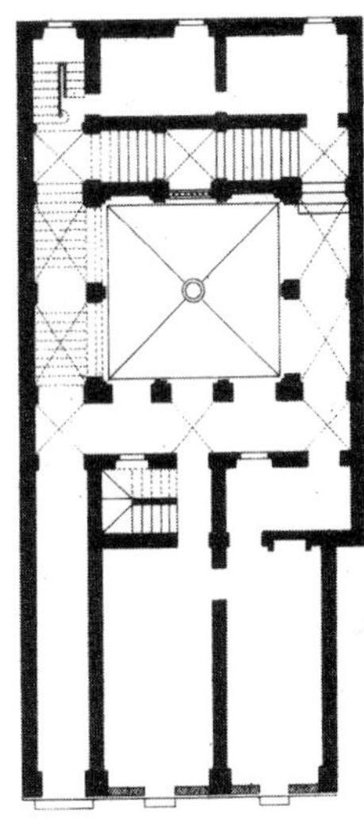

2.10 Small palazzo in Rome drawn by Letarouilly.
From Letarouilly, *Édifices de Rome Moderne.*

development. When the *palazzo* was extended, its main entrance was moved to a small *piazza* away from the street.[10] Thus, the family and its visitors could remain completely separate from the income-producing shops. The building type has strong connections to those of ancient Rome where social classes were mixed on the street. But because the residential entrance was not necessarily adjacent to the shops, the building could now be used in the service of a stronger physical separation between classes.

Shops could easily be included in *palazzi* because the formal receiving rooms and family quarters started on the *piano nobile* level, one story up from the ground floor, leaving the ground floor for service functions of different kinds. Shops could therefore be placed in spots where they did not interfere with the organization or function of the dwelling (Figs. 2.10, 2.11). The work of Fabrizio Nevola in Siena and Patricia Waddy in Rome has shown that families gained additional income from the rental of shops. In Renaissance Siena, *palazzi* typically had the most prestigious residential space on the *piano nobile*, leaving the ground floor free for service functions – and for rental shops, when the location was right.[11] These shops were sometimes run by the families who owned the *palazzi*, and in some cases they were rented by people who lived elsewhere in the city. There was most likely a variety of approaches to ownership, rental and use, and the kinds of businesses that occupied the shops often corresponded to the prestige of the family and its *palazzo*.[12]

10 Waddy, *Seventeenth-Century Roman Palaces*, 132–172.
11 Nevola, "Palaces, Shops and Clientage," 374.
12 Nevola, "Palaces, Shops and Clientage," 374.

2.11 Eighteenth-century engraving of Rome by Vasi.
Courtesy of Vin Buonanno with thanks to James Tice.

In at least one Siena example, the development of the Piccolomini family on the Strada Romana, the shops included mezzanines and perhaps dwelling rooms accessed by stairs from the shops[13] – a direct translation of the ancient Roman form. Siena was distinguished partly by the pragmatic attitude that builders of *palazzi* had toward the inclusion of shops. They did not feel a strong need for the *palazzo* to be a pure type, with a more "dignified" ground floor.[14]

The *palazzo* with shops had a dual role in the morphology of the city. The *palazzo* is a building that is highly ordered, allowing the family to project its identity and power. The positions of the *cortile*, *piano nobile*, main rooms of the *piano nobile* overlooking the street, stair leading upstairs to the *piano nobile* are all highly codified. Ideally, the cortile has an axis of symmetry that passes through the *portone*, or entrance, and helps give the building an inward focus. Because *the piano nobile* is raised, and accessible only after entering the *cortile*, the building is often understood as a kind of "urban fortress" in which the family enjoys autonomy and privacy.

But the existence of shops adds morphological complexity. With shops, the ground floor becomes an important contributor to street life, and helps knit the *palazzo* into the city at ground level. The row of shops is an essential part of the connectivity of the city, in which coherent open space alternates between the cortile and the street – and in which human activity alternates between the privately owned *cortile* (which may, however, have acted at times as semi-public space) and the more public activity of the street. So, like the ancient Roman building, the *palazzo* included shops – but the building interiors were more private.

[13] Nevola, *Siena*, 128.
[14] Nevola, *Siena*, 127.

2.12 Rome.
Photograph by author.

In Rome, Florence and other cities, smaller, linear party-wall buildings housed artisans, retail shopkeepers, and other people – the bulk of the city's population – who were not part of the *palazzo*-owning nobility or who did not occupy shops and connected apartments in *palazzi*. This building type existed in medieval times, is similar to the merchant's house of northern Europe in its narrow frontage and existence of a shop at its front, and was flexible in the way its front room could be used (Fig. 2.12).

These narrow buildings usually had between four and six stories, and often had two doors, or one door and one shop opening, on their façades. In some cases the stair leading upstairs is in the shop, and in others it is part of an entrance hall that is to the side of the shop. The shop may be connected at the ground floor to other parts of the building, or not connected; some shops still have internal connections to dwellings upstairs.

This is a flexible building type, which allows for different positions of the stair, different uses of the ground-floor front room and different ways of connecting to the street. When the stair is pulled to the façade, the ground floor may be easily used independently of the upstairs rooms; when the stair is deeper into the building, one must pass through the front room to get to it. But even here, one of the two doors may allow for the construction of a passage along one side of the front room, leading to the stair – and allowing the front room to be used independently.

Many eighteenth-century illustrations show a characteristic shopfront, consisting of a low masonry wall with an opening above it, adjacent to a door. This is virtually identical to shopfronts found in ancient Roman cities. These illustrations represent clear evidence of retail shops with the kinds of goods that could be easily sold over the counter. But many front rooms of houses were also shops, without an open shopfront, into which the customer had to enter. These were the workshops of artisans or shops in which finer goods were sold – goods such as clothing or jewelry, for which the sale took longer and where a more private interaction between buyer and seller was needed.

Houses and *palazzi* were part of a rich and connected texture of neighborhood life. Individual neighborhoods had a strong identity, with considerable interactions of people on the streets. Families were concentrated in the same neighborhood, with overlaps of family ties and commercial ties.[15] Buildings, with their own multiple functions of building and dwelling; multiple populations of building owners, servants and shop workers; and duality between the inward-looking *cortile* and outward-looking shops helped give physical form to a social place that was connected, intense, and multi-layered – the continuation of the socially rich, urban street life that existed in ancient Rome.

15 See, for example, Eckstein, "Neighborhood as a Microcosm," 219–239.

Venice

The Venetian house is a locally specific variation of the Italian *palazzo* (Fig. 2.13). The basic type has a tripartite organization with three long parallel bays, perpendicular to the street or canal. This arrangement is uniquely Venetian: the bays arise from the parallel bearing walls that help distribute

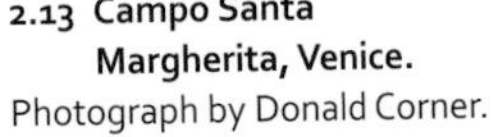

2.13 Campo Santa Margherita, Venice.
Photograph by Donald Corner.

loads evenly onto a subsoil that lacks bedrock. Wooden beams span between these parallel walls, so the front of the building facing the canal could be open, allowing for the large, ornamented windows that are typical of Venetian buildings. As Ruskin described, shopfronts were sometimes spanned with wooden beams, allowing the shops to have a maximum opening to the street.[16]

[16] Goy, *Venetian Vernacular Architecture*, 84.

When they were on canals, the buildings' lowest floors were used for shipment and storage of goods. The next floor, the *piano nobile*, was accessed from the land side via a stair in a small entrance *cortile*. Although the *cortile* might have been the only courtyard, it was not necessarily in the center of the building, and did not have the formal primacy it had in the Roman *palazzo*. At the *piano nobile*, the central bay was occupied by a large, reception room/parlor, which faced the canal at one end.

There are numerous variations on the basic organization, and Venetian architects and builders were particularly clever in organizing complex layouts and stair arrangements. Apartment houses, sometimes built to house workers in Venice's large shipbuilding industry, maintained the party-wall organization of larger *palazzi* while incorporating layouts that allowed each apartment to be serviced by its own stair. Shops at the ground floor – sometimes included in the original building and sometimes the result of later conversions – were incorporated within the bay system of the apartments above. The system could be quite flexible in the way the shop was connected to adjacent apartments.

A number of examples illustrate the unique way Venetian buildings incorporated stairs (Fig. 2.14, a–d). One seventeenth-century building in the Campo Ruga (a) incorporates a ground-level passage between the stairs and the bay in which the shop is located, making it impossible for the shop to be directly connected to any of the apartments on upper floors. The building nevertheless demonstrates a clever intertwined stair arrangement. A door from the *campo* enters into a room with an L-shaped stair that leads up to an apartment that occupies the entire first floor. Another door, from the passage and away from the one on the *campo*, leads to an entrance room facing the *cortile* at the back of the building that further leads to a stair that occupies the vertical space of the first stair, after the first floor. This stair, which has no outlet to the first floor, leads to a second apartment that occupies the entire second floor.

This typical Venetian arrangement of nested, independent stairs gives each apartment independence and its own connection to the ground, with the shop neatly incorporated into the building.

Other examples (b, c) also provide no connection between the shops and the apartments above: in both cases the shops are open only to the street. In one case (b), the shops are on a different street from the symmetrical *palazzo* front, and in the other (c), they are on the same square, and help to reinforce the symmetry with windows on either side of the building's central axis.

Houses in the fifteenth-century multi-dwelling building in the Salizzada S. Lio (d) are organized in a similar way to buildings of the same era elsewhere in Europe. They are single-bay buildings, each about five meters in width. The only door to the building is into the shop, and the apartments upstairs are accessed by means of a stair that begins in the shop. The head of the

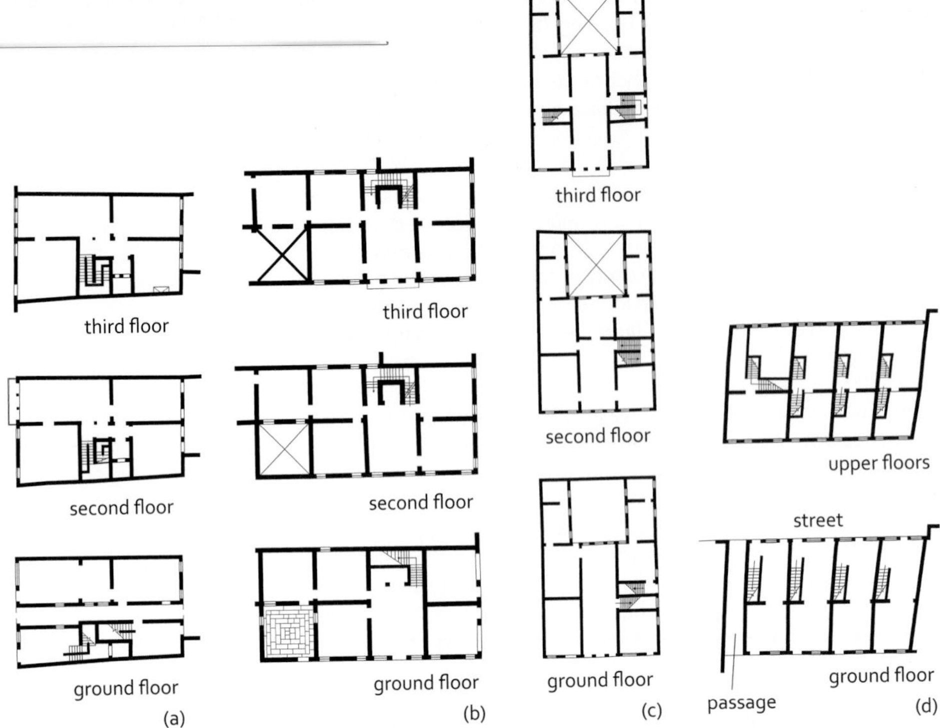

2.14 Plans of four Venice shop/houses.
Drawing by Will Krzymowski based on drawings in Trincanato, *Venezia Minore*.

first flight of stairs is near the wall between a front room and a back room, and the flight of stairs begins at this wall. Because the stair landing is at this division between rooms, there is flexibility in how the building may be subdivided.

The complexity of these Venetian buildings – and indeed of most of the Italian examples – is indicative of a place in which dwellings and shops/workplaces are finely intertwined, in which daily life makes little distinction between what many regard today as opposite poles of existence.

Shops and houses in the traditional Islamic city

There is one group of cities, historically connected to those of ancient Rome, in which the shop/house did *not* typically exist.

Islamic cities of North Africa and the Middle East are characterized by houses that often represent typological transformations of the courtyard buildings of the cities of the Roman Empire. In these cities, in which Roman rule was replaced by that of different Islamic caliphates, Islamic religious and cultural ideas helped to shape urban form and the design of houses.[17] They did this through transformations of Roman street patterns and Roman houses, and through new construction.[18]

The residential quarters of typical Islamic cities in North Africa and the Middle East did not include shops. These quarters often had only one entrance, with gates that were closed at night, helping to protect women and the privacy of family life. Different from Rome, the house was not strongly connected to the

[17] Hakim, *Arabic–Islamic Cities*, throughout.
[18] Elisséeff, "Damas a la Lumiere des Théories de Jean Sauvaget," 165–176.

public realm, and commerce largely took place in the bazaar and adjacent streets, leaving residential districts free of strangers and business.

The North African/Middle East Islamic house has parts and relationships in common with the Roman atrium house (Fig. 2.15). These include the centrality of the courtyard and the arrangement of major rooms around it; the existence of an arcade around the courtyard; and an arcaded porch (called the *tablinium* in the Roman house and the *taktaboosh* in the Islamic house) more or less opposite the entrance.

But the houses also differ in two telling respects. First, the Islamic house eliminated the symmetry of the axis leading to the atrium, and replaces the symmetrical *fauces* with an asymmetrical *skifa*, to prevent views into the courtyard. Furthermore women's quarters were put deep into the Islamic house, further isolating women from the public realm. Second, the Islamic house did not incorporate shops, and the ground-floor front wall is solid, without shop openings. The Islamic house rejected the public idea of the Roman house by putting privacy foremost in the organization of the house and district.

Finally, buildings in the old city of Ahmedabad, in the west Indian state of Gujarat, provide a demonstration of typological diffusion and the ways in which cultural and geographic influences intermingle. Ordinary urban buildings in Gujarat and the nearby state of Rajasthan (influenced by the Muslim conquests that began in the seventh century) are variations of courtyard buildings, with some similarities to the courtyard buildings of the Middle East, as well as to the nearby rural vernacular. There is likely a distant typological connection to the courtyard buildings of southern Europe, as well as to some

2.15 Comparison between large Roman house and large house in Islamic city.
Roman house from Smith, *Dictionary of Greek and Roman Antiquities*, 430; Bayt El Suhaymi Documentation, Restoration and Conservation Project, Arab Fund for Economic and Social Development, 1997, drawing by Will Krzymowski.

traditional Hindu houses, which are based on the form of the square mandala and organized around courtyards.

The houses of Ahmedabad respond in different ways to ethnicity and local urban geography in their economic use. Although the city was founded as Muslim, there is a Hindu population as well. Houses owned by Hindus are often less private than those owned by Muslims, with front rooms more open

2.16 Inside a *pol* in Ahmedabad, India.
Photograph by author.

2.17 Businesses on the outside edge of a *pol* in Ahmedabad, India.
Photograph by author.

to the street. Sometimes the Hindu-owned houses had small workshops, located in the front room behind the raised platform on the street (*otla*).[19]

But the ability to use the house for economic purposes is not restricted to one ethnic group. The *haveli* (houses) in the historic Muslim center are party-wall buildings organized in *pols*, small neighborhoods that had a single gate that gave them privacy. The individual buildings were organized around *chowk* or small courtyards that were located in the middle of the house, and entered through a series of layers, beginning with an *otla*, or raised porch. The buildings and their neighborhoods were hybrids of imported Islamic ideas and local Hindu ones.

By and large, these buildings were not shop/houses. The *pol* interior was almost exclusively residential and commercial activity was kept to bazaars on the outside (Figs. 2.16 and 2.17). But today, buildings at the edge of the *pol* may take on a hybrid function, when they have frontages both to the outside and inside. On the outside, there may be a shop at the ground floor, with a staircase beside it leading to rental apartments above. The building took on three functions – the family house, with privacy maintained on the inside of the pol, shop space and rental apartments. Nowadays these rental apartments have been converted to storage space for the shops.[20]

This hybrid arrangement may be compared to *palazzi* in Rome. In both cases, the private courtyard on the interior is reserved for residential use, while the building owner can take advantage of the economic value of the space facing the outside. Although the *cortile* of a *palazzo* belongs to a single family, and the semi-public courtyard of a *pol* belongs to a number of families, the contrast between private or semi-private residential space and public commercial space corresponds to an architectural arrangement that allows the building to serve each of those spaces in differing yet appropriate ways.[21] Again, the economic imperatives of commercial life result in complex, hybrid architectural configurations.

19 Pramar, *Haveli*, 96.
20 This information was provided by Akbar Nazim Modan in a private communication, January 2009.
21 See also Davis, *Culture of Building*, 163, for illustrations of how buildings of different sizes and of differing economic bases work together in the urban environment. In these cases, small buildings with a lot of interaction with the street surround large ones that otherwise would present blank façades to the street.

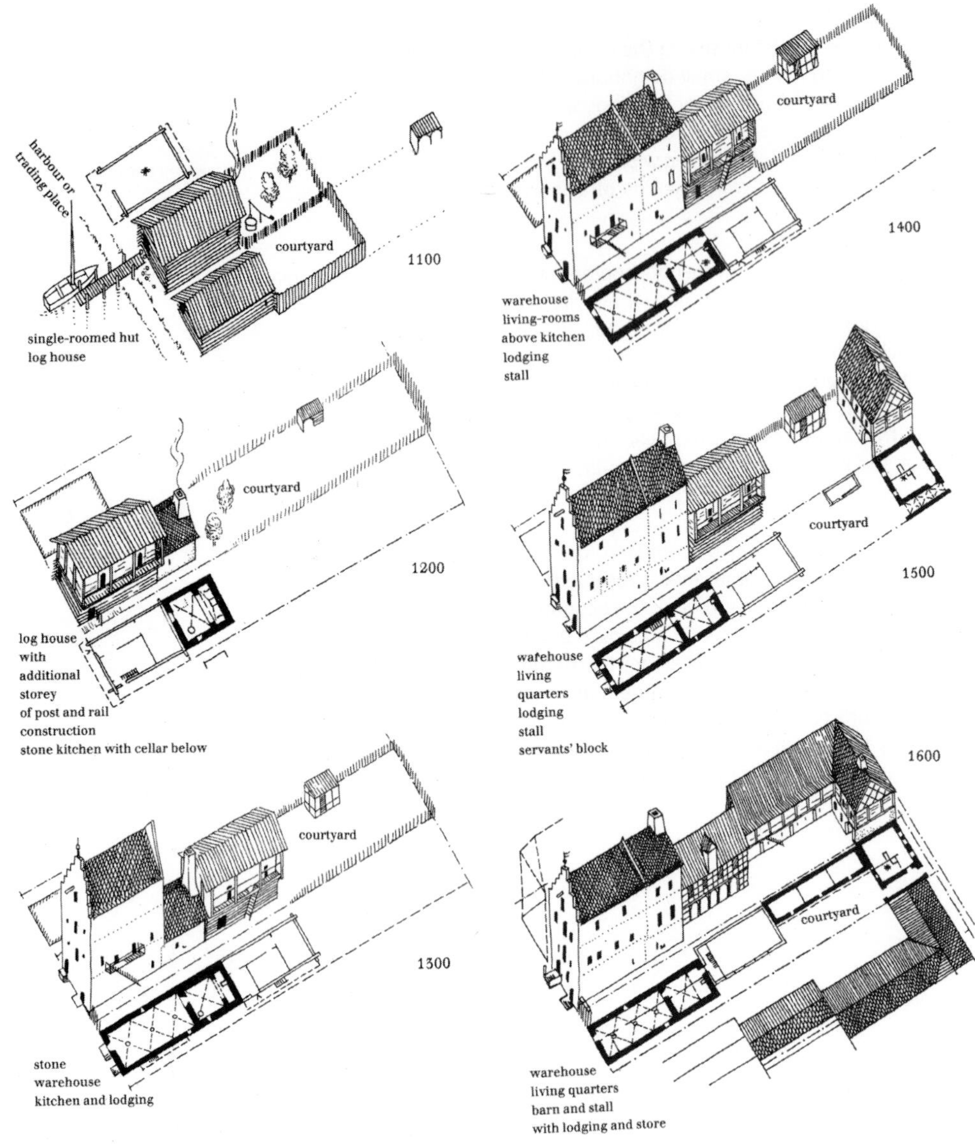

3.01 Hypothetical evolution of typical northern European merchant's house.
From Büttner and Meissner, *Town Houses of Europe.*

3

MERCHANTS' HOUSES OF NORTHERN AND WESTERN EUROPE

Stairs led to the third floor, where the consul and his family had their quarters, but there was also another row of rooms along the left side of the hallway. The gentlemen smoked their cigars as they strode down the wide staircase with its openwork railing of white-enameled wood. The consul halted on the landing.

"There are three more rooms on the mezzanine," he explained, "a breakfast room, my parents' bedroom, and another room, open to the garden, though it's not used much. A little hallway serves as a corridor along one side. But – straight ahead! – as you can see, the delivery wagons can drive right through the passageway and on across to Becker Grube, at the rear of the property."

The wide, echoing passageway below was paved with large, square stones. There were offices both to one side of the vestibule door and at the far end of the passage, whereas the doors to the cellar and the kitchen, still fragrant with tart shallot sauce, were to the left of the stairway. On the far side, somewhat higher up, newly painted wooden galleries jutted from the wall: the servants' quarters, the only access a flight of open stairs rising from the passageway. Next to the stairs stood a couple of enormous old cupboards and a carved chest.[1]

(Thomas Mann, *Buddenbrooks*)

Many cities of northern Europe – from France through the Low Countries to the Baltic, and including the southern cities of Scandinavia – have been critical to world trade, and their shop/houses are central to the topic of this book. Although buildings differ from region to region, they share various characteristics, including locations on long lots perpendicular to streets or canals, the use of upstairs floors for warehouse storage and the use of the lower floors for both dwelling and commercial purposes.

The medieval urban merchant's shop/house has one origin in the linear form brought about by timber-frame construction. The width of traditional timber-framed buildings arises from the span of wooden beams, and its length comes from repetition of structural/spatial bays. In Germany, archaeological evidence dates such buildings back to the seventh century,[2] and there was continuous development of the type since then. In this development, rural types were transformed into urban ones, and farm functions were replaced by craft, manufacture and trade (Fig. 3.01).

The use of the timber frame emerged with rural buildings, and indeed the farmhouse, including the accommodation of food processing, may be seen as the "original" shop/house. It is a building in which family life and productive work are strongly intertwined; and in which, even if food is processed for the use of the family itself, the integration of work and domestic life is important to the economic bottom line. There is, furthermore, not a clear conceptual boundary between the farmhouse and the urban house. This ambiguity came from occupational fluidity that was necessary to make ends meet. Rural people

[1] Mann, *Buddenbrooks*, 34. *Buddenbrooks* was originally published in German in 1901. The novel is set in the city of Lübeck, and describes several generations of a mercantile family.
[2] Chapelot and Fossier, *Village and House*, 72–81.

3.02 *Gehoeft*. Illustration from early twentieth-century children's book showing multiple domestic and farm activities in the courtyard.
From Wallenstein, *Stadt, Wald, Hochgebirge, Bauernhof*, n.p.

engaged in artisan trades other than farming, and people maintained kitchen gardens and animals even after they moved to the city.[3]

A rural/village type, the *gehoeft*, found in southern Germany, is a building complex organized around one or more courtyards, and may include dwelling rooms, workshops, spaces for farm functions and spaces for animals. While the *gehoeft* may have arisen partly because of south German inheritance practices, in which properties are divided among the various sons, it shares characteristics with other house/barn clusters and buildings that are found throughout central and northern Europe – and the buildings that emerged out of them, in North America (Figs. 3.02 and 3.03).[4]

In the centuries preceding medieval urbanization, linear farmhouses based on the repetition of structural bays became more elaborated in plan and differentiated in function. Single-room structures housing people and animals transformed into multi-roomed buildings for people alone. In these houses, the arrangement of rooms was still generally linear, partly because it was easier to build a partition wall directly under a transverse beam or truss, than perpendicular to it. The timber-framed farmhouse in England, the *laenge* in Denmark and the early canal house in Amsterdam are all examples of this linear form.

When urbanization began to increase, this structural idea fit well with requirements of increasing density. Medieval towns and cities developed long and narrow burgage plots – the result of a common desire by traders and merchants to be in the same place near the town center. This led naturally to the use of a building plan that was itself long and narrow, and the timber frame was a perfect fit.

[3] During medieval times Lübeck, along with many other cities, grew much of its food within the city walls.
[4] Thanks to Esther Hagenlocher for describing this building type to me.

3.03 Pelster house barn, Franklin County, Missouri. This building was built between 1860 and 1864 by a German immigrant.
From Library of Congress/Historic American Buildings Survey.

The construction and plan of the timber-framed building evolved to meet urban conditions. Wooden houses, with roof ridges parallel to the street, originally stood freely on their lots, with land around them continuing to be used for agricultural purposes. As agricultural pursuits gradually declined in importance, and urban occupations gained, houses began to take up the full width of their lots. Masonry party walls replaced wood, and gables turned to face the street, allowing for their future elaboration to show wealth and status. The hall of the farmhouse became the center of a unit of urban economic production. Since the short front façade was the only part of the house exposed to the public, it had the primary role in expressing the importance of the house or wealth of its family and did so largely through the elaboration of the gable. It also had to be the commercial frontage of the building, particularly after the development of the glazed shopfront.

A building type that makes direct and obvious use of the repeating timber bay, flexible in the way it transforms over time to incorporate businesses and dwellings, is the Danish *laenge*, appearing largely in smaller towns and cities (Fig. 3.04). Unlike other urban buildings that depend on the narrowness of the street frontage, the *laenge* is often oriented parallel to the street. This allows good light to all the rooms; it allows for sufficient frontage when there is a desire for more of the ground floor to be used for commercial space; and the structural repetition makes it flexible, allowing for easy combination with adjacent buildings or for internal reconfigurations (Fig. 3.05).[5]

The shallow depth of the *laenge* allows, in some houses, for an entry hall to pass through the building from front to back, permitting access to a back garden or outdoor work space. When the building is divided into a front and back zone, the front room may be larger, allowing it to be more flexibly used

[5] The best source in English on the Danish *laenge* is Orum-Nielsen, *Dwelling*.

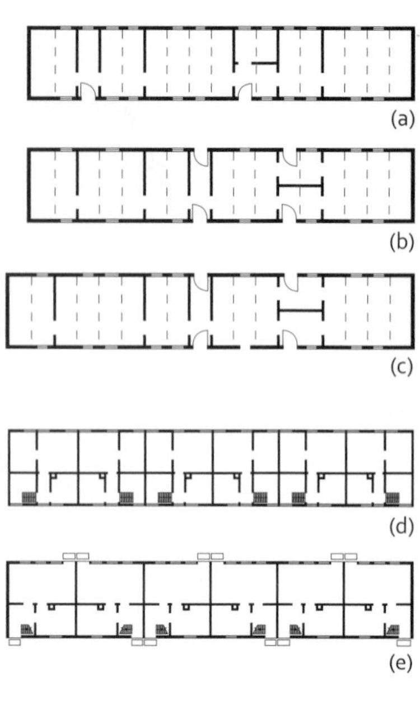

3.04 Building based on *laenge* typology, Helsingor, Denmark.
Photograph by author.

3.05 Plans of *laenge*. The top three drawings show the various ways that the basic units may be combined. The bottom two drawings are of Filevaerket (file works) at Raadvad. In each unit of this building, an entry hall allows access to a downstairs workshop or to an upstairs dwelling. The flexibility of the *laenge* type allowed the workshops to be turned into dwellings. The position of the stair allows for the two levels of the building to be connected to each other or used independently.
Drawings by Will Krzymowski after originals in Orum-Nielson, *Dwelling*.

for a shop. *Laenge* line the streets of many traditional Danish towns, containing shops and dwellings equally easily.

The Amsterdam canal house

It was, however, in the large trading cities of northern Europe that the narrow-fronted urban shop/house, that emerged partly out of rural precedents, was developed to its full potential (Figs. 3.06 and 3.07). During the seventeenth century, the growth of the Dutch empire led to the rapid development of Amsterdam as an important mercantile and financial center. A major new extension to Amsterdam's canal system was built, leading to the three "ring canals" of Keizersgracht, Herengracht and Prinsengracht. They were originally planned as major commercial arteries, to be lined by buildings containing the

3.06 House with shop outside Amsterdam. *Rembrandt, Two Cottages, ca. 1636.*
The Metropolitan Museum of Art, Robert Lehman Collection, 1975 (1975.1.801).

3.07 Buildings in the small town of Oudewater, shown on the right and painted by Willem Koekkoek in about 1867, have similar organizational and stylistic features as larger houses in Amsterdam.
© The National Gallery, London.

dwellings and businesses of merchants, shippers and manufacturers. By today's standards most of these buildings were small. But what we now know to be the pleasant, tree-lined canals of Amsterdam, lined with dwellings and not too many businesses, was, in the seventeenth century, an active extension of the port, with goods being loaded and unloaded and the canal edges acting as wharves for adjacent buildings.[6]

There was some distinction in land use within the area of the canal extensions. Obnoxious industries and shop/houses of small-scale artisans were in the Jordaan, an early urban extension, and the Prinsengracht had a higher per-

6 Komossa et al., *Atlas of the Dutch Urban Block*, 17–24.

3.08 Plans of seventeenth-century Amsterdam houses. In one (a) it is necessary to cross the *voorhuis* (entrance room or shop) to access the stair, and in the other (b) the stair comes forward to the façade.
Drawn by Will Krzymowski after original in Meischke et al., *Huizen in Nederland*.

3.09 Houses in Amsterdam, showing large windows, and one door leading into the *voorhuis*, and one leading to the stair.
Photograph by author.

centage of buildings that were only warehouses without residential functions than the two inner canals. But there was commerce throughout the city, and many houses maintained their function as warehouses, even behind façades that took on the latest architectural styles, designed by stonemason/ architect Philips Vingboons and his contemporaries.

The houses had one principal frontage, along the canal or street, and almost always had plan dimensions that were shorter along the canal, or at least no wider along the canal than perpendicular to it. The earliest versions of the buildings were direct descendants of the timber-framed rural buildings found all over northern Europe. Each house had its own complete timber frame, and there likely would have been a small space between adjacent houses. But as more brick construction was introduced to the city and party walls were built, the use of structural wood began to be restricted to transverse spans and roofs.[7]

Early houses had a door entering into an entrance room known as the *voorhuis*, that in turn led to a back room and a stair (Fig.3.08a). This room was a place to receive guests or conduct business. Architecturally, there was no difference between houses in which business was conducted and houses in which it was not – other evidence must be used to make that determination. The cellar and area under the roof would have been used for storage, sometimes with a separate entrance from the outside, and people ate and slept on the ground and first floors.

A variation of this plan, built originally or as a later transformation, has a stair just inside the entrance leading to upper floors (Fig. 3.08b). If there was an interior door just inside the main entry, leading to the *voorhuis*, this stair would have given flexibility to the house and allowed it to be used either entirely by the family or by a separate family or business upstairs.

Large, multi-pane windows into the *voorhuis* (Fig. 3.09), allowed light penetration deep into the house, including to a balcony/mezzanine floor that often overlooked the *voorhuis*. These windows (shown from the interior in several of Vermeer's paintings set in Delft) were the same whether or not the *voorhuis* had a commercial function.

As the wealth of merchants increased during the prosperous seventeenth century, there was a gradual transformation of canal-house architecture. Architects designed houses with elaborate façades, and larger house plans incorporated corridors and formal symmetries. Over the decades, as buildings were replaced or rebuilt, they incorporated current architectural styles, and the extant houses in Amsterdam's canal district are of varied styles and periods.

Building transformations also existed that could not been seen from the street. For example, there were smaller buildings in the passage that, on long narrow lots, led to the back of the lot, and the subdivision of some houses into apartments. Early houses were reconstructed, with the stair at the front, to allow independent access to upper floors, and to allow the shop to be rented independently of the rest of the house. And, particularly in the streets perpendicular to the canals that led to the city center, there was also the gradual transformation of façades, beginning in the nineteenth century, to install large plate-glass windows in shops (Figs. 3.10 and 3.11).

Today, there is little mercantile activity on the principal ring canals. There are some businesses at the intersections with cross streets and minor canals, along

[7] Some of the most detailed work on seventeenth-century canal houses has been done by the Hendrik de Keyser Foundation. Their Amsterdam work is published in Meischke et al., *Huizen in Nederland*. I am grateful to Paul Rosenberg, architectural historian with the Hendrick de Keyser Foundation, for explaining the buildings and their history to me.

3.10 Corner house in Amsterdam showing shopfront as full width of façade.
Photograph by author.

3.11 Street in the Jewish quarter of Amsterdam.
Collection Jewish Historical Museum, Amsterdam (Collection J. van Velzen).

with banks, public institutions and offices. The canals have a strong residential character. The boats that ply them are almost all pleasure boats of one kind or another, and most commercial activity near the three canals is on perpendicular streets. This functional transformation took place without an essential architectural transformation of the buildings or the street pattern. The flexibility was possible, over almost four hundred years, because of the narrow, party-wall building type, and a street pattern that incorporates a variety of street widths within a clear, connected geometry.

The Lübeck merchant's house

In larger houses in other cities, the party-wall arrangement, along with the narrow frontage, forced the development of a plan incorporating a strong public-to-private gradient beginning at the street. In the Lübeck house, the public realm effectively continues from the street deep into the house, in an arrangement that is considerably more complex than that of the Amsterdam canal house. This arrangement traditionally put commerce and domestic life – including cooking – into a large room that faced the back garden rather than the street.

Near the Baltic Sea, Lübeck, one of the great cities of the Hanseatic League, was an important port of trans-shipment of grain, salt, fish and wood – trade that kept the city prosperous for several hundred years. Considered an archetypal medieval city, Lübeck appears often in histories of urban form. The historic core is surrounded by water, including a man-made channel dug to make shipping easier and to provide more docks, which line the waterfront. The city plan features a cathedral and cathedral square, a town hall and market square, several main streets, several churches other than the cathedral and a system of streets that lead from the city center to the water. Many of these streets are still lined with merchants' houses. Although about one-third of the historic core of the city was destroyed by Allied bombing in World War II, many houses remained, and many of those have since been documented and restored.

Lübeck was the birthplace of the German writer Thomas Mann, whose great novel *Buddenbrooks: The Decline of a Family* takes place in a fictional but accurately described Lübeck merchant's house. The novel describes how mid-nineteenth-century life was given expression by the house, and how the house acted as a symbol for the family itself. Scholars in Lübeck have examined the relationship between *Buddenbrooks* and the houses Mann lived in, and although Mann exercised artistic license with details, there is enough accuracy in the novel for it to act as a guidebook to Lübeck houses of that period (Fig. 3.12 and Plate 30).[8]

One house, at Mengstrasse 31, is typical in its architecture, and in the way domestic life and economic life were intertwined. The history of the house extends back as least as far as the twelfth century: archaeological evidence indicates two small, wooden houses on the site, with roughly square plans, set back from the street. Hazelnuts found in the yard suggest that it may have been a place for animals. The present house was built in 1612, and it was owned successively by a writer, a merchant and finally by a family of prominent glass painters. (The present owner, an architect, who is a member of the family of glass painters, restored the house following the final closing of the glass shop in 1995.) When the house was used by glass painters, different rooms were used for different purposes connected with the business: for showing

[8] Some of the insights on Lübeck houses come from conversations with architectural historian Michael Scheftel in Lübeck, December 2004.

3.12 Lübeck merchants' houses.
Photograph by author.

glass to clients, for painting glass, for proofing colors, for making lead frames, for baking stained glass, for puttying glass into frames. The rooms for painting and proofing needed special light, and were located adjacent to the back garden.

This was typical of houses belonging to wholesale merchants, artists, craftsmen and professionals located in districts away from the main marketplace. These houses were not built for everyday retail trade, which was located in and around the marketplace. In that location, temporary stalls sheltered people such as vegetable sellers, and permanent buildings ringing the perimeter housed jewelers and dealers in fine goods. In a clear zoning of businesses, wholesalers were located in streets that led up from the water's edge, and retailers were at the city center.

The houses have four or five stories plus a cellar (Fig. 3.13). The principal room is the *diele*, a large hall occupying the entire width of the ground floor, as high

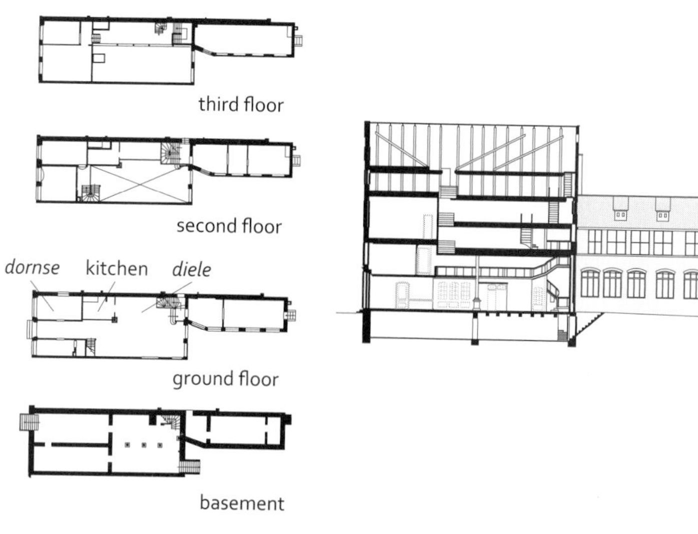

3.13 Plans and section of typical Lübeck house. Drawings by Will Krzymowski.

3.14 The *braudiele*, or brew hall, in a Lübeck house. Painting by Hermann Linde. © Museen für Kunst und Kultergeschichte der Hansestadt Lübeck.

as sixteen feet tall. The *diele* housed multiple activities of business and family life. In early houses with an open fireplace, and later with a glassed-in kitchen, it was the place of cooking, heat and the comings and goings of tradespeople and customers (Fig. 3.14; Plates 31 and 32).

An entrance hall from the street led into the *diele*, after passing by the *dornse*, a private room for the head of the household. In contrast to the openness of the kitchen and *diele*, the *dornse* was an office and place from which the householder could see the street, the entrance, as well as the *diele*, while remaining private. In the *dornse* at Mengstrasse 31, customers looked at samples of glass, accounts were kept and orders were written.

A glass-enclosed kitchen, adjacent to the *diele*, allowed light into the kitchen. It also allowed surveillance of the kitchen staff and visibility from the kitchen to the table at the end of the *diele*, and helped the fireplace maintain its role as the principal source of heat for the *diele*.

Beyond the kitchen was a stair leading to a balcony overlooking the *diele*, providing access to rooms above the *dornse* and above a rear extension, in which people slept. Depending on the business, upstairs rooms were used for storage and workshops, and the cellar was likewise used for storage. Access to the upper floors was by a small circular staircase; goods were hoisted up through openings in the floor in the interior of the house, using a large hoist-wheel just below the roof.

A large window onto the back garden was the principal source of light for the *diele*, and the place for a large table. House reconstructions during the eighteenth century placed that window symmetrically in the wall, giving a symmetry to the rear façade, and transformed the gardens into places of pleasure rather than only service.

Interior windows visually connected rooms and helped bring light into them. These included a window between the *dornse* and the entrance hall so that visitors could be seen, and windows between the kitchen and the *diele*. The balcony in the *diele* was open to below or glazed, and interior windows from rooms off the balcony looked down into the *diele*. Even after the eighteenth century, as there began to be greater separations of use between rooms, and a spreading-out of domestic functions from the ground floor, there remained a desire to maintain visual connections between the rooms.

These connections, that put the *diele* – the place where commercial and family life were intermixed – at the symbolic and functional center of the house, extended to the public realm as well. The *diele* acted as an extension of the street and people could enter it without knocking at the front door and would be easily seen by people in the *diele* or in adjacent rooms. In this sense, the *diele* and the passage leading to it were similar to the passage in the Japanese *machiya*. In both cases, the public realm extended into the building, allowing commercial activity to maintain a strong connection to the street.

Until the eighteenth century, domestic life happened only on the ground floor, among the family business, and the upper rooms were used for storage of goods. During the eighteenth century, the floor above the ground floor began to be used for domestic uses. Sitting and sleeping rooms were placed there, and with them, wooden stairs leading to a gallery overlooking the *diele* supplemented the small circular stair that allowed access to the upper, storage floors. At Mengstrasse 31, the back rooms on the ground floor changed from living rooms to working rooms in about 1840, when some dwelling functions moved upstairs.[9]

Although businesses did not leave houses entirely, the eighteenth-century transformation of the Lübeck house happened during a time when many businesses were expanding and establishing other locations for some of their operations. This was similar to other cities, where new middle-class sensibilities accompanied a growing fragmentation of urban functions.

The basic typology of *diele*-as-center was also present in smaller artisans' houses (Figs. 3.15 and 3.16).[10] These artisans included people who worked away from home, such as ship carpenters, and those who worked at home in minor crafts. The houses were developed as investments on the rear properties of larger houses, forming small lanes (*gange*), entered from major streets via passages beside the larger houses. Although these tiny houses may have had a ground area of only around 200 square feet, they included the elements of the much larger house: a *dornse*; a *diele*, which because the house is so small is smaller than the *dornse*; a large fireplace in the part of the *diele* that is at the back of the house; and a stair, also in the *diele*. These buildings and their narrow back lanes helped form a complex and hierarchical urban morphology. They helped maintain a mixture of social classes on the same block, and provided a place for independent artisans who were not necessarily employees

[9] Much of the evidence on use of the rooms comes from probate inventories.

[10] Michael Scheftel has done an extensive study of this. See his *Gange, Buden und Wohnkeller in Lübeck*.

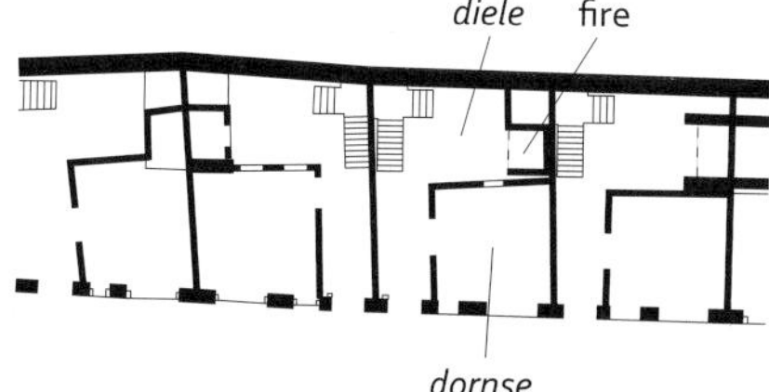

3.15 Plan of *gange*.
From Scheftel, *Gange, Buden und Wohnkeller in Lübeck*. Drawing by Will Krzymowski.

3.16 *Gange*, rear houses, in Lübeck.
Photograph by author.

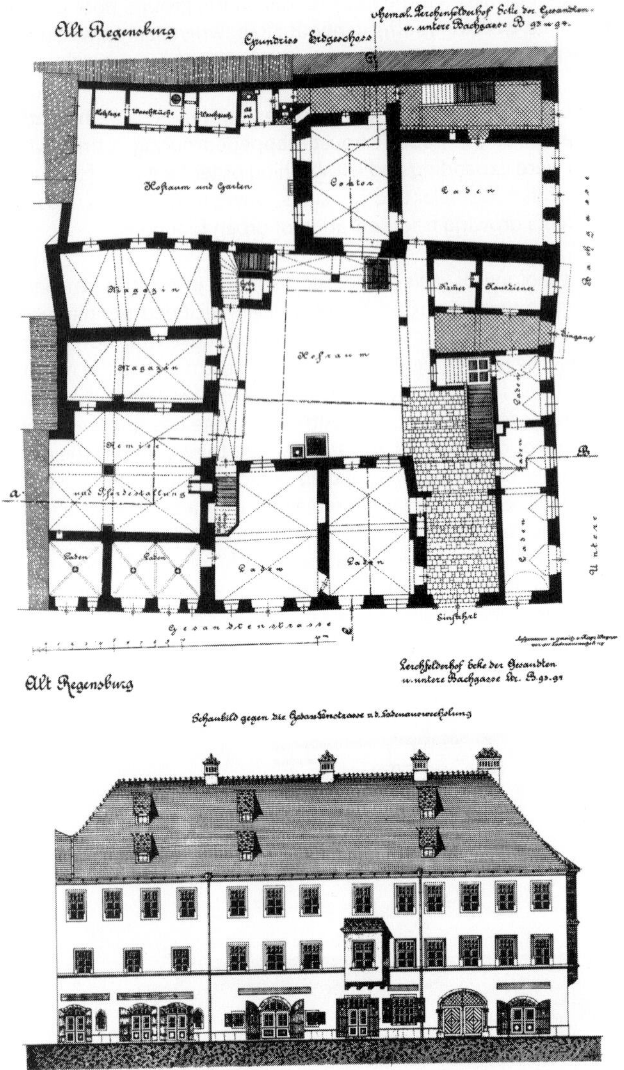

3.17 Ground-floor plan and elevation of Regensburg courtyard house with shops on street.
From Strobel, *Bürgerhaus in Regensburg*.

of the merchants who occupied the front houses. Many of these *gange* survive, and contain houses, which, like mews houses in London, are highly prized.

As many examples have so far made clear, the shop/house is not a single building type but rather a social/economic idea manifested in a wide variety of types. This variation may exist within a particular city or a relatively small geographic region. There is a large difference, for example, between northern and southern Germany – a difference that partly emerges from a different history.

Regensburg, in an area of southern Germany that was colonized by the Romans during the time of the Roman Empire, has houses that are organized around courtyards, as opposed to Lübeck where linear buildings have no courtyards but gardens at the rear. Large Regensburg houses have a variety of ground-floor rooms that serve the business, including stores facing the street and storerooms on the interior, with dwelling rooms beginning on the first floor. In the case of one of these buildings, the wide entranceway leads to a place where one might either go up the stair to the first floor, or enter the courtyard (*hof*) underneath an arcade (Fig. 3.17). In this case, one may access the private quarters with only a glance at the business activity on the ground floor, and bypass that activity almost entirely. In this respect, the Regensburg house is similar to the complex courtyard house near the Campo de' Fiori in Rome that was described in the previous chapter.

Paris and the commercial/residential building

So far, this chapter has dealt mostly with family shop/houses rather than multi-family buildings with independent shops. During the nineteenth century, as urbanization increased and the structure of industry changed, residential location also changed. More workers in cities, now company employees rather than apprentices, were no longer living in family houses but instead on their own, sometimes with their families. New building types emerged that were initially transformations of single-family houses, containing dwellings for multiple families and with commercial space at the ground floor. Cities such as Paris, Berlin and Vienna began to be characterized by streets and districts full of such buildings.

The typical Parisian apartment building of the nineteenth century was organized around or in front of a courtyard, and entered from the street through a portal that was typically closed at night. Shops were located on either side of this portal. Inside the portal, and adjacent to it, was a stair that led to apartments on upper floors, arranged with the highest-rent apartments lower down, and cheaper accommodations higher up. A person of means would live on the first floor. "He pays perhaps 300 [pounds] per annum for the rent of his share of the edifice. Above him are tenants possessed of different gradations of fashion or opulence, to the sixth or seventh floor, which are inhabited by the milkman, the cobbler or the scavenger, and who pay only a rent of ten pounds."[11] This was the modern equivalent of the old medieval tenement – the buildings not only mixed uses, but mixed classes.

These buildings have multiple origins. One is the vertically zoned medieval building that took full advantage of available land on the site. In the eighteenth century, buildings that maintained the street wall existed in the old medieval core of Paris as well as in the immediately adjacent *faubourgs* (suburbs) (Figs. 3.18, 3.19 and Plate 49). In these suburbs, buildings might have been originally built to only three stories, but then added to as density and land values increased. The process of urban growth was one in which increases of density moved outward from the center – so that many neighborhoods that are now part of "central Paris" were once on the outskirts, and where the pressure on principal streets forced new development on adjacent streets.

In Paris, the mezzanine with the shopkeeper's dwelling was not as strong a tradition as in Rome. More common was the dwelling behind the shop, when the shop was not directly connected to the dwelling at all,[12] even in buildings that had multiple stories of apartments above. Adjacency to the street was critical, but functions such as storage were taken care of in the middle of blocks.

[11] From Edward Planta, *Pictures of Paris, The Stranger's Guide*, quoted in Tindall, *Footprints in Paris*, 51.
[12] Loyer, *Paris Nineteenth Century*, 92.

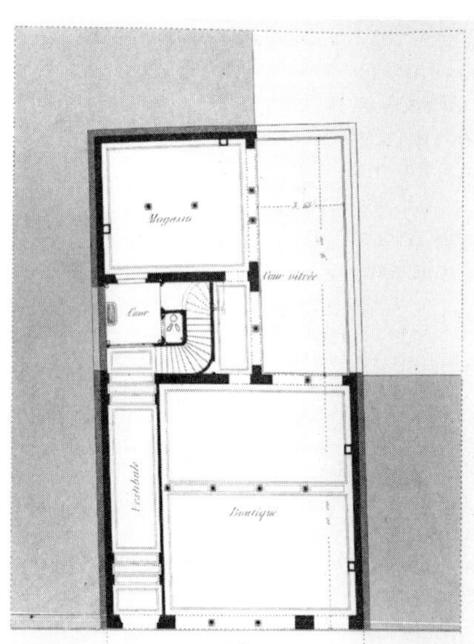

Plan du Rez-de-Chaussée.

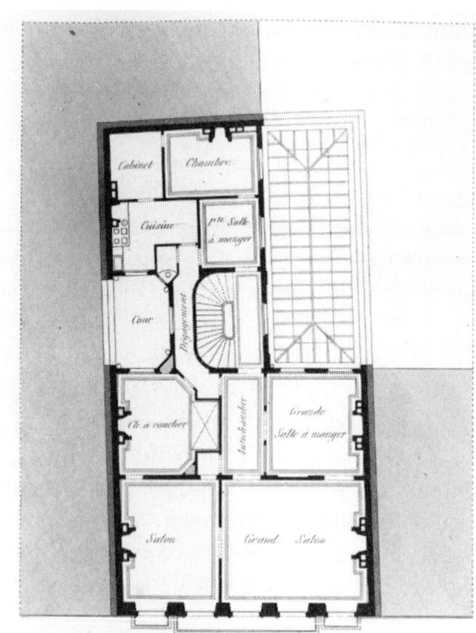

Plan du 1.er Etage.

MAISON BOULEVARD DE SÉBASTOPOL.

par Cusin, Architecte

ECHELLE DE 0,005 P. M.

The second origin was the larger house, often found in the *faubourgs* farther out that were originally settled by people who wanted to be away from the density and noise of the center. These buildings were set back from the street, forming an entry courtyard in front and a garden at the back. The entry courtyard had a wall between it and the street, for privacy. As density and land values increased, buildings were erected at the street edge, replacing the wall and reducing the size of the courtyard, and then connecting to the original building. This arrangement allowed the site to be densely built up while still providing daylight to dwelling rooms – and providing a hybrid between courtyard buildings and vertically organized tenements.

Nineteenth- and early-twentieth-century cities such as Paris, Vienna and Berlin were characterized not only by aesthetically pleasing streetscapes. They also had a diverse social mix that came from the proximity of businesses at the streets, different kinds of dwellings and businesses within buildings, at different floors, that did not require direct street frontage. This rich mixture happened within architecturally solid buildings, with strong spatial order and often with fine details that adapted to their uniquely urban social demands.

3.18 (left, top) Paris.
Photograph by Aluin Comiter.

3.19 (left, bottom) Ground- and first-floor plans of a small building on Blvd de Sébastopol, Paris, designed by Cusin. The ground-floor plan, on the left, shows a shop connected to a storeroom in the back, and a separate passage that leads to a stair that serves upper-floor apartments.
From Calliat, *Parallele des Maisons de Paris*, 1857.

4.01 Butcher Row, Exeter.
Courtesy of Devon County Council.

4

FROM LONDON TO MAIN STREET

Our Little Store rose right up from the sidewalk; standing in a street of family houses, it alone hadn't any yard in front, any tree or flowerbed. It was a plain frame building covered over with brick. Above the door, a little railed porch ran across on an upstairs level and four windows with shades were looking out. But I didn't catch on to those . . . Of course, all the time, the Sessions had been living right overhead there, in the upstairs rooms behind the little railed porch and the shaded windows; but I think we children never thought of that.[1]

(Eudora Welty, "The Little Store")

North American shop/house types include the two-story brick building with an apartment above on old commercial streets of Philadelphia or in the outer boroughs of New York, the New York apartment building with shops below, the San Francisco corner Victorian with a grocery store built in, the semi-detached house in an immigrant neighborhood, which has had its ground floor converted to a shop, and many others.

Few buildings can trace their ancestry to only one place or culture, as different attributes of buildings – plan, construction, ornamental motifs – may have different origins. But many urban buildings of North America can trace much of their lineage to England – and English urban buildings have some of their own roots in buildings of the countryside.

The English urban shop/house has its origin in the farmhouse, itself a descendant of the longhouse that existed all over northern Europe. A linear building that originally housed people and animals, the longhouse evolved into a more complex building after the animals were moved into buildings of their own. This developed into the linear "hall-and-parlor" plan, with different variations of entrance and position of fire somewhat dependent on geographic location. Sometimes rooms were added to the two-unit plan, at the ends or in transverse wings. The basic linear configuration remained, however, even when incorporated into a more complex plan.

Initially, buildings in towns were variations of village houses, with variations of the same linear plans[2] – and it was easy for a shop to occupy one of the rooms (Fig. 4.02). In low-density towns, the two-unit plan maintained a parallel relationship to the street, with one of the two rooms used for the shop and the other the parlor, or with small shops added along the length. In denser places, the linear plan turned to become perpendicular to the street. Here, only one room fronted the street, and this was naturally the shop.[3] In one variation, shops were added – either during initial construction but more likely later – to the side of the house.[4]

[1] Welty, "Little Store," 822, 825.
[2] For an accessible and illustrated account of how construction types and details in English vernacular architecture diffused, see Brunskill, *Illustrated Handbook of Vernacular Architecture*. Particularly interesting are Brunskill's charts showing how large houses, small houses and cottages underwent transformations of different kinds at different times; this may be extended to the difference between city and country.
[3] Platt, *English Medieval Town*, 67.
[4] Pounds, *Culture of the English People*, 362.

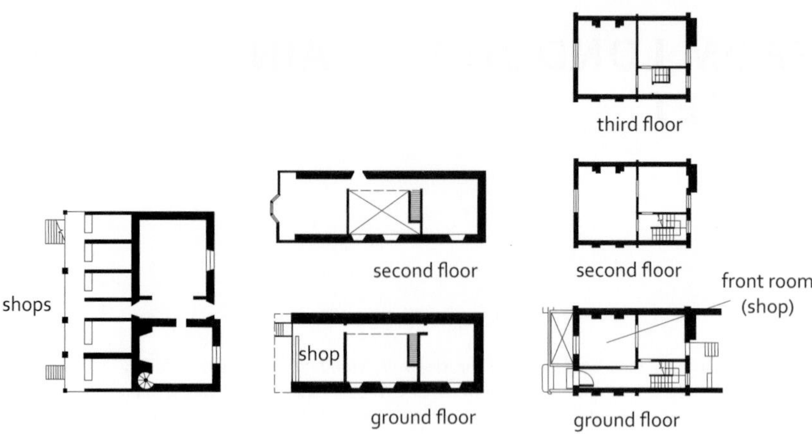

4.02 Sequence of drawings showing the possible evolution of the English terraced house from the medieval urban building. In each case the street is to the left. In the first house, the main rooms are in a line parallel to the street, and small shops front the house. In the second house, the main rooms have been turned so they are perpendicular to the street. The plan suggests a side passage. The third house is a typical terraced house.
Drawn by Will Krzymowski.

This is supported by archaeological evidence that indicates houses in towns in which the lower floor was used as a shop, and the flexible use of other rooms. In a row of three houses in Southampton, "none show any evidence that the ground floor had other purposes than warehousing and display."[5] This is supported by the fact that the stairs to upper floors were external. Some building contracts specified that the lower floors of houses were to be shops;[6] there is evidence of sixteenth-century rural houses with shops, often as part of businesses related to the textile trade;[7] and probate records also indicate that houses contained shops. In post-medieval buildings in London, there is evidence of people having slept in all rooms of the house, including the shop.[8]

Early retailing was centered around the marketplace, which consisted partly of stalls occupied on market days for the sales of farm produce, and partly by permanent shops, often dealing in more expensive goods or staples that did not deteriorate over time. Retail shops were largely along the principal street and adjoining streets, and included front rooms of dwellings as well as sheds and more temporary structures that might have been attached to the fronts of dwellings.

How commerce was accommodated varied with the kind of business. Sales naturally took place in a ground-floor front room, but if manufacture happened in the house it took place either in that room – if the amount of space required was not great – or in another room, or even another building on the lot. Storage could be in a different room or in a loft above the shop.[9] The front room might have been modified, with the addition of a shutter that could be folded down, or with a simple stall erected outside. But these functions and modifications were in a building that was still essentially a dwelling house.[10]

Access to the back room(s) was either through the shop, or by means of a side passage, which developed to allow access to the back room(s) without going

5 Platt, *English Medieval Town*, 70.
6 Salzman, *Building in England*, 483, 554, 598.
7 Johnson, *Housing Culture*, 125–126.
8 See, for example, Brown, "Continuity and Change," 578–580.
9 Portman, *Exeter Houses 1400–1700*, 33.
10 Pounds, *Culture of the English People*, 363.

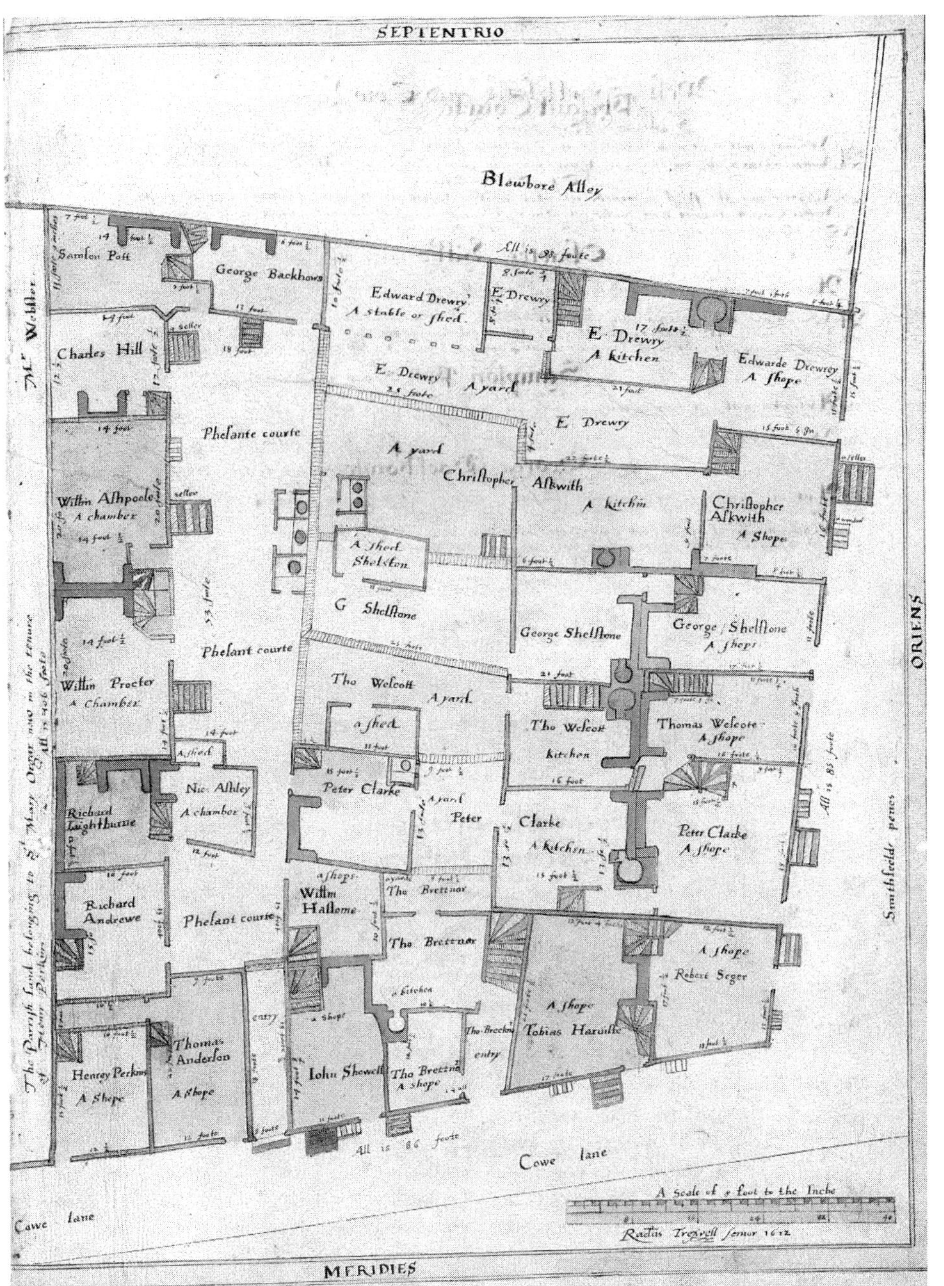

4.03 Map of London houses by Ralph Treswell.
Reproduced by kind permission of Christ's Hospital.

through the front room/shop. A more complex organization, and the addition of rooms above, was allowed by the elimination of the high central hall that was open to the roof. This permitted a greater density of rooms on a particular site. Medieval and post-medieval towns became very dense with great competition for frontage; in some cases plots may have been as small as six feet wide.[11]

In London, these features are shown in detail with a remarkable series of ground plans. In the decades around 1600, Ralph Treswell carried out surveys of houses owned by various London institutions. These institutions sublet land for building – a process that characterized London development for several centuries – and carried out periodic surveys of their properties.

Treswell's maps provide a detailed description of early party-wall houses in London (Fig. 4.03 and Plate 12). Houses often contained a front room, which Treswell characterized as a shop and through which one had to pass to get to the rest of the house. On some streets, virtually all front rooms were indicated as shops, and on others only some of the rooms were so indicated. Although Treswell only drew the ground-floor plans, the existence of stairs, along with other documentary evidence, makes it clear that many buildings had three or more floors. In some cases the shop was entered from the street and in some cases from a passage; sometimes the room immediately behind the shop acted as a warehouse. Often the kitchen was also on the ground floor.

Terraced (row) houses, designed and built as identical party-wall units, already existed in England at this time; they were sometimes built as almshouses or as workers' housing. The buildings measured by Treswell are also antecedents to the terraced house that became the most common building type in urban England during the eighteenth and nineteenth centuries.

The buildings show the essentials of the party-wall house organization, in which a shop may easily be incorporated into the front room. This building could be built as a single unit in small groups, or as long terraces (Fig. 4.04). It could have shops initially built in, or could have front rooms transformed later.[12] And if the building were built with a front garden adjacent to the street, it could be extended forward with a one-story shop if the street developed into a commercial street.

The details of house plans varied: by width, stair (sometimes parallel to the party wall and sometimes perpendicular) and by section (when the stair was perpendicular to the party wall, the front and back parts of the house were sometimes separated by half a floor level, so that it took two half-runs of the stair to go up a whole floor level). Styles varied and changed over time. But virtually all these variations maintained the basic terraced-house configuration, within which the ground-floor front room could easily be a shop. Indeed, any room could easily take on a productive or commercial function, since the narrow circulation zone that included the stair made any room easily accessible without disturbing the activities in other rooms.

London, of course, responded to urbanization differently from cities such as Paris or Berlin in which thousands of multi-family apartment houses were built in the nineteenth and twentieth centuries. In London, the individual family house was always the norm, so even districts close to the centre like Mayfair (for the rich) or the East End (for the poor and working classes) were characterized by individual terraced houses.

[11] Aston and Bond, *The Landscape of Towns*, 99. See also Conzen, *Alnwick, Northumberland*, 27–28.

[12] See, for example, Guillery, *The Small English House*, 64. Guillery writes that it would be "anachronistic to isolate the shophouse [sic] as an architectural type," because of the frequent transformations that were undertaken in houses.

4.04 Early wooden terraced houses with shops in London.
Reproduced by permission of English Heritage/National Monuments Record.

Tens of thousands of these buildings were built during the eighteenth, nineteenth and early twentieth centuries, helping to form the present character of London (Fig. 4.05 and Plate 18).[13] Most were constructed by little-known builders, but even in the eighteenth century there was architects' involvement. George Dance the Younger designed numerous shop/houses that included both the side passage arrangement, and arrangements where it was necessary to pass through the shop to get to the stair.[14]

Terraced houses contained thousands of family-owned businesses located in their front rooms or ground floors. An examination of a 1925 London city directory[15] yielded the following list of businesses located in houses for just one section of the south side of Barnsbury Street in Islington (north London):

Barnsbury Street, Islington

3 Charles Hungate, confectioner

5 Thomas Richards, dairy

7 John Ford, picture frame maker

41 Lawrence Webster, credit draper

British Syphon Manufacturing Co., Ltd

. . . here is Milner Square . . .

"Masta" Patent Pipe Co. (Milner works)

Richford & Co., ironfounders (Milner works)

[13] The best book on this house type is Muthesius, *English Terraced House*. See also Summerson, *Georgian London*; Cruickshank and Wyld, *London: Art of Georgian Building*; and Rasmussen, *London: Unique City*. The various volumes of the *Survey of London* illustrate variations through the city. For accounts of house and property development in London see Olsen, *Town Planning in London*, Dyos, *Victorian Suburb*, and Clarke, *Building Capitalism*.

[14] Kalman, "Architecture of Mercantilism." In Fritz and Williams, *Triumph of Culture*, 72–82.

[15] Kelly's Directories, *Post Office London Directory*, 1925. This directory was accessed in 2006 at the Guildhall Library, London.

4.05 Small London terraced houses with shop conversions.
Photograph by author.

45 Giovanna Grassi, confectioner

47 William Frankham, grocer

Post, Money Order and Telephone Call Office and Savings Bank

49 Thomas Profit, chemist

51 James Duggen, furniture dealer

53 Edward Wood, butcher

. . . here is Liverpool Road . . .

57 Thomas Wade, boot repairer

59 Mrs. Elizabeth Harrold, chandler's shop

61 Arthur Churly, furniture broker

69 Robert King, chimney sweeper

71 Frank Hubbard, beer retailer

. . . here is Prospect Place . . .

. . . here is Lonsdale Square . . .

These businesses, representing the necessities of daily life, include retailers, artisans and small-scale manufacturers. Although by 1925 large-scale industrial production and wholesale distribution were, of course, well established in Britain, and it was clear that individual artisan production was seriously declining, there was still a wide variety of family businesses in terraced houses.

None of these businesses still exist (in 2010), Barnsbury Street has few businesses on it, and the neighborhood is now an upscale place where most businesses are concentrated around Upper Street and immediately adjacent streets.

One variation of the terraced house is a result of the particular requirements of the textile industry. Before the growth of factories during the Industrial Revolution, much textile manufacturing happened in houses. Manufacturing does not need street exposure, and the high level of light required for textile operations such as weaving or sorting wool helped contribute to the development of a building type in which workshops were located *above* dwellings. These dwellings still stand in Spitalfields, where houses for immigrant Huguenot weavers were built with large windows at their upper floors. In some cases separate external stairs allowed workers to access workshops so that they would not have to go through the dwelling, in an interesting twist on many buildings described in this book. Sometimes the upstairs workshops of several adjacent houses were linked together into what was the germ of a larger factory.[16] And even in 1925, shop/houses with related businesses still existed, but now owned largely by Jews, and on some streets mixed in with shopkeepers selling the essentials of everyday life:

[16] Burnett, *Social History of Housing*, 80–81. This is also described in a detailed history of working at home in the U.K. by Holliss in "The Workhome," 101–223.

Fournier Street, Spitalfields:

11 Solomon Rosen, manufacturing furrier

13 S. Kaufman & Co., wholesale drapers

. . . here is Wilkes Street . . .

15 British Society for the Propagation of the Gospel among the Jews (Gilead Medical Mission House to the Jews)

17 Marks Eker, fur and skin merchant

19 Abraham Piratinsky, silk merchant

19 Israel Bilkus, furrier

23 Mrs. Annie Schneiders, fur and skin merchant

25 Jacob Rosen, manufacturing furrier

27 London Dispensary

29 Max Kouffman, fur and skin merchant

Brick Lane, Spitalfields:

12 Louis Gordon, tobacconist

14 Sam Phillips, fried fish shop

. . . here is Finch Street . . .

18 Joseph Kitsberg, milliner

22 Circus & Benjamin, wholesale drapers

24 B. Levin & Sons, butchers

26 & 122 Charles Bernstein, baker

28 Mrs. Rachel Harris, leather [?]

17 Bridenbaugh, *Colonial Craftsman*, 127.
18 Wood, *New England Village*, 120–121.
19 Hofstra, *Planting of New Virginia*, 300–301.

30 Benjamin Goldberg, ladies' tailor

30 Julius Heiler, dentist

32 Israel Levenstein, confectioner

34 A. Adler & Co., booksellers

36 Daniel Kekovnick, drug stores

38 Mark Gales, woollen merchant

. . . here is Osborn Place . . .

These businesses were all in terraced houses that were several stories tall. Some of them may have occupied the entire building, but most of them likely did not. Today Brick Lane is lined with ground-floor shops, many of them south Asian restaurants run by Bangladeshi immigrants. Fournier Street, west of Brick Lane, is largely residential. The houses, some of which are almost 400 years old, have demonstrated a remarkable level of resilience over the years.

Buildings in American towns

The original farm buildings of New England were direct translations of English precedents, modified for the New England conditions of greater availability of wood – used for siding as well as framing – and of colder winters, which led to the inclusion of house cellars. But after the very early period, settlement patterns became quite different from the English nucleated village (which itself was changing as the result of land enclosure) and incorporated dispersed farmhouses and loosely organized village centers.

Village houses were often typologically the same as farmhouses, and people's occupations were village occupations, serving the farms. Most businesses, in city and village alike, were family businesses, and there were strong similarities between buildings in different places.[17] People had multiple occupations, so that the farmer might also have been a manufacturer of furniture and equipment – at least for his own use – and people in towns maintained gardens and animals.

In this context of occupational fluidity, it was easy for the front room of a building to be a shop, or for a shop to be included somewhere else on the property, since properties were often large. A series of maps of Sturbridge Center, Massachusetts shows the growth and change of the village over thirty years, including the appearance and disappearance of stores and shop/houses (Fig. 4.06).[18]

Mixed uses did not exist only within a particular building, but extended to the house lot. Based on an analysis of insurance policies for Winchester, Virginia in 1800, Warren Hofstra analyzed the building types on six properties on a major street. Including minor buildings such as sheds and storehouses, and buildings attached to others but counted as separate buildings, there were a total of forty-seven buildings on these six lots (Fig. 4.07). They included five buildings classified as "store and house" but also three situations where the store was close enough to the house to suggest that they were used together. The properties also included warehouses, storehouses, sheds and stables.[19] These were very large lots, subsequently subdivided, and able to accommodate new economic initiatives, whether or not they were included in the dwelling.

4.06 (above left) The changing distribution of functions in Sturbridge, Massachusetts.

Redrawn by Sam Yerke and Will Krzymowski from Joseph Wood, The New English Village, 120–121, figure 5.4. © 1997 The Johns Hopkins University Press. Reprinted by permission of Joseph Wood and The Johns Hopkins University Press. The original illustration was drawn by Joseph Wood and based on Levine, 1971.

4.07 (above right) Six lots in Winchester, Virginia.

Courtesy of Warren Hofstra. Image by Professor Paul McDermott and Mr. Philip Mobley.

Colonial and Federal houses lent themselves to commercial use. In the simple hall-and-parlor plan, one of the two rooms could easily accommodate a business use – a shop, a tavern, a doctor's office or the office of a businessman whose main place of business was elsewhere (Fig. 4.08). The central-chimney or central-hall plan easily allowed members of the household to come and go – into the other downstairs room, through the other downstairs room to a back kitchen or up the stair – without disturbing the activity in the shop or office. If the building were transformed to include a shopfront with a separate door and large window, people could enter the shop without entering the house at all, but the person working in the shop could go back and forth between the shop and the house. Even when retail buildings were not exclusively dwellings they still retained the form of dwellings and may have included space for employees to sleep.[20]

Artisans also added on rooms for their shops. A shoemaker in Winchester, Virginia had a:

> two story wooden house [with] two rooms separated by a central hallway on each floor. A fifteen-foot addition to the north gable wall served as a shoemaking shop, and a fifteen-foot-square kitchen was connected to the rear of the central passage by a covered walkway. A free-standing wooden stable also occupied the back lot.[21]

Many houses, particularly in rural places and small towns, were wooden, and brick construction in towns increased in the nineteenth century after fires destroyed closely packed wooden buildings and as fashion and civic pride

[20] Martin, "Commercial Space as Consumption Arena," 206–211.
[21] Hofstra, *Planting of New Virginia*, 300.

4.08 Central-hall house/ tavern in Annapolis Royal, Nova Scotia.
Photograph by Alvin Comiter.

4.09 Nineteenth-century New York shop/houses. Grand Street, #511–513, 1937. Photograph by Berenice Abbott. Museum of the City of New York, Gift of the Federal Arts Project, Works Progress Administration.

began to call for more substantial buildings. But wooden buildings with land around them on their lots were easy to add onto, and this flexibility allowed people to easily and cheaply respond to economic opportunity.

The next typological step was the transformation, in tighter urban conditions, of the two-room-separated-by-central-hall farmhouse into the "2/3 house" – the side-hall building, with its long dimension perpendicular to the street, and with major/minor spatial organization. This is essentially the plan of the English terraced house or the New York row house.[22] The side hall allowed the front room to easily become a shop, communicating directly with the street, while allowing a family member working in the shop to communicate directly with the rest of the house. As it did in England, this transformation allowed a farmhouse to transform into an urban house with the principal dimension perpendicular to the street – and for the shop to begin to find its place in a clearly understood location on a city street (Fig. 4.09). These buildings accommodated businesses along with dwellings.[23] They may have included three functions: dwelling, manufacture, and sales; the shops themselves may not have been finished in any special way, as fancy display was still not prevalent.[24]

In eighteenth and early nineteenth-century Boston, most shops – places for retail trades and crafts – were located in the front rooms of houses. In 1800, these shops included 22 druggists, 1 armorer, 17 booksellers and stationers, 65 grocers, 14 jewelers, 9 lemon-and-lime dealers, 24 lumber/board merchants,

[22] Glassie, "Eighteenth-Century Cultural Process," 402–405.
[23] Bridenbaugh, *Colonial Craftsman*, 127.
[24] Upton, *Another City*, 149–150.

[25] Sawtelle, "Commercial Landscape of Boston," 28, 40.
[26] Sawtelle, "Commercial Landscape of Boston," 202.
[27] Blumin, *Emergence of the Middle Class*, 45–46.
[28] Bailey, *Main Street Northeastern Oregon*, 90–91, 129, 175.
[29] Information from Sanborn maps and from photographs in the Oregon Historical Society, Portland.
[30] Hayward and Belfoure, *Baltimore Rowhouse*, figure 91, 132.

293 retailers and shopkeepers (with unspecified goods), 5 seedsmen, 30 shoe stores, 4 toy shops, 90 bakers, 41 hatters, 113 tailors, 44 cabinetmakers, 5 mathematical instrument makers, and many others.[25] These home-based businesses represented a large part of the retail and craft economy of what was then the fourth-largest city in the United States.

The exact configuration of the business relative to the residence depended on the kind of business and the prosperity of the artisan or shopkeeper. There were a number of functions: production, custom sales (which presumably did not require a shop, but could happen in a deeper room of the house) and retail sales. With silversmiths for example, actual production could have happened in a building on the back of the lot, or in a production facility elsewhere, but sales were in a front-room shop.[26] Conditions within the building may have been cramped, as in some cases the entire ground floor may have been occupied by the business, and production functions may have taken place within otherwise "residential" rooms.[27]

The form of these buildings was influenced by the growing density of towns and cities. Buildings began to be as wide as their lots, with two or more stories (Figs. 4.10, 4.11 and 4.12). Although gable roofs may still have been visible from the street, the lines of eaves began to be continuous. Buildings were still wooden; there were still outside stairs leading to upper stories in some places, but the appearance of streets began to be distinctly "urban." There was a continuous transformation from rural house types to the urban street – and in like manner, the wooden-house, two-story streetscape was eventually to be supplanted by taller buildings of brick.

Late nineteenth- and early twentieth-century commercial/residential buildings in American small towns

The familiar two-story streetscape in towns all over the country is the result of a decades-long process of transformation that often began with simple wooden shop/houses. The development of main streets in towns of northeastern Oregon followed cycles of increasingly intensive land use (Fig. 4.13). The first cycle was one in which shops were located in what were essentially houses – sometimes with dwellings and sometimes without. In subsequent phases, additional lots were developed, buildings were expanded, and two-story buildings were built, with office space or apartments on their upper floors.[28] Eventually brick buildings replaced wooden ones.

In Albany, an important agricultural center in the Willamette Valley of Oregon, people lived next to their businesses in the downtown and in houses on lots that also had shops, scattered throughout the blocks surrounding the downtown. In the late nineteenth- and early twentieth-centuries, downtown buildings that included shops were typical of those all over the country. Apartment entrances were to the side of the shopfronts or at the back of the building, particularly if the building was at a corner (Fig. 4.10). In some cases internal stairs connected the shop with the apartment above.[29]

Larger variations of this idea were to be found in cities, in which development came to be characterized by multiple dwellings, sometimes built in rows like English terraced houses, and sometimes as larger apartment buildings. In Baltimore, as in England, houses at the ends of rows were sometimes built as shop/houses, and were wider than the other dwelling houses in the row.[30]

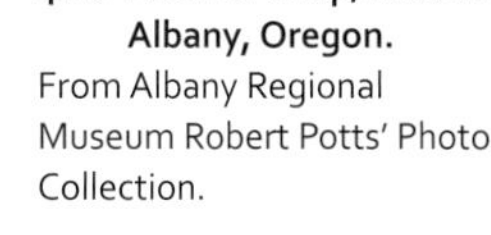

4.10 A corner shop/house in Albany, Oregon.
From Albany Regional Museum Robert Potts' Photo Collection.

4.11 Shop/house in Petersburg, Virginia.
From Library of Congress/ Historic American Buildings Survey.

4.12 Corner building in south Portland, Oregon, 1941.
Courtesy City of Portland.

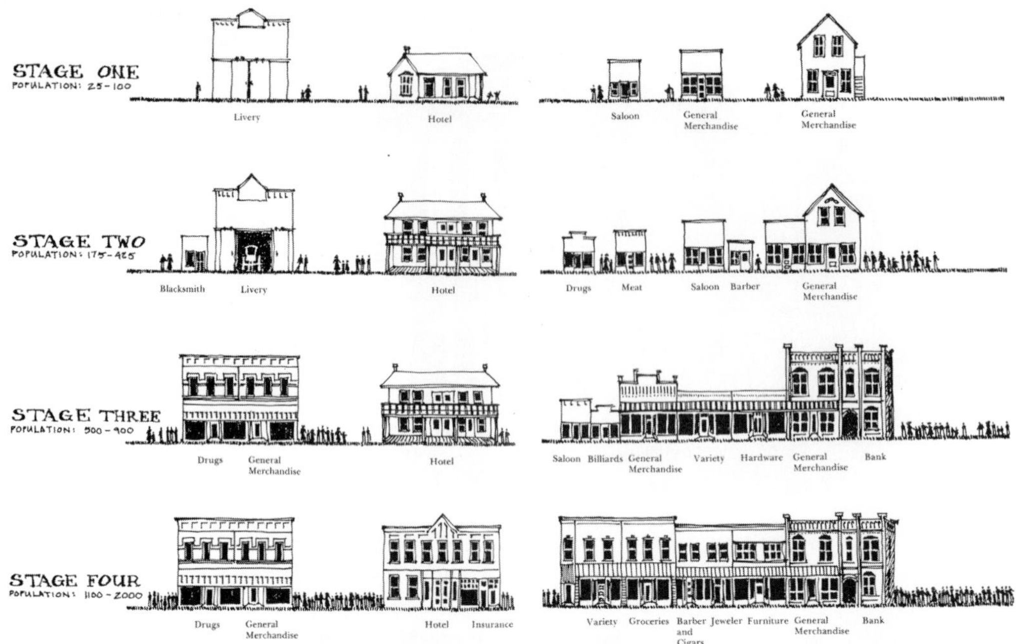

4.13 Increasing densities of main street development in Oregon. In the first stage, buildings were simple modifications of dwelling houses and may have contained living quarters upstairs or on the back of the lot. In subsequent stages, offices began to compete for second-story space.

Barbara Ruth Bailey, *Main Street, Northeastern Oregon: The Founding and Development of Small Towns.* Reproduced with permission of the Oregon Historical Society.

But the shop/house type most associated with North America is perhaps the simple corner grocery store in residential neighborhoods in small towns and cities all over the continent. Often, with grocery stores owned by immigrants serving the needs of people in the immediate vicinity, these buildings served as dwellings, stores and neighborhood centers. They were in scale with neighboring buildings, had a corner door to the store, side door to the stair, and an internal connection from the store to the stair hall. Although living quarters were upstairs, the kitchens were often downstairs next to the store. As Eudora Welty wrote, these humble buildings were central to the life of their neighborhoods.[31]

New York apartment houses with ground-floor retail uses

Chapter 3 described how the nineteenth-century transformations in European cities necessitated a new form of dwelling – the apartment house. The same was the case for North America, and particularly in New York, where land values were high partly because of a restrictive geography, and the multi-family apartment house became a primary building type.[32] This type also emerged gradually out of colonial precedents.

The Dutch colonial urban house in New Amsterdam shared features with the Amsterdam house, described in the last chapter. It was built by Dutch

[31] An exhibition and catalog sponsored by the National Building Museum focused on these buildings and the life of people in them, in Galveston, Texas. See Beasley, *Corner Store*.

[32] See for example Elizabeth Collins Cromley, *Alone Together*, and Richard Plunz, *History of Housing*.

craftsmen (and with bricks imported from Holland until brick kilns were established on the island). Like the Amsterdam house, it used the front room as a shop, and in some cases the projecting bracket at the top of the gable was used as a hoist. Dutch immigrants to New York regarded themselves as Dutch, and maintained their language, habits, ways of commerce and ways of building.[33] But beginning with the transfer of the city to the English in 1664, and immigration from England during the eighteenth century, English building practice began to have a larger influence.

Through the nineteenth century, New York City grew as a great port, as a financial and publishing center and as a center for clothing manufacture, an industry that relied on immigrant labor. To accommodate the growing population, housing types were developed that could incorporate commercial and residential uses in the same building, in particular New York variants of the shop/house (Fig. 4.14).

Early houses in New York were wooden and, when in dense situations, had blank side walls and a row-house organization, able to easily incorporate shops into their front rooms. By the early nineteenth century, the existence of shops in houses became undesirable for the upper classes.[34] This was exacerbated by the increasing immigrant population, and by the growing practice of converting single-family houses into rooming houses and front rooms into stores (Fig. 4.15).

[33] See, for example, Rothschild, *New York City Neighborhoods*, 10–11.

[34] Lockwood, *Bricks and Brownstone*, 46.

4.14 Prince and Marion Streets, New York, 1896.
Collection of the New-York Historical Society.

4.15 Mulberry Street, New York, 1895. The street includes wooden buildings with eaves parallel to the street, and the lower wooden building on the left, toward the viewer, has gables characteristic of older Dutch buildings.
Collection of The New-York Historical Society.

A new building type, the tenement, emerged for the working classes. These buildings took their place in neighborhoods like the Lower East Side, away from the wealthier districts that remained with single-family row houses and apartment buildings with larger flats. Typologically, many tenement buildings are simple repetitions of the row house, mirrored side-to-side and front-to-back. Tenement buildings could easily incorporate shops, and were originally built with them or converted later to include them. In some cases the shop was directly connected to the kitchen of a ground-floor apartment (Fig. 4.16).

Most New York lots were multiples of 25 feet wide, a width that could accommodate a tenement building with four apartments per floor: two in the front, two in the back and a stair/circulation hall in the center. Early tenements had light and air only from the front and back, leaving rooms in the center without daylight or fresh air. Increasingly strict building regulations, notably the "New Law" of tenements in 1901, increased the amount of required light and ventilation. Simple transformations led to the 50-foot-wide building and then the 100-foot-wide building. Although there were numerous variations, they all pushed major living and dining rooms to the front and back, and relied on internal light courts for kitchens, service rooms and minor bedrooms. Depending on location, the first floor was adaptable enough so that it could be configured into either apartments or stores. And in neighborhoods such as the Lower East Side, many apartments housed productive work, so that money-generating activity was not restricted to the ground-floor shops.

The typical New York block above Fourteenth Street – the majority of Manhattan – is 200 feet long in the north–south direction, and this meant that

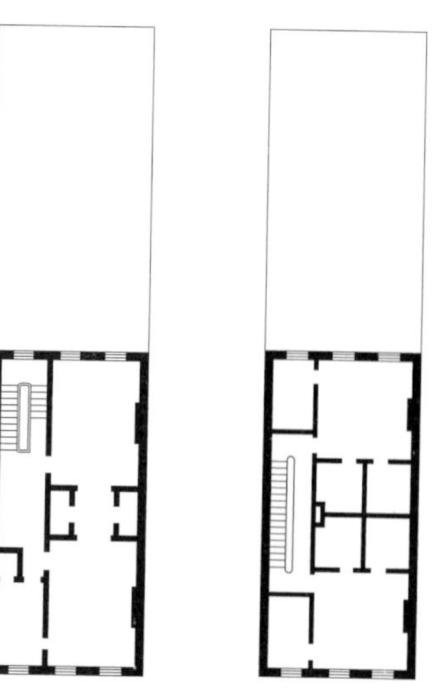

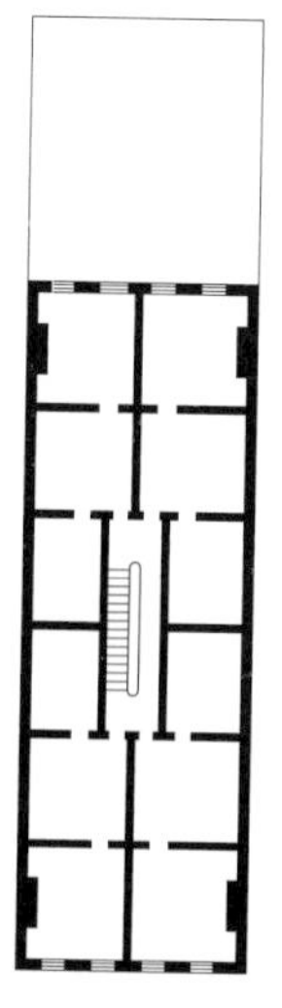

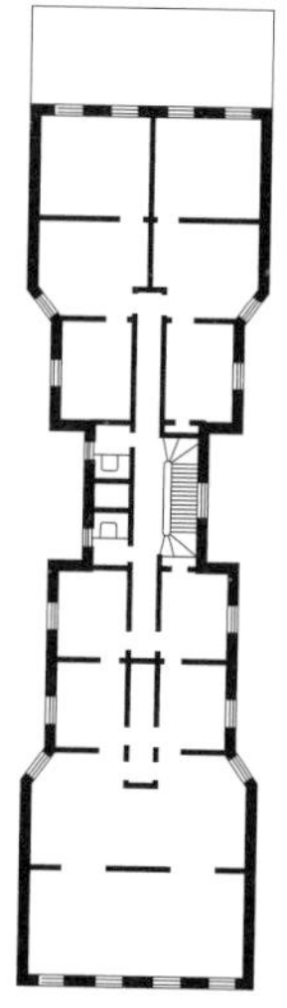

4.16 Upper-floor plans showing the evolution of the New York tenement building beginning with a one-family row house and proceeding through stages in which the basic row house unit was first subdivided and then repeated, front and back, and side-to-side.
Drawing by Will Krzymowski.

4.17 Small New York buildings with ground-floor shops.
Photograph by author.

4.18 New York apartment buildings of different sizes and different eras. The two buildings to the left of the corner building each have shops at the base and two apartments across the front.
Photograph by author.

when the size of buildings increased in the late nineteenth century, many of them were corner buildings, with storefronts along the commercial street and residential entrances on the residential street. New York had developed its own version of the commercial/residential building – to be discussed further in Chapter 8 (Figs. 4.17, 4.18; Plates 29, 57).

By the beginning of the twentieth century, a wide variety of American types – ranging from the general store/dwelling at a country hamlet, to the corner grocery, to the packed New York tenement – had emerged. And in New York, there has been continuity of the idea of the mixed-use residential building, even if the idea is less usual in other cities. In Manhattan at least, the high population density makes ground-floor commercial space viable, so apartment buildings that have frontages on commercially zoned avenues naturally include such uses.

* * *

The intention of Part I has been to describe some of the variety of shop/houses in the world, along with some common factors that formed these types and that are generally applicable. A few basic principles, that will be elaborated on in Part II, apply:

- concentration in the urban fabric, putting shop/houses together on particular kinds of streets in the city;
- continuity of shop functions and potential shop functions with the public realm;
- flexibility of use, so that the basic building type incorporates commercial and productive functions in different ways;
- architectural flexibility over time, so that buildings may be transformed for different economic functions without fundamentally altering their structure or that of the urban fabric in which they exist.

Part II

THE FABRIC OF EVERYDAY LIFE

Part II: THE FABRIC OF EVERYDAY LIFE

The ordinariness of the shop/house comes largely from its purposefulness. The design and organization of these buildings are highly contingent on the details of family and economic life. These buildings are pragmatic. They use the three-dimensional volume of an urban site in the most efficient and lucrative way. Their internal functions can adjust relative to each other, during use. They make little apology for the commerce and work that happen inside them. And they add up to a street that has the same features of purposeful function, repeated dozens of times.

These architectural attributes allow the buildings to house a kind of daily life that has existed in cities since cities began. It is family- and locally based, contributing to an active and fine-grained local economy, inclusive of children, respectful of small talk and neighborly gossip and buying a half-dozen eggs. It is a kind of ordinary daily life that has largely disappeared in many wealthier places and "advanced" economies, but that needs to be looked at not with nostalgia but as a potentially useful, hyper-modern form.

Part II deals with how the purposefulness of shop/houses is manifested in their location in the city, their design and their flexibility over time and within architectural space. Since one of the assumptions of this book is that shop/houses share essential characteristics from culture to culture, these four chapters represent a synthesis and analysis of the four chapters of Part I, in which cultures and places were presented in ways that were distinct from each other, and to some extent historically.

Furthermore, the characteristics shared by shop/houses allow for a blurring of the distinction between vernacular buildings, which are often designed by builders according to commonly understood types, and buildings designed by architects, which may have a level of inventiveness in addition to their adherence to common ideas. In this book, the work of various architects in history is mentioned: George Dance the Younger in London; Philips Vingboons, Aldo Van Eyck and Theo Bosch in Amsterdam; Otto Wagner in Vienna; Maxwell Fry, Jane Drew and Pierre Jeanneret in Chandigarh; Auguste Perret in Paris; and a number of others.

Although these architects were working within the context of vernacular shop/houses that had developed over hundreds of years, the projects of many of them were innovative. The Chandigarh projects incorporated strategies for cooling and shading in the summer Punjabl climate that were not necessary with European row-house precedents. Van Eyck and Bosch, in their Amsterdam project, incorporated a second-story entrance gallery that allowed dwellings to be separated from shops without taking up room on the commercial front for an entrance. Wagner and Perret incorporated contemporary construction techniques and Dance developed interpretations of the plan that recognized the subtlety of the relationship between dwelling and commercial space.

But at the same time, the shop/houses designed by these architects owe their basic organizational features to the vernacular building cultures in which they designed, or which influenced them – and because shop/houses are also formed by economic forces that differ little from culture to culture, have similar organizational features, and similar attributes of location within the city, to each other.

They are also dynamic over time, in their organization and use. This flexibility is not automatic – it is not necessarily the case that any building, designed according to any organizational type or method of construction, is equally flexible. Many of these buildings are narrow, or have narrow sub-units, allowing them to have strong connections to the street. Many of them are variations, one way or the other, of row-house plans, with major/minor organizational schemes, allowing for easy access to all rooms from semi-public space and therefore the ability to change occupancy or use of any room or of any group of rooms without affecting the occupancy of the others. They often have plans that do not require a sharp boundary between commercial and residential space – so to some extent, the clear use distinctions that came about in the eighteenth century are once again minimized.

This architectural flexibility over time allows for the family or the building owner to have the confidence to stay in the building, or remain with the building as an investment. In turn, this flexibility supports the both the physical continuity and the social stability of the neighborhood, as families can go through different stages of their life cycle in place. At one scale, that of the building, things may be in continual flux – rooms have their uses changed, doors are added or blocked off, small building additions are made. But at another scale, that of the neighborhood, there may be more of a sense of permanence, and slower change over time. As buildings slowly change, streets and the sense of place in the neighborhood seem to change much more slowly.

So in the end, the building, the neighborhood, and the city – and the inhabitants of the city – form one interconnected system, in which the boundary between the building and its social and material contexts is blurred. The four chapters of Part II, dealing with the meaning and function of the shop/house, its location in the city, the flexibility that it exhibits over time, and finally its architectural attributes, need to be understood together, in the same way that architecture, urbanism and geography need to be understood together. And although cities are in some ways very different from place to place, they contain within them functions and processes of transformation that have deep similarities.

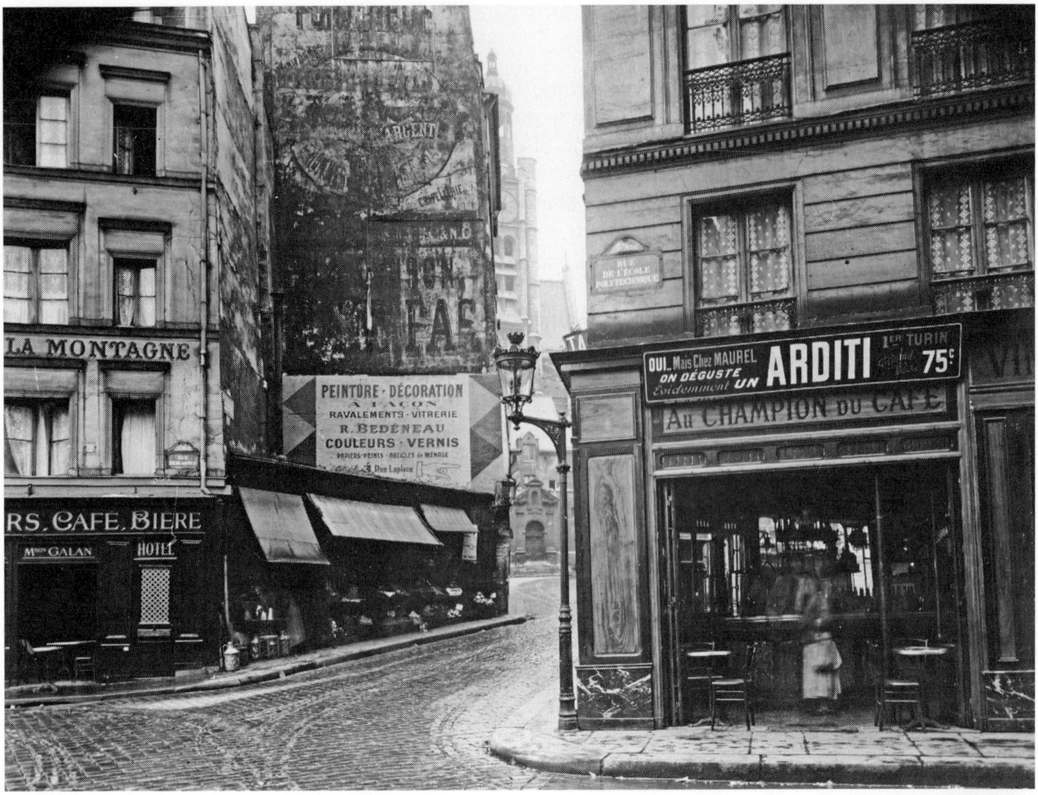

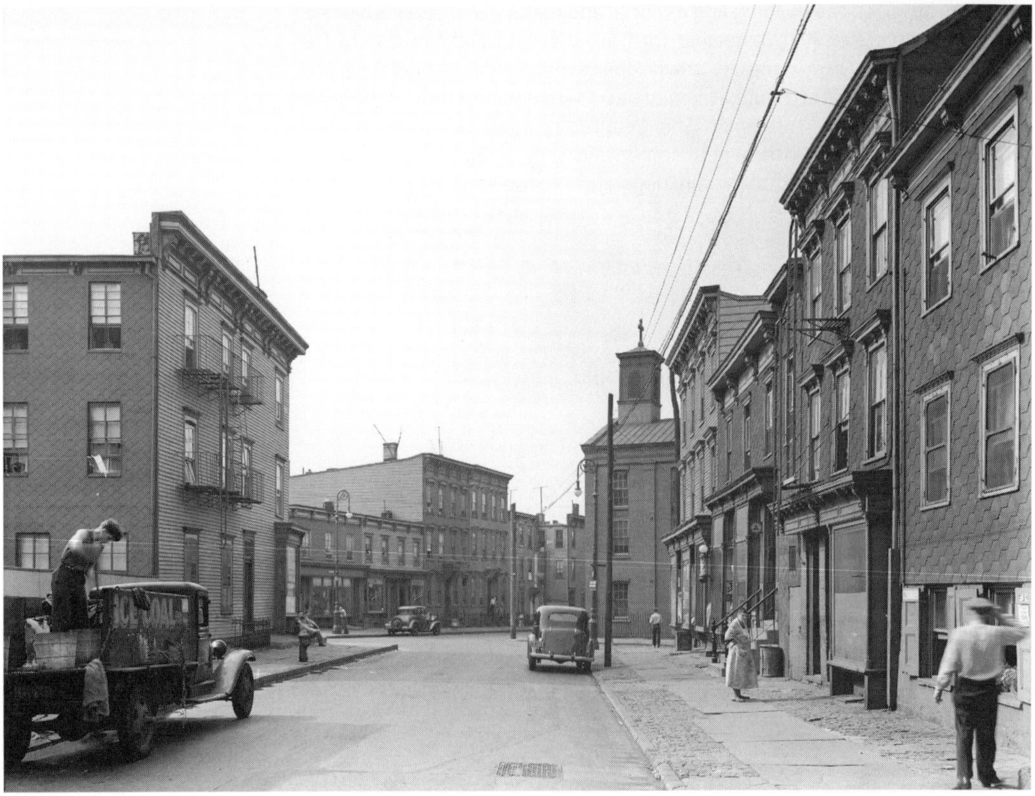

5

LIVING AND WORKING IN THE CITY

Transmission from one generation to the next was ensured by the everyday participation of children in adult life.[1]

(Philippe Aries, *Centuries of Childhood*)

[1] Aries, *Centuries of Childhood*, 368.

In contemporary urban design discourse, the idea of "mixed use" is almost always understood in terms of the social vitality of the neighborhood – having active streets day and night, having uses in dwellings and shops that can support each other, reducing car use and increasing pedestrian life.

But in addition to supporting urban life in these ways, the shop/house also traditionally harbored economic and social relationships that were connected to family life itself. It is not the intention of this book to propose moving back in time to the days of apprenticeship or much more permeable boundaries between public and private life. Nevertheless, there are ample enough criticisms of modern life to suggest that the urban world may benefit from the social integration and economic fluidity that were represented in the shop/house.

The shop/house is useful because it supports everyday life, in the most ordinary and common sense. Everyday life – reading the newspaper with a cup of coffee, chatting with a neighbor on the street, putting the key in the front door when arriving home, working hard to meet a deadline, buying bread and a quart of milk, taking children to school, meeting friends, going to the bank on a lunch break, stopping at the dry cleaners on the way home – is the ground of people's experience. It is overlaid with inner lives of thoughts and dreams, and punctuated by the surprising moment, the special occasion, and the beautiful. It is always present, sometimes in the background and sometimes in plain view – and it is lived more than it is thought.

5.01 An ordinary Paris street in 1925.
Atget, Eugène (1857–1927). Rue de la Montagne-Sainte-Genevieve, Juin 1925. Digital Image © The Museum of Modern Art (I. 1969.1447) Licensed by SCALA/Art Resource, N.Y.

5.02 An ordinary New York street in 1937. Powers and Olive Streets, 1937.
Photograph by Berenice Abbott. Museum of the City of New York, Gift of the Federal Arts Project, Work Progress Administration.

The relationship between the shop/house and everyday life is supple. On a day-to-day basis, work may be easily done in the house or in easy access to the house; workplace and dwelling are sometimes the same, sometimes together, easily intertwined and overlapped. Moving back and forth between domestic and economic uses, the shop/house may accommodate functions that readily expand and contract. Economic uses may include the rental of space to people outside the family – a boarder, a student renting a basement room, a rental apartment in a multi-unit building. The family can stay in place by allowing the building to be used in ways that are diverse and easily changeable.

This smooth relationship between daily life and its environment has been, at various times in history, typical of cities. Until relatively recently, the locus of daily life was largely local, not governed by remote economic or political institutions. While larger economic and political forces always affected what happened locally in cities, people's actions, work and decisions were happening within local structures and institutions, and characterized by immediate relationships between individuals. Although life might not have been easy, it was personal rather than bureaucratic – and the shop/house, with its spatial hybridity and resilience over time, was connected to and supportive of this constellation of personal relationships.

Contrast the hybrid shop/house with the monofunctional and spatially pure approaches to building type, which are strongly connected to the Enlightenment ideas of taxonomy and categorization. Pure building types, as they were defined and transmitted in theory, were largely idealizations that did not necessarily take into account hybrid social realities.[2] The gradual emergence of large institutions that replaced small ones – factories and schools replacing workshops, large companies with functionally distinct departments replacing family businesses, municipal government providing local services, "housing" replacing houses – were all connected to new building types that had uniquely defined functions. The increasing scale and resultant abstraction of institutions in the eighteenth and nineteenth centuries, removing individual agency from many aspects of daily life, were supported by buildings that made their categorization, abstraction and economic functionality easy.[3] The shop/house, on the other hand, was never defined theoretically and was often a messy reality. That is why it has many names in this book, and why it is described with so many individual manifestations in Part I. But that messiness is a sign of life – of the ability of a particular socio/economic phenomenon to find its physical form in a myriad of different ways. The typological complexity and variety are, in fact, results of an organic social process that is perhaps analogous to the emergence of biological species diversity, in which many different building types transform to accommodate similar needs.

Today, planners and designers are struggling against the effects of twentieth-century urbanism, which ruptured the ground on which ordinary everyday life happens. The ability to live close to one's work, the ability of children to naturally experience the world of adults, the nearby availability of everyday goods and services, the ability to easily start a small business – all of these are now more difficult. It is a curious fact that many innovative projects in design and planning need to struggle against bureaucracies, and the mentalities that have grown around them, to simply reintroduce opportunities to live ordinary, everyday life.

The shop/house is an important architectural symbol and framework for ordinary life. It is an ordinary building that often sits humbly in the background. But everyday life happens in it and next to it, and without pretension it acts as a ready armature for that life.

Supporting the life of families and children

Buddenbrooks is the epic of four generations of a merchant family in Lübeck, northern Germany, in the nineteenth century, tracing the rise and fall of the family's personal and business fortune. The book begins with a housewarming party, celebrating both a new house in Meng Strasse and the emergence of the family firm as an important wholesale grain business in the city. The family house contains living quarters as well as the firm's offices; the family also owns warehouses in another part of the city, and boats for the shipment of grain.

2 Villari, *J.N.L. Durand*, 63. With regard to J.N.L. Durand, who along with Quatremère de Quincy is regarded as a founder of modern typological theory, Sergio Villari writes that "... the building types described by Durand are not – however much one would like to believe it – the result of an analysis of the functional necessity of the new city at the end of the *ancien regime*, but rather of city as capital. They are for the most part derived from the classical code; in all of them temples, followed closely by triumphal arches, gymnasiums, slaughterhouses, law courts, baths, and so on, predominate." Durand himself, in his *Leçons*, does not mention shops in his discussion of the functions of urban buildings, but does include, in the illustrations, residential buildings that incorporate shops. Durand, *Précis des Leçons*, 172–174, Plates 25, 26.

3 "Formal, geometric simplicity and functional efficiency were not distinct goals to be balanced; on the contrary, formal order was a pre-condition of efficiency." Scott, *Seeing Like a State*, 106.

The house has several floors that allow for different generations to live together, for the family to entertain in style and for the family's business to be conducted from the house.

The Buddenbrooks family, its business and its house were intertwined and practically indistinguishable. And the integration of different aspects of life found in this fictional nineteenth-century upper-middle class German family still exists in many cultures. Among immigrant Chinese people in London, children are not only expected to help out in the business, but accept those responsibilities as a normal part of growing up. When asked about how work in the shop started, one child said: "I don't know. They've never asked us. It's almost as though it's just expected. We just watched and learned when we were young. There was no training course or anything . . . When we came back from school, we came back to the shop and hung around. That's where the TV was, at the counter, in the shop. We didn't have a TV upstairs." Here, children's work roles expanded gradually, from working in the kitchen to serving customers at the counter. For these children, this was not "work" but an ordinary part of family life.[4]

Historically, this kind of integration was strong. Philippe Aries strongly relates the multi-functionality of rooms before the eighteenth century with the lack of distinction between different aspects of life, in both large and small houses. Before the café, the house was the place for social life as well. Today's categories did not exist: "A lawyer's clients were also his friends and both were his debtors. There were no professional premises, either for the judge or the merchant or the banker or the business man . . . in the same rooms where they ate, people slept, danced, worked and received visitors."[5]

In this description, even the idea of the "shop/house" – that a separate shop and house were somehow combined in the same building – itself seems to represent a functionally fragmented typological form. In Aries' description, everything was part of a seamlessly unified daily life. This extended to the finances of the family and the business: in the early eighteenth century in England, there was not a distinction between household expenses and business expenses: the two were understood as part of the same economic unit.[6]

This interaction was not limited to the life of lawyers, merchants and bankers. Writing about the lives of poor women in New York between 1789 and 1860, Christine Stansell observed, "In the first half of the nineteenth century, the boundaries between public and private life were fluid and permeable. Laboring women made their lives as wives and mothers on the streets as much as by their hearthsides."[7]

Or consider the life of children. Children profit by being part of the adult world, seeing adults at work, being in situations in which they are at the edge of adult activities and perhaps gradually venturing into them. Children's education profits, at least partly, from "learning by doing," and by observing the real world. Children's self-confidence grows when their world is allowed to expand naturally – when they can take increasing risks, as they grow, in an enlarging and more complex environment. As David Nasaw put it:

> The children of the city grew up listening to the peddlers cry their wares in the street. They were watching when the pots-and-pans merchant paraded his utensils across the kitchen table; they listened to the insurance man

[4] Song, "Chinese Children's Work Roles," 59.
[5] Aries, *Centuries of Childhood*, 393–394.
[6] Alexander, D., *Retailing in England*, 185–189.
[7] Stansell, *City of Women*, 52.

[8] Nasaw, *Children of the City*, 52.
[9] Aries, *Centuries of Childhood*, 368.
[10] Gladwell, *Outliers*, 151.
[11] Song, "Chinese Children's Work Roles," 292–293.

and the undertaker as they sold their goods and services; they stood by as their mothers haggled with the vegetable man and their fathers bargained with the tailor over the price of a new suit – with an extra pair of pants thrown in.[8]

Along with the fragmentation of institutions that marked the Enlightenment and the Industrial Revolution, the last 200 years have seen the gradual removal of children from ordinary urban life, and the development of institutions – schools and a vast targeted economic market – that have had as one of their effects the isolation of children from certain kinds of learning and certain kinds of socialization. The idea that a child might learn by doing, directly from adults either formally or informally, has been largely lost. In the words of Philippe Aries:

> Generally speaking, transmission from one generation to the next was ensured by the everyday participation of children in adult life . . . Everyday life constantly brought together children and adults in trade and craft, as in the case of the little apprentice mixing the painter's colors; Stradan's engravings of trades and crafts show us children in the workshops with older companions . . . In short, wherever people worked, and also wherever they amused themselves, even in taverns of ill repute, children were mingled with adults. In this way they learnt the art of living from everyday contact. The social groups corresponded to vertical partitions which brought together different age groups.[9]

By living in the same house where a business is being conducted, or even by living on a street where businesses are nearby, children rub shoulders with those businesses and their activities. If they happen to be living in the same place where their parents are working, they may develop an understanding of the business – and even if they do not eventually take the business over, learn practical things about the world.

This is normal life. The modern substitute for this kind of acculturation of children is either nothing, or else a whole raft of educational and social mechanisms – trade schools, after-school programs, business courses – that developed during the nineteenth and twentieth centuries. It is perhaps a benefit of the digital world that children can again "learn by doing" – albeit sometimes without interaction with adults.

Connecting children to the work of their parents may be a factor in children's future success. In *Outliers: The Story of Success*, Malcolm Gladwell describes the career trajectories of numerous people with parents who were garment workers, and who often did piecework at home, on the Lower East Side of Manhattan. Many of these people grew up to be doctors, lawyers and engineers, and in some cases every child in a large family became a professional. Gladwell attributes the children's success partly to being close to the work of their parents, who were exercising skills of bargaining, of risk-taking and of simple hard work. They would not necessarily have seen this if the work were separated from daily life.[10]

And transmission of knowledge is not only from the older generation to the younger. Among Chinese immigrants in London, children helped their parents with tasks that required knowledge of English – and this was facilitated by parents and children working side-by-side in the shop.[11]

Enhancing the social and economic life of neighborhoods and their streets

The symbiotic roles of family members within the house may be a microcosm of similar relationships among people in a neighborhood.

Shop/houses in which families are living and working in the same building, as well as those in which unrelated people are living and working, help support neighborhoods that are diverse and alive. People living and working in the same place usually have a sense of responsibility and service with respect to their business, which fosters personal connections with customers. And families, children, shopkeepers together in the same place, along with customers who come to the businesses that are not the same as the residents, foster a healthy diversity that is not present in single-use districts.

This is not only a question of lifestyle, or the physical vitality of the street. It has to do with the economic functioning of neighborhoods, in the sense that was described by Jane Jacobs and some more recent authors.[12] A local economy that includes shop/houses supports interchange that recycles money within the community. If the building is architecturally flexible, it supports the building's ability to produce income during the entire life cycle of a family, allowing the family to stay in the neighborhood. These economic ideas are a foundation for the relative stability of neighborhoods.

As will be described in the following chapters, the shop/house is itself a manifestation of the idea of architectural and urban flexibility – a building for which a specific function is not as important as the ability to take on a variety of functions, and to change fluidly from function to function. The ability of the building to change is an element of the relative stability of the neighborhood. A vital neighborhood changes, but more slowly than the individual buildings within it. It is not a static entity, frozen in time, a postcard image of a place. It is an organism, pulsing with life, its prosperity changing, with buildings being added to, others fully occupied and stable for generations, a few empty and abandoned, with people and businesses gradually transforming. This life is palpable in the interactions of people, in the activity on the sidewalk and in day-to-day economic transactions. Within this dynamic entity, the shop/house may be a vital element.

In *The Death and Life of Great American Cities*, Jane Jacobs conjectured that the "conditions for city diversity" are mixed primary uses, small blocks, aged buildings and concentration.[13] Taken as a group, these four attributes deal with form (small blocks and concentration), use (mixed primary uses) and economics (aged buildings) – suggesting that effective urban practice is not only a matter of physical design.

Mixed primary uses bring different kinds of people together and promote day-and-night use of a district. Small blocks mean more intersections and therefore more opportunities for crossing paths and social variety on the street. Aged buildings, with lower rents, allow start-up businesses and families/people of lower income levels to establish themselves in neighborhoods. And concentration guarantees that people and uses will rub shoulders enough to promote interaction and interchange.

The shop/house, in its different forms, strongly contributes to Jacobs' criteria. It is not the only kind of building that does so, and indeed, urban diversity

[12] See, for example, Johns, *Moment of Grace*, 47–90, and Rae, *City: Urbanism and its End*, 73–140.
[13] Jacobs, *Death and Life*, 143–221.

requires a wide variety of buildings: row houses and apartment buildings, schools and supermarkets, service stations and shop/houses. But shop/houses, and neighborhoods of shop/houses, do incorporate formal, functional and economic interchanges, and are often the background fabric of neighborhoods that are vital and diverse.

A block of shop/houses automatically brings primary uses together and promotes concentration (including the residences that Jacobs says must be included). For reasons of economic geography, shop/houses are often associated with short blocks. And because shop/houses are often variations of building types like the row or terraced house, their basic architectural organization is so strong that they easily and flexibly transform over time. This ability for flexible transformation allows for their longevity, which helps contribute to a district that has buildings of different ages.

A different but consistent formulation comes from Christopher Alexander and his colleagues. *A Pattern Language* – first published in 1977 but based on work that began at the beginning of the 1960s, just as *Death and Life* was being published – lays out 253 patterns – relationships between parts of a healthy environment – ranging from the regional/urban scale down to the design and details of buildings.[14] Alexander wrote specifically about the opposing social forces that are resolved in the shop/house:

> A man wants to live in his work and he wants to be close to his family; but in a town where work and family are physically separate, he is forced to make impossible choices among these desires. He is exposed to the greatest emotional pressure from his family, at that moment when he is most tired – when he just comes home from work . . .
>
> A woman wants to be a loving woman, sustaining to her children; and also to take part in the outer business of the world . . . But, in a town where work and family are completely separate, she is forced to make another impossible choice . . .
>
> A young boy wants to be close to his family, and to understand the workings of the world and to explore them . . . But, in a town where work and family are separated, he, too, is forced to make impossible choices. He has to choose to be either loving to his family, or to be a truant who can experience the world . . .[15]

While not every boy who experiences these forces will actually become a truant – people cope and adapt to their circumstances – the opposing forces that Alexander describes are real. A pattern is a way to arrange the physical environment to mitigate or eliminate such opposing forces. Patterns relevant to this discussion are mostly those at the urban and neighborhood level, and those dealing with the relationship between the building and the street. The following patterns, from *A Pattern Language*, are all consistent with the idea of the shop/house; one mentions it explicitly.

> *9/Scattered work*
> Use zoning laws, neighborhood planning, tax incentives, and any other means available to scatter workplaces throughout the city. Prohibit large concentrations of workplaces without family life around them. Prohibit large concentrations of family life, without workplaces around them.

[14] Alexander et al., *Pattern Language*.
[15] Alexander, C., *Timeless Way of Building*, 108.

26/Life cycle
. . . each community include a balance of people at every stage of the life cycle, from infants to the very old; and include the full slate of settings needed for all these stages of life.

35/Household mix
No one stage in the life cycle is self-sufficient . . . Encourage growth toward a mix of household types in every neighborhood, and every cluster, so that one-person households, couples, families with children, and group households are side by side.

48/Housing in between
Build houses into the fabric of shops, small industry, schools, public services, universities – all those parts of cities which draw people in during the day, but which tend to be "nonresidential." The houses may be in rows or "hills" with shops beneath, or they may be free-standing, so long as they mix with the other functions, and make the entire area "lived-in."

57/Children in the city
If children are not able to explore the whole of the adult world round about them, they cannot become adults. But modern cities are so dangerous that children cannot be allowed to explore them freely . . . As part of the network of bike paths, develop one system of paths that is extra safe – entirely separate from automobiles, with lights and bridges at the crossings, with homes and shops along it, so that there are always many eyes on the path. Let this path go through every neighborhood, so that children can get onto it without crossing a main road. And run the path all through the city, down pedestrian streets, through workshops, assembly plants, warehouses, interchanges, print houses, bakeries, all the interesting "invisible" life of a town – so that the children can roam freely on their bikes and trikes.

85/Shopfront schools
Instead of building large public schools for children 7 to 12, set up tiny independent schools, one school at a time. Keep the school small, so that its overheads are low and a teacher-student ratio of 1:10 can be maintained. Locate it in the public part of the community, with a shopfront and three or four rooms.

87/Individually owned shops
Do what you can to encourage the development of individually owned shops. Approve applications for business licenses only if the business is owned by those people who actually work and manage the store. Approve new commercial building permits only if the proposed structure includes many very small rental spaces.

89/Corner grocery
Give every neighborhood at least one corner grocery, somewhere near its heart. Place these corner groceries every 200 to 800 yards, according to the density, so that each one serves about 1000 people. Place them on corners, where large numbers of people are going past. And combine them with houses, so that the people who run them can live over them or next to them.

[16] This is a recurrent theme in Christopher Alexander's work. It was first articulated, perhaps, in his paper "The City as a Mechanism for Sustaining Human Contact," and further developed in the now-classic, "A City is Not a Tree" which dealt with the morphological character of healthy urban structure.
[17] Jacobs, *Death and Life*, 428–448.
[18] Alexander, C., *Nature of Order*, Books 1 and 2.
[19] Ellin, *Integral Urbanism*.
[20] Lewis, Paul et al., *Lewis. Tsurumaki. Lewis*.

> *127/Intimacy gradient*
> Unless the spaces in a building are arranged in a sequence which corresponds to their degrees of privateness, the visits made by strangers, friends, guests, clients, family, will always be a little awkward . . . Therefore: Lay out the spaces of a building so that they create a sequence which begins with the entrance and the most public parts of the building, then leads in to the slightly more private areas, and finally to the most private domains.
>
> *130/Entrance room*
> At the main entrance to a building, make a light-filled room which marks the entrance and straddles the boundary between indoors and outdoors, covering some space outdoors and some space indoors. The outside part may be like an old-fashioned porch; the inside like a hall or sitting room.
>
> *165/Opening to the street*
> In any public space which depends for its success on its exposure to the street, open it up, with a fully opening wall which can be thrown wide open, and if it is possible, include some part of the activity on the far side of the pedestrian path, so that it actually straddles the path, and people walk through it as they walk along the path.

"Living Over the Store" is not a pattern of its own, although it is mentioned in the pattern "Corner grocery" and strongly implied in such patterns as "Scattered work", "Housing in between" and "Individually owned shops". One of the recurring themes in *A Pattern Language* is that of reunifying what is seen to be a fragmented contemporary existence. Solutions to functional problems of alienation and social separation are intended to be reinforced through spatial relationships that would "mend the fabric" that had been torn as the result of modern processes of land use and zoning.[16] Such spatial relationships are reinforced by small size, local ownership and individual control.

Jacobs and Alexander both understood their specific observations to be aspects of broader theory. At the end of *The Death and Life of Great American Cities*, Jacobs wrote a chapter titled "The kind of problem a city is,"[17] in which she foresaw the systems theory of the 1960s and 1970s, more recent work on generative codes and writings about organized complexity and the need for urban theory to go from the particular to the general. Alexander went on from *A Pattern Language* to the development of deeper geometric ideas that embody the patterns, and ideas about the generative process of urban formation.[18]

Contemporary theoretical approaches are saying the same things with different words. As mentioned in the Introduction, there is a strong correspondence between Nan Ellin's ideas of "hybridity, connectivity and porosity" and the ideas of Jacobs and Alexander. In her book *Integral Urbanism*, Ellin provides evidence of a new attitude toward the making of cities in which the overlapping and interpenetration of urban spaces gives life to cities, in opposition to the modernist ideas of zoning and functional separations.[19]

These ideas are finding their place in speculative and even actual practice, by architecture firms that are seen as progressive and forward-looking. The New York architecture firm Lewis Tsurumaki Lewis has designed hybrid urban buildings that combine work and dwelling.[20] The architect Teddy Cruz, who works near the San Diego/Tijuana border, recognizes the importance of hybridity in ordinary tract-house development, and has designed physical prototypes and proposals for zoning changes that recognize and accommodate the sorts of commercial transformations that ordinarily happen in low-income, immigrant neighborhoods.[21] Many Latin American governments, understanding the importance of weaving poor populations into the formal economy, are investing in transit systems, including aerial gondolas, which connect *favelas*, or informal urban settlements, with established neighborhoods.[22]

The designers of these contemporary initiatives would agree with Jacobs and Alexander about the importance of the city providing a physical frame, with supportive institutions, for ordinary urban life – and for respecting that life as it is lived, rather than redesigning it as a new ideal.[23] Architectural modernism was to a large extent utopian – working toward an ideal world that did not exist, projecting how people should live rather than recognizing and supporting how they actually did live.

It may be claimed, in rebuttal, that our present, fragmented environment of strip malls, four-lane clogged arterials and single-function zoned cities is how people actually want to live, and that the argument being made here is therefore also a utopian one. But the paradigms that produce the unsustainable city are clearly breaking down, and both long-standing and innovative ideas about how to order the city are beginning to (re-)emerge. At the very least, it seems worthwhile to provide the seeds of a different choice.

[21] "Casa Familiar: Living Rooms at the Border and Senior Housing With Childcare" in Lepik, *Small Scale, Big Change*, 93–102.

[22] See, for example, "The Gondola Project," http://gondolaproject.com/2010/10/13/the-complexo-do-alemao-teleferico/, accessed January 16, 2011; "Manguinhos Complex" in Lepik, *Small Scale, Big Change*, pp. 113–122.

[23] In several visits to the University of Oregon, the South African architect Jo Noero talked about seeing architecture as a supportive "frame" for human life.

6.01 West Fourteenth Street, Manhattan.
Photograph by author.

6

THE GEOGRAPHY OF MIXED USES

The block: my block. *It was on the Chester Street side of our house, between the grocery and the back wall of the old drugstore, that I was hammered into the shape of the streets.*[1]

(*Alfred Kazin, A Walker in the City*)

Urban shop/houses are distributed in patterns that depend on density, street layout and economic activity. They are not only independent buildings, but collective phenomena, explained through architectural understandings as well as through interactions with their economic and social contexts.

The importance of the shop/house as a collective phenomenon is revealed with the numbers of these buildings that exist, or once existed. In some eighteenth-century English towns, merchants and craftsmen represented around half the enumerated population,[2] mostly living in family shop/houses. In the center of Paris and Vienna, multiple-unit shop/houses appear on street after street. In Asian cities such as Bangkok and Hanoi, neighborhoods of shophouses are still dominant, even in the midst of economic booms that are resulting in the construction of high-rise buildings. American cities are more functionally segregated. But shop/houses were common until at least the early nineteenth century and even as recently as 1928, in Cook County, Illinois – the county including Chicago – shop/houses were almost five times as prevalent as stores without dwellings,[3] representing almost 9 percent of all buildings that were either stores or residential buildings (Table 6.1). Shop/houses persist in older neighborhoods in large cities such as San Francisco, New York, Boston and Toronto, and in many smaller ones.

The prevalence of significant numbers of urban shop/houses suggests the need for systematic explanations of location and distribution. This is not only an academic matter, since the success of new projects depends on their location as well as on their architecture. This chapter is concerned with the shop/house as a collective phenomenon, dealing with the place of shop/houses in the overall urban pattern.

A look at one New York neighborhood begins to reveal these patterns. One origin of this book lies in Brooklyn, in the dense Crown Heights neighborhood I visited every Saturday for about ten years as a child. Populated by first- and second-generation Jewish immigrants, the neighborhood was a whole world, and I came back to it in my thoughts again and again over the years, thinking about the nature of cities. In July 2006, when I walked the neighborhood for the first time in over forty years, going past buildings that I still knew, I found both the familiar and the surprise of what I did not properly remember.

1 Kazin, *Walker in the City*, 83.
2 Borsay, "English Urban Renaissance," 182–186.
3 Hoyt, "One Hundred Years", 291.

Table 6.1
Numbers of buildings in Cook County, Illinois in 1928

Building type	No.
Residential buildings (total)	468,119
Residential buildings (with stores or offices)	41,517
Stores	8,963
Office buildings	808
Service stations	1608
Hospitals	72
Factories and loft buildings	7130

Source:
Hoyt, "One Hundred Years of Land Values in Chicago," 291.

6.02 Eastern Parkway, Brooklyn, showing entrance to Utica Avenue subway station and the mixed-use buildings on Schenectady Avenue at left.
Photograph by author.

6.03 St. Johns Place, Brooklyn. The tenement building at 1292 St. Johns Place is second from left; the buildings on the left once had shops at their ground floors.
Photograph by author.

6.04 St. Johns Place at left and Troy Avenue at right, Brooklyn.
Photograph by author.

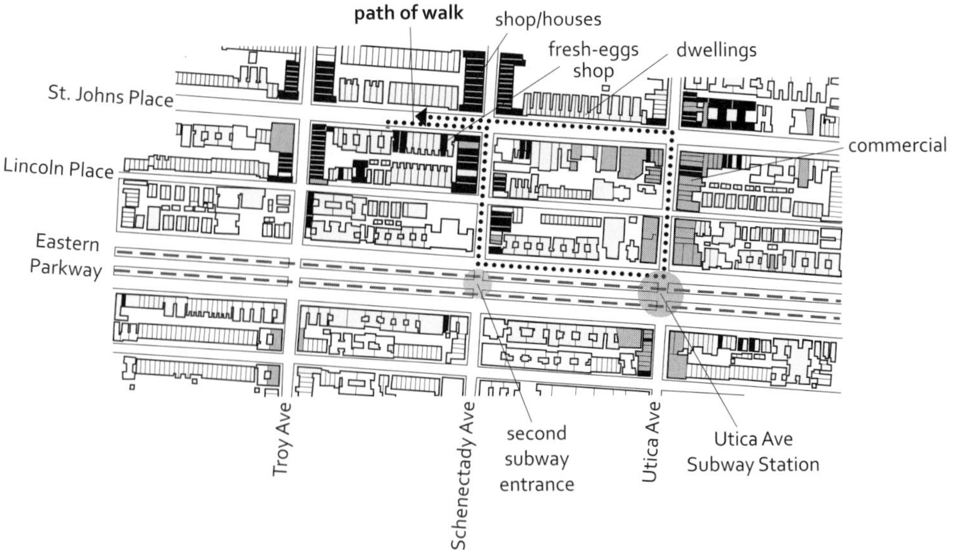

6.05 Diagram of a part of the district of Crown Heights, Brooklyn. A dotted line marks the path of the imaginary walk that began and ended at 1292 St. Johns Place.
Diagram by Matthew M. Brown, Will Krzymowski and Sam Yerke.

My childhood experience of the neighborhood was centered on a few square blocks, from St. Johns Place south to Eastern Parkway, and from Troy Avenue east to Utica Avenue. This was a whole world, as small areas often are to children. But it also contained within it a variety of environments, linked together in what turns out to be an ordered way.

Eastern Parkway, one of the great boulevards of the world, is one of Olmsted's extensions of Prospect Park, stretching east into the neighborhoods of immigrants in Crown Heights, East Flatbush and Brownsville. In *A Walker in the City*, Alfred Kazin described Eastern Parkway as the place for middle-class Jews, " . . . alrightniks, making out 'all right' in the New World, they were still Gentiles to me as they went out into the wide and tree-lined Eastern Parkway."[4] In *The Boulevard Book*, Allan Jacobs, Elizabeth MacDonald and Yodan Rofé write about Eastern Parkway's easy-going, graceful character, the way it absorbs a lot of automobile traffic without being overwhelmed, the clusters of commercial buildings around subway stops along its length.[5]

Eastern Parkway skirts neighborhoods that have residential streets with four-story tenements and two-story row houses, commercial streets, combined residential and commercial streets. This is an ordered structure, the pieces of which support each other in their life, and the entirety of which supports the life and character of Eastern Parkway (Figs. 6.02, 6.03, 6.04 and 6.05).

The tenement building at 1292 St. Johns Place, one of four adjacent four-story buildings built in 1919 in the middle of the south side of the street between Troy and Schenectady Avenues, has nineteen apartments: four on the ground floor and five on each of the upper three floors. Let us imagine it is 1958, and that we are children taking a walk from this building around the neighborhood.

Turning right out of the front door, we find narrower tenement houses. The first two include three ground-floor shops – a small grocery store, a candy store and a Venetian-blind repair shop. Proceeding eastward are more tenement buildings without shops, but at the ground floor of one of the

[4] Kazin, *Walker in the City*, 9.
[5] Jacobs, *Boulevard Book*, 44–53.

tenement buildings near the corner is a tiny shop selling farm-fresh eggs. Turning south, onto Schenectady Avenue, we find a busy commercial street, with pharmacies, 5 and 10s, groceries, shoe-repair shops, the London and Fishberg fruit-and-vegetable market – many of these stores in buildings with apartments above.

Looking westward on narrow Lincoln Place, we see two-story row houses and an occasional larger apartment house, most without shops. We do not turn into Lincoln Place, but proceed south on Schenectady Avenue, to find an elementary school on the right, fronting onto Eastern Parkway, and the neo-classical building of a branch of the Brooklyn Public Library diagonally across the boulevard. Also at this intersection are clusters of shops, the stairs leading down to the western entrance of a subway station, the gracious rows of trees, park benches and people out for a weekend stroll along Eastern Parkway with the autumn leaves underfoot.

Crossing Schenectady Avenue and heading east on Eastern Parkway, we accompany the strollers under the trees, past row houses with tall stoops, an occasional apartment house, schools and synagogues. We come to Utica Avenue with its own clusters of shops at the boulevard and another entrance to the block-long subway station, and turn north toward Lincoln Place and St. Johns Place beyond. Utica Avenue, which gives its name to the subway station, is the place not so much for "everyday" shopping as for clothing, jewelry, the Sam Ash music store. We arrive at St. Johns Place and turn west, toward home, passing all-commercial buildings for a good part of the block, including the local A & P. Finally we reach Schenectady Avenue, cross the street, and we are almost home.

How can this experience be analyzed? The design of Eastern Parkway made it a desirable place to live, and a gracious setting for institutions such as schools, libraries and synagogues. The subway – a Brooklyn extension of the Lexington Avenue and Seventh Avenue/Broadway lines in Manhattan – reinforces the boulevard by establishing a series of nodes at the subway stations, with commercial uses and public institutions.

The commercial uses make their way up Utica, Schenectady and Troy Avenues, often mixed with dwellings. The other east–west streets, St. Johns Place and Lincoln Place, remain largely residential. But St. Johns Place had pockets of commercial activity near the avenues – more so near Utica Avenue on which commercial activity was greatest – where stores could take advantage of pedestrian activity. The few mid-block shops on St. Johns Place served people in immediately adjacent tenements.

The builders who formed this neighborhood were deliberate in the separation of different classes.[6] But land uses were not so separate that people in different economic circumstances did not rub shoulders with each other – and there was considerable mixing of different classes on the shopping street, in the school and in day-to-day encounters on all the streets.

Houses without shops are concentrated on the most exclusive street – Eastern Parkway and on east–west streets away from the north–south avenues. Buildings that combine dwellings and shops are mostly on the north–south avenues that link the residential streets to the subway stations. And buildings that contain only commercial functions are only on the avenues, particularly the busiest one, or very near them on the east–west streets.

[6] Moore, *At Home in America*, 52. See also pages 66–75 for a description of the social and economic variety of this neighborhood and others like it.

This is an ordered structure, in which the shop/house plays a key role. This neighborhood shares characteristics of shop/house location and distribution with many other places. The structure emerges as a result of individuals and builders acting according to their own interests. Although it may be distorted in cities with strict functional zoning or centralized economic control, the structure is similar in places as diverse as Brooklyn and London, Amsterdam and Kyoto, where local economic forces act on the distribution of functions and building types.

A response to economic forces in the city, applied at a local level

The distribution of shop/houses is neither uniform nor random. An ordered pattern emerges partly as a result of individual, local economic decisions, each one an attempt to gain maximum use out of a piece of land. These decisions interact with the street pattern, with the existing structure of uses, and with each other to continually remake the city. It is a process of emergence, as that word is used in contemporary science, in which large-scale order grows from local actions.[7] The detailed structure of the city is the result of hundreds of thousands of individual actions.

The question of location and distribution helps illuminate the idea that the small family-owned shop/house is part of the same phenomenon as the multiple-unit building with independent shops and apartments. Within a framework in which buildings are architecturally flexible, the exact mix of uses they take on is partly dependent on relative location within the city. This is a dynamic process, and will not necessarily result in a building that is "purely" a family shop/house or "purely" a building with completely independent units. The decisions that families and other economic actors make naturally include a full range of hybrids, with different amounts of, and relationships among, commercial and residential space. These proportions and relationships are influenced partly by location.

The location of buildings that combine commercial and dwelling functions is determined partly by an overlapping of the factors that determine each function separately.[8] Retail shops need enough dwellings within an acceptable distance for the particular kind of business – the "catchment area."[9] In a pedestrian city, depending on the kind of business, it also requires being on a street with ample foot traffic – a place of pedestrian concentration for people within the larger catchment area. This often means commercial streets that are well connected to residential ones. Density and street pattern interact and are both important in the equation.

Dwelling location is guided by a different set of variables, including the proximity or cost of transport to work, and the quality of location, including the nearby availability of retail services, parks and schools. Sometimes the quality of the dwelling environment means immediate removal from the public realm, or the ability to have a garden, or peace and quiet.

Commercial and residential uses may therefore be located according to opposing forces. Retail buildings need residential density nearby and exposure on streets with pedestrians – but density and street exposure are not necessarily desirable for housing. To some extent, this explains the location of the Georgian squares of London and the east–west residential streets of New York. In these situations, dwellings are on different streets and in separate buildings from businesses, on quiet streets that are physically near but morphologically removed from more public streets.

[7] See for example Johnson, S., *Emergence*, and Alexander, C., *Nature of Order*, Book 2.

[8] The argument of the following several paragraphs was published in Davis, "Commercial-Residential Building and Local Urban Form." The discussion is based partly on the value of street frontage, which is of course more important to retail trade than to other commercial activities. The distribution of buildings that combine dwellings and work in general is much less constrained by factors of retail location – and many people work at home. But at the same time, retail businesses and many others are still place-dependent – and the analysis is intended to point up the nature of the relationship between those place-dependent shop/houses and the geography of urban districts.

[9] For one classic account of retail location, see Berry, *Geography of Market Centers*.

[10] Warner, *Streetcar Suburbs*, 98. The relationship between streetcar lines and land values in Chicago is described in Hoyt, "One Hundred Years", 191.

The shop/house emerges when residential and commercial uses compete for the same real estate. The architectural result is not one use winning out over the other, but a building in which both can co-exist.

This is the case in dense urban environments. In nineteenth-century Boston:

> Though the streetcar opened to the lower middle class more land than it [had] ever before been able to reach, the supply was too little for so large a number of families. These families not only competed with each other, but with industrial and commercial users who were also attracted by the convenience of the inner suburbs.[10]

In general, when competing uses are on the same street, and land values are high enough to force more intensive use than just one story, two uses may be combined in the same building (Figs. 6.06 and 6.07). This explains buildings like the New York avenue apartment building, Parisian buildings with vertical organization around courtyards, as well as more modest cases, such as the corner store in small towns, where people live upstairs. So it is not only in densely populated places that this competition is present. With the corner store, within the family's economic situation, the need to reconcile costs and income means that the family needs to make maximum use of its piece of land. It resolves the competition between the two uses by putting them together in the same building. A family is using a piece of real estate intensively, for both dwelling and business, but it is optimizing its location by putting it in a place that is both within a residential neighborhood (for family life) and in a place in that neighborhood where it will get maximum foot traffic (for the business).

When residential density increases beyond that which can support only the corner store, the commercial/residential building may still appear as an only occasional event in an otherwise all-residential building fabric. In these places, the shop/house is distinct: it stands out, and may act as a node or important social center on an otherwise quiet street.

In the overall urban plan, density interacts with street pattern and transportation infrastructure. Shop/houses are located on streets that help "funnel" people from all-residential streets toward urban centers, local neighborhood centers or transportation lines (Fig. 6.08). This explains the linkage between shop/houses and streetcar lines (many of which are now bus lines) in many cities, and the north–south New York avenues, where the short blocks help concentrate foot traffic from the longer residential blocks to north–south transportation lines that lead to midtown and downtown Manhattan.

This locational distribution is reflected in building types. It puts family shop/houses in areas of least density and more complex multi-unit buildings in areas of greater density. Land values, rents and uses are constantly jostling with each other, in a process that optimizes total return. This dynamic process is one of location *as well as of building transformation*. So, in addition to the initial locations of buildings being specified by their types, buildings that are architecturally flexible may transform, because of their locations, to contain particular uses. The result may be that buildings of the same type will evolve differently at different places within a district, resulting in a variety of configurations and modes of use, beyond those suggested by the initial types (Table 6.2).

The transect in Fig. 6.08 applies to small towns as a whole, as well as to districts within larger towns and cities that are centered at important intersections or

6.06 (left) Competing uses on Madison Avenue, on the Upper East Side of Manhattan.
Photograph by author.

6.07 (below) Competing uses in Hong Kong.
Photograph by author.

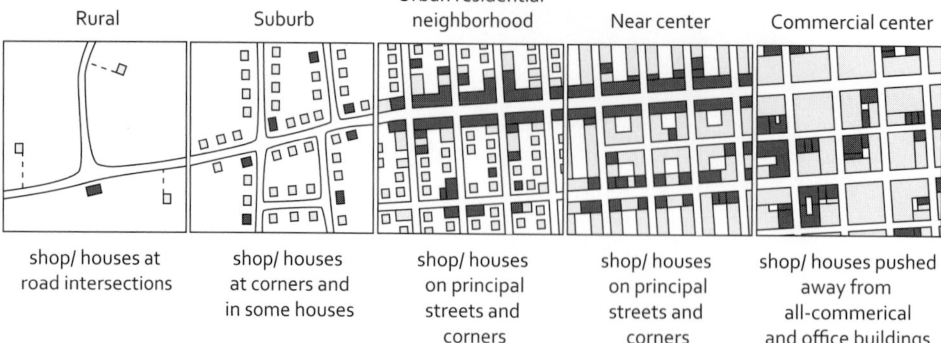

6.08 This diagrammatic transect summarizes the locational issues of shop/houses. There are more shop/houses when residential density is higher. Since they may need retail frontage, they are densely packed on streets that are collector streets with respect to residential streets. When residential density is lower, shop/houses are only at intersections. In the commercial center, where residential uses are excluded, shop/houses are pushed to less intense streets.
Diagram by Matthew M. Brown and Sam Yerke.

Table 6.2 A typical gradient of shop/houses and shop/house locations

Building	Typical location	Typical scenario associated with this building and location
Single-family house with shop in room	Street corner in residential neighborhood	A family maintains a business with a minimum of capital investment
Single-family house with connected shop below	Street corner in residential neighborhood; part of row of buildings on neighborhood commercial street	The business needs its own space, but in the same building
Single-family house with connected shop below, and second rental shop and/or rental room in the dwelling	On or near neighborhood commercial street; increasing density	The family maintains the shop, and is able to rent out more space in the building as needs for domestic space decrease
Multiple-family dwelling where one apartment has a connected shop below and there are also one or more independent rental shops and one or more independent rental apartments	On busy commercial street, at the corner of a residential street	The owner-family lives and has a business in the building, and is taking advantage of land values for investment
Multiple-family dwelling with multiple, independent shops	On a busy commercial street, such as a north–south New York avenue	The building owner/family may or may not live in the building, and is maintaining the building as an investment

transit stops. The overall pattern of shop/houses in the city therefore has multiple centers, some more intense and some less so, each exerting its own influence on the territory around it.

The importance of these dynamics of land value and density can be seen in situations where shop/houses do not exist. Where commercial rents are very high, as in midtown Manhattan, there may not be any shop/houses. Multi-story department stores became profitable when pedestrian density was so high as to make multi-story commercial buildings desirable and viable. Likewise, where residential rents are very high, as in east–west streets on New York's Upper East Side, there will typically not be shop/houses. In other words, shop/houses exist where both uses can contribute together to the site's and building's value.

Within the framework of these ideas, different cities have different characteristic arrangements of streets with shop/houses. In London, many residential squares are designed for privacy, removed from through streets. Lonsdale Square in Islington, for example, is a mid-nineteenth-century square that is removed from the surrounding urban fabric,[11] in an arrangement that makes through traffic almost impossible. The houses on the square are four-story terraced houses, without shops. Shop/houses are located on busier streets that are fed by the square and other residential streets (Figs 6.09, 6.10 and Plate 19). Like the buildings in the square, they are buildings that are variations of terraced houses, but in which the front room or the entire ground floor is devoted to commercial uses.

In the large area of Manhattan first laid out in 1811 – generally, the grid above Fourteenth Street – shop/houses tend to appear on the north–south avenues rather than the east–west cross streets.[12] (They do exist on some major east–west cross streets such as 79th Street and 86th Street, which are east–west public transit routes.) The building types that accommodate shops on the east–west streets and the north–south avenues are the same – row houses and larger apartment buildings. But in many cases there are more apartment buildings on the avenues, allowing the residential streets to maintain a lower scale (Figs 6.09 and 6.11).

In Amsterdam, in the district of the three concentric canals laid out during the seventeenth century, shop/houses are located in streets that run perpendicular to the canals and lead to the city center.[13] As described in Chapter 3, the buildings along the canals were originally mercantile buildings that combined dwellings and warehouses. But this pattern began to change in the eighteenth century, and the buildings along the canals gradually became residential-only.[14] Now the canals accommodate pleasure boats rather than commercial shipping, and their streets – with blocks that are much longer than the commercial streets that run perpendicular to them – are tree-lined and peaceful (Figs 6.09 and 6.12).

In modern Kyoto, shophouses are located on commercial streets and secondary streets of intermediate intensity within districts (Figs 6.09 and 6.13). Some portions of major arterials are too heavily trafficked and noisy for dwellings, and the small streets in the middle of districts are not busy enough for commercial activity to survive.[15] On these streets, the houses are not necessarily traditional *machiya*, but more modern free-standing or connected houses.

11 Hillier and Hanson, *Social Logic of Space*, 123–126.

12 Information from observations by Howard Davis and analysis of data in reverse telephone directories by Steven Miller.

13 Information from observations by Howard Davis in 2003.

14 Komossa et al., *Atlas of the Dutch Urban Block*, 17–24.

15 Information from observations by Nicholas Venezia in 2009.

Left column:

6.09 Maps showing shop/house location in sections of (a) Islington, London; (b) New York's Upper West Side; (c) Amsterdam; (d) Kyoto; and (e) Macerata, Italy. In all five cases, shop/houses are on neighborhood commercial streets that are fed by quieter residential streets and squares.

Photographs (Figs. 6.10–6.14) show typical streets in these areas. Research by Howard Davis, Steven Miller, Matthew M. Brown, Nicholas Venezia. Maps drawn by Matthew M. Brown and Sam Yerke.

In Macerata, a hill town in the Marche region of Italy, shop/houses are located on principal streets that lead toward the urban center, but tend not to be located on less accessible residential streets, nor on the principal streets in the urban center itself, which contain commercial and institutional buildings.[16] Shop/houses and houses without shops are variations of the same types (Figs 6.09 and 6.14).

These places all demonstrate similar patterns. In streets where shop/houses predominate, they are located "in between" all-residential streets and busier, more important streets or places. This is the case whether the street layout is a grid, a distorted grid, an "organic" form or some hybrid, and whether the density of buildings is high or low. Most critical is the place of the shop/house within the street hierarchy.

A subtlety of location

In places with high pedestrian traffic, retail or commercial uses may move slightly up the residential streets, often where they can still be seen from the commercial streets. This is the case, for example, on many east–west streets in Manhattan, where restaurants and other businesses occupy the ground and basement levels of brownstones, in locations near the avenues (Fig. 6.15). In England, where speculative developers from the eighteenth to early twentieth centuries built long rows of party-wall terraced houses, the buildings at the ends – where they meet major through streets – are often shop/houses. This location puts the shop/house in between the residential street – helping to form the retail catchment area – and the main road, where it has additional visibility and may help to form a small cluster of shops or even a retail district (Fig. 6.16).[17]

Right column, p. 108:

6.10 An intersection in Islington, London.
Photograph by author.

6.11 Broadway on the Upper West Side of Manhattan.
Photograph by author.

6.12 View of Amsterdam showing street with shop/houses, at center, perpendicular to residential canals.
Photograph by Donald Corner.

6.13 Street with shophouses in Kyoto.
Photograph by Nick Venezia.

6.14 An intersection in Macerata showing shop/houses on the busier streets and residential-only buildings on quieter ones.
Photograph by author.

[16] Information from observations by Howard Davis in 2007.
[17] Muthesius, *English Terraced House*, 68.

6.15 (left) Side street in Manhattan showing commercial function occupying row-house basement.
Photograph by author.

6.16 (right) Lincoln, England, showing shops at the end of house terraces.
Photograph by author.

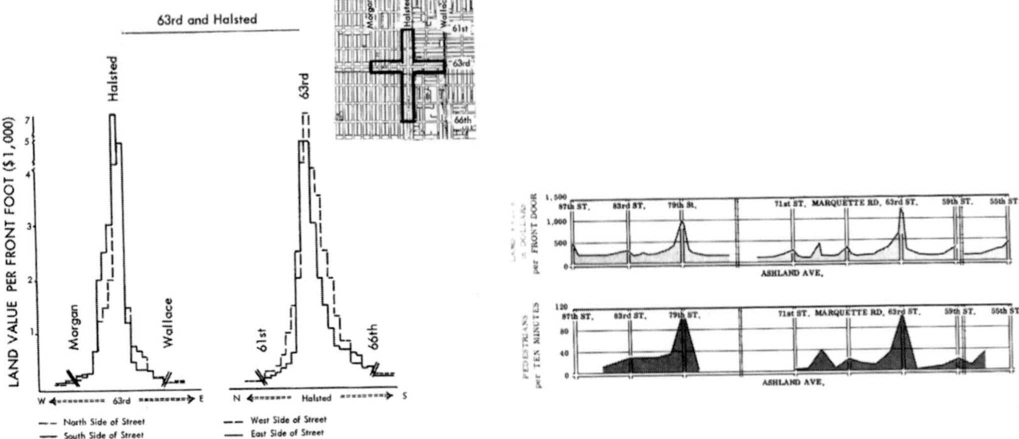

6.17 Graphs of a street in Chicago, showing the strong correlation between pedestrian densities and land values; and land values relative to a particular intersection.

From Berry, *Geography of Market Centers and Retail Distribution*, 1st Edition, © 1967, pp. 49–50. Reprinted by permission of Pearson Education, Upper Saddle River, N.J.

Table 6.3
Estimated Premium of Corner Lots in the CBD of Chicago

Year	Average corner premium (percent)
1836	20
1856	25
1873	25
1896	60
1926–32	100–300

Source:
Hoyt, "One Hundred Years of Land Values in Chicago," 433.

The fact that corner sites are particularly desirable for business also makes them suitable for shop/houses, particularly in situations where office uses, for example, do not trump residential uses at upper floors. The neighborhood corner store is in a position where it may get business from both streets, but where the dwelling may still enjoy amenities such as privacy and a back garden. This can be seen not only in American towns, but also, for example, in the map of Kyoto shown in Figure 6.09, where even within the residential area, away from the intensely commercial street, there is a cluster of shophouses at the intersection of two streets.

In Kyoto, during the Edo period, the corner was regarded as the best place for commerce, and shops in those locations were often larger and more elaborate.[18] In Renaissance Siena, certain locations near the center of the city were appealing for the *palazzi* of prestigious families, because of the symbolic power of such locations. Shops selling fancy goods were also located in the ground floors of those *palazzi*, because of the intensity of street life near the center of the city.[19] In his work on Chicago land values, Homer Hoyt quantified the premium of corner lots in the central business district (Fig. 6.17, Table 6.3).[20]

The American corner store and the Kyoto shophouse were both built in situations with a minimum of zoning constraints, or where zoning rules reflected local economic forces that already existed. In these cases, people were able to act based on their own desires and judgments about their economic situations. These are tiny examples of "urban emergence" – of large-scale, organic order in the city coming about as the result of small, individual decisions. In the framework of a fine-grained street geometry (Jane Jacobs' small blocks, for example) and small lots (that may make opportunities available to people with less available capital), a vibrant urban structure may naturally emerge.[21]

18 Lofgren, *Machiya*, 183.
19 See Nevola, *Siena*, 126.
20 Hoyt, "One Hundred Years", 433.
21 These ideas have been carefully described by Christopher Alexander. One of his first elaborations of them was in a public lecture at Berkeley in 1974, "The Growth of Order from Small Acts." Book 2 of Alexander, *The Nature of Order*, lays them out in detail.

A detailed historic example, using evidence of rents, helps confirm the ideas of this chapter (Fig. 6.18). On the Lower East Side of Manhattan in 1900, density was extremely high and most buildings had commercial uses at their ground floor. But even here, corners were more valuable than mid-block buildings for commercial rentals, and the shorter east–west blocks were more valuable than the north–south longer blocks (in this neighborhood of Manhattan, blocks had a different orientation than the usual east–west orientation farther north). Although residential densities on the Lower East Side were among the highest in the world, commercial space was valuable enough that cellars might have been rented separately from stores above, and many buildings had two levels of shops – one or two shops a half-level up from the street, and one or two a half-level down (Fig. 6.19). The value of the commercial space came partly from the extremely high residential density.

In the above discussion, economic factors have been paramount, and factors of lifestyle choice and housing quality, which are more difficult to quantify, have only been mentioned. Location may be affected by a host of factors in addition to economic ones – proximity to other members of a family or ethnic group, emotional attachment to a neighborhood that comes from a history of residence or business there, particular qualities of buildings and their ability to take on different functions. These factors interact with economic ones, giving variety and local specificity to the urban fabric.

And as mentioned, externalities such as zoning have also affected location, exerting constraints on what might otherwise be more continuous gradients of value and uses. At the same time, in cities such as New York, zoning of some neighborhoods was done based on pre-existing patterns of use. That is one reason New York zoning has a fine grain compared to the zoning of other cities. In many places it was done after uses had been determined, and reflected the existing uses. Some of these existing uses were maintained in the new zoning and some were "grandfathered" in and allowed until the uses changed.

But geography, even affected by contingencies such as zoning, is not enough. The ability of urban districts to flexibly accommodate a mix of functions depends on the presence of buildings whose architecture allows for this mix, and for the flexibility of buildings to allow commercial and residential functions to expand and contract as needed. Shop owners established in a neighborhood know what is going on around them – whether there are more or less potential customers, what customers want, where space is available, how much space costs. They intuitively understand commercial and residential vacancy rates and rents, and how these numbers are changing. That sensitivity can lead to changes in the building that allow the businesses and families freedom to change as well.

In use and transformation, shop/houses and their urban contexts form a single, indivisible unit, in which the meaning of the word "context" itself needs to be questioned. The word "context" implies a duality between a building and what is around it – as if the building and its context are neutral with respect to each other, and do not affect each other. But like many buildings, and perhaps more than some, the shop/house and its street and neighborhood work together, in their formation and in their day-to-day function, in a symbiotic way. The shop/house depends on the neighborhood for business and for social associations. The neighborhood depends on its shop/houses for its economic and social vitality, and even for its identity. When the shop is an active retail business, its activity intermingles with the activity of the sidewalk. The people

hotel
store
jewelry
dry goods
cellar
cutlery store
clothing store
dry goods store
jewelry store
dry goods store
milk store
whole sale goods
corner store
undertakers store
Canal Street
dairy
saloon
butcher
grocery
trimming store
grocery
store
picture frame store
synagogue
grocery
butcher
grocery
trimmings store
lunch room
chair store
clothing store
Chrystie Street
cart storage
cellar
candy store
grocery
restaurant
grocery
shoe store
coffee store
candy store
milk store
cloak shop
glass store
butcher shop
butcher
grocery
laundry
hairdresser
grocery
barber
store
store
crockery
delicatessen
Forsyth Street
Bayard Street
drug store
store
private home
picture
frames
book store
grocery
butcher
dry goods
cellar
grocery
cellar
liquor store
% 53 49 45 41 37 33 29 25 21 0
60 40 20 0

6.18 (previous page) On this map of a block of the Lower East Side at the beginning of the twentieth century, the darker grays indicate a higher percentage of rent that came from commercial uses.
The data for this map is from DeForest and Veiller, *Tenement House Problem*, 439–458. Diagram by Will Krzymowski and Sam Yerke.

6.19 (left) Orchard Street, Lower East Side, New York, showing commercial activity at the lower floors of tenement buildings.
Berenice Abbott photograph. Photography collection, Miriam and Ira D. Wallach Division of Art, Prints and Photographs, The New York Public Library, Astor, Lenox and Tilden Foundations.

living in the dwellings support other businesses nearby, and children and adults form social ties with others in the neighborhood. As in the relationship of a biological organism to its habitat, the physical boundary belies the interactions that cross it.

7.01 Corner store belonging to the Tropeas in Galveston, Texas.
Photograph by Betty Tichich, The Corner Stores of Galveston project.

7

ADAPTABLE BUILDINGS AND FLEXIBLE ECONOMICS

We live up over the store . . . It makes it very convenient for me and for my customer because, you know, when it comes to closing time, I don't have to be particular to watch the clock because all I have to do, I just have to close the door when my customer's ready, and then I go home.[1]

(Angelina Tropea)

He reads several papers, eats breakfast with his family and helps pack his daughters, Malia, 10, and Sasha, 7, off to school before making the 30-second commute downstairs – a definite perk for a man trying to balance work and family life. He eats dinner with his family, then often returns to work; aides have seen him in the Oval Office as late as 10 p.m., reading briefing papers for the next day . . . Mr. Axelrod said "The chance to be under the same roof with his kids, essentially to live over the store, to be able to see them whenever he wants, to wake up with them, have breakfast and dinner with them – that has made him a very happy man."[2]

(Sheryl Gay Stolberg on President Obama's life after a week in the White House)

The terms "adaptability" and "flexibility" may refer to the ability of a building to incorporate different uses, or to take on different functions over time without a change in its configuration, or to be able change its physical configuration with the use of moveable walls in order to assume different functions, or to easily make renovations, to help the building adapt to new demands.[3]

Housing flexibility is usually discussed in contexts such as changing family size, or the ability of a house to allow for the semi-independent dwelling of elderly parents or teenagers. But the accommodation of business occupies a relatively small part of the literature. One recent book, although describing dozens of projects, [4] includes only one or two in which flexibility is intended to allow for commercial activities. The housing work of John Habraken[5] and of Avi Friedman[6] does not explicitly deal with work or commercial functions.

Even less is written about architectural flexibility and urban form. Much of Jane Jacobs' work is concerned with the fine grain of the city and its responsiveness to economic change.[7] In *The Death and Life of Great American Cities* she wrote that buildings with different ages in a district ensures different levels of rent, and therefore the ability for new businesses to co-exist alongside established ones. Older businesses need the innovation and good prices that newer businesses offer, and depend on services that are offered by businesses that pay cheaper rents. Likewise, newer businesses may find their markets in established firms.

1 Beasley, *Corner Store*, 33.
2 Stolberg, "From the Top."
3 See, for example, Brand, *How Buildings Learn*.
4 Schneider and Till, *Flexible Housing*.
5 Habraken, *Variations*.
6 Friedman, *The Grow Home*.
7 See for example, Jacobs, *Economy of Cities*, and Jacobs, *Nature of Economies*.

[8] Sawtelle "Commercial Landscape of Boston," 64; Innes, *"Lower Sort,"* 126–149.
[9] Song, "Between 'The Front' and 'The Back'," 289.

This chapter describes how people use their houses in hybrid situations of work and dwelling. The inventiveness of people in the use of their houses leads to a wide range of configurations, ranging from the informal and temporary to the designed and permanent.

The flexibility of economic life: oiling the engine of economic improvement

Families all over the world need to respond to changes in their economic fortune, their aspirations, and their expanding and contracting positions in the world. Children are born, grow up and move away; businesses are formed and are successful, or stagnant, or failures; jobs are won or lost; the neighborhood revives, or declines, or remains stable. The shop/house provides physical settings that can expand or contract in ways that optimize financial investment. By harboring a business or by providing the basis for a real-estate investment in the same place as the dwelling, the shop/house allows the dwelling and the family's economy to "breathe" relative to the other.

In early nineteenth-century New England the investment required to start a business prevented many journeymen from doing so,[8] and their ability to combine workplace and residence was a factor in being able to move from journeyman to master status. In contemporary London, the shophouse with a takeout food business provides a means for immigrant Chinese families to begin a path of upward mobility in a new country. They use the shop/house not only for economic reasons, but also for the family to stay together.[9]

7.02 House and shop in Santiago, Chile. This is the first building one encounters on a road leading into a squatter settlement.
Photograph by author.

Informal settlements in developing countries are populated by people for whom the house represents a springboard to economic advancement. People may start out with no house or with a makeshift house, and when more permanent housing becomes possible, then the family's work is still part of the housing decision, as the house may serve as a place to store items being hawked in the market, or to cook food for sale, or as a small shop. Until there is sufficient income, the house with an exclusively residential purpose is not a priority.

According to Graham Tipple, the house remains flexible in its daily use:

> [Time] spent in domestic activities can be converted to time spent in the [home-based enterprise] as the ebb and flow of domestic work permits; food intended for sale can be consumed for the family's evening meal; space which is used for, say, sleeping during the night can be utilized for making paintbrushes during the day and, if a person is ill and needs to lie down, can be converted back to sleeping space even in the daytime; money can be spent on improvements in living conditions or in working conditions (or both at the same time). All these changes can be made virtually without cost and inconvenience.[10]

When the family's fortunes change, a workshop can easily be turned into a bedroom or vice versa.[11] Furthermore, moving out of a home/work situation on the part of a parent, for example, may mean a loss of employment for other members of the family who may themselves be able to combine work with other activities, but who could not do so without the business being in the house.[12]

Athough the overlap of activities may be physically uncomfortable,[13] interchangeable barriers between different categories – between money spent on the house and money spent on the business; between food eaten at work and food eaten at home; between time of work and time of family life; between space of work and space of family life – allow time, money, food and space to be used to maximum advantage.

In Dharavi (in the city of Mumbai), the largest slum in Asia, conditions are as crowded as they get, with people living in tiny houses, some a few square meters in area, on lanes so narrow that it becomes difficult to walk, lanes onto which little daylight can enter. Yet, "Every square inch of Dharavi is being used for some productive activity . . . Everyone is busy, doing something. There are few people hanging about . . . Hindu, Muslim, south, north, food, jewellery, hardware, health care, all down one street."[14]

Slums in cities like Mumbai (formerly Bombay) exist partly as results of exploitative, global economic policies.[15] Of course those policies exist, but so do the hundreds of millions of people who are living their lives and trying to make their way in the world. In Gillian Tindall's words:

> Today Bombay, with a density of population about four times that of modern New York, probably resembles more nearly, in social and economic ethos, the New York of a hundred years ago. Certainly it contains grinding mills, both metaphorical and actual; it contains wickedness, ruthlessness and heartlessness. But it is also for many people, including some of the poorest, a place of endeavour, activity, chances, succour, a place to seek your fortune and even find it.[16]

[10] Tipple, *Extending Themselves*, 53. Thanks to Tareef Khan for pointing out this book to me.
[11] Lipton, "Family, Fungibility and Formality," 208.
[12] Lipton, "Family, Fungibility and Formality," 218.
[13] Kellett, "Exploring Space," 10.
[14] Sharma, *Rediscovering Dharavi*, 78–79.
[15] Davis, *Planet of Slums*.
[16] Tindall, *City of Gold*, 22–23.

A hundred years ago, conditions on New York's Lower East Side were crowded, unsanitary and unhealthy. But tenement apartments were used as workplaces in piecework arrangements with clothing manufacturers. These home workshops made the Lower East Side the stepping stone to economic advancement. Most people, or their offspring, moved on – to Williamsburg, to Brownsville, to Harlem, to the Bronx. And *their* offspring, the third generation, moved into the American mainstream. People, or their children, moved from being a peddler, to opening a shop, to being an entrepreneur, to being a professional. Charles Bernheimer wrote "One year may see a clothing or cloak worker in a shop; in few years there will be a sign at the residence of this same man, '______ M.D'."[17]

And this upward mobility began to change neighborhoods:

> To one who has had an opportunity to watch the economic development of the district south of Houston Street, the formation of a well-to-do class in the midst of the Russian Jewish colony has been a very interesting phenomenon. The general improvement in the character of the stores, the sudden appearance of a dozen or more commercial banks, the well-furnished cafés of a type utterly unknown five or six years ago, the modern apartments "with an elevator and a 'nigger boy' on the stoop" all tell eloquently of this growth.[18]

The neighborhood was dynamic. The area had unhealthy living conditions – but it also provided pushcart peddlers with a ready market. The apartments were small – but people made space in them for piecework. Rents in the shops were out of reach for people who lived in the apartments above, but some of those people did eventually open businesses for themselves. The physical structure of the neighborhood embodied a range of possibilities that eased people's upward mobility.[19]

A similar process works in contemporary Chinese cities. One shophouse in Guangzhou is rented by a small-scale entrepreneur from the city of Haifeng, who left a communist work unit to establish a clothing business in Guangzhou (Figs. 7.03 and 7.04). After he rented the shophouse, his wife joined him, and they now live upstairs from the shop with their two children, a woman from their home town who cooks and takes care of the children, and two brothers, not related to the family but also from Haifeng. The brothers work in the shop, take meals with the family and have ideas of opening a shop of their own someday. The cook is near the end of her working life and the two brothers at the beginning. The shophouse allows each of them to benefit from the others' presence.

The Guangzhou shophouse described in Chapter 1 changed over the course of the twentieth century, flexibly adapting and helping its family make ends meet. The three houses were separated early in their lives, each occupied by one of three brothers. The chestnut-powder manufacturing business was closed in 1958, and the present owner of the central house went to work in a state-operated textile mill until it was closed in 1995. From 1958 on, the house was used only for residential purposes and in 1986 it was split into two units, one of which the owner let to two sisters. This became his sole source of income after the factory closed. And in 2001, commercial life returned to the house when an antique seller rented the ground floor for his house and business.

[17] Bernheimer, *The Russian Jew*, 406–407.
[18] Bernheimer, *The Russian Jew*, 104–105.
[19] This discussion is not intended to imply that there was neither exploitation nor sexism in the productive function of the slums. Indeed, because productive work was taken out of the workshop or factory and into the home in the garment industry, this helped to perpetuate the idea that women might be paid less for their work. See Stansell, *City of Women*, 119, and throughout.

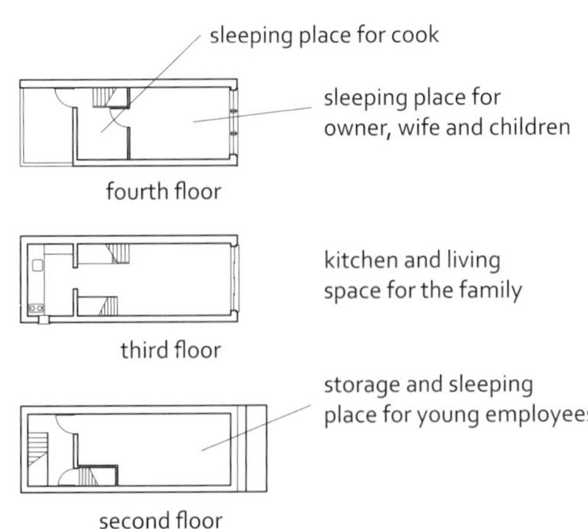

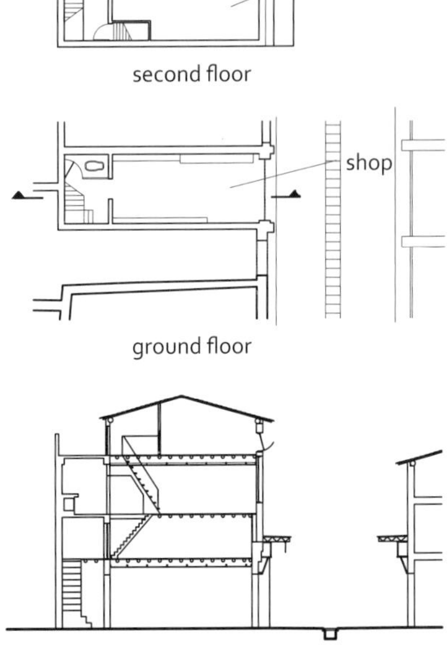

7.03 Intensive use of space in Guangzhou shophouse, which makes it possible for several families to earn a living there.
Drawings by Matthew M. Brown.

7.04 Street where Guangzhou shophouse is located.
Photograph by Matthew M. Brown.

Circumstances in developing countries – in the Lower East Side 100 years ago and in contemporary China – are not so different from those in the contemporary West.

In *The Rise of the Creative Class*, Richard Florida describes how modern life is increasingly characterized by a different attitude toward time. People no longer compartmentalize their activities into clearly distinguishable blocks of time – work, play, family. Instead, activities overlap each other, so that someone's day may include work, for example, interspersed with exercise, or coffee with friends; and a weekend is no longer a weekend in the traditional sense, but includes work and other activities.[20] This represents a perhaps unprecedented kind of flexibility – and not the least of these changes is the increasing importance of buildings in which people both live and work, and neighborhoods that put the venues for different activities near each other.[21]

But this need is not restricted to web designers or business consultants. Michael Pyatok writes:

> . . . not so obvious . . . are those who earn their additional incomes not by word processing or by speculating on the stock market via the web, but by repairing appliances, making clothing, running catering businesses, manufacturing and assembling toys, dolls or plaster figurines or providing all manner of services from hair and nail cosmetics to body-building personal training – all undertaken in the confines of the homestead.[22]

So at opposite ends of the contemporary economic spectrum there may be the desire to begin a business with as little capital or bureaucratic difficulty as possible – a desire that may be facilitated by similar kinds of buildings.

The flexibility of space and time: from the informal to the designed

> In a small English village shop, [at] Bishopsbourne in Kent, where an old lady kept shop in her cottage, shoppers waited in the front room while the things they asked for were fetched through from the back. On Saturday night the shop's trappings were pushed aside, and the front room, complete with piano moved into its centre, was converted to a parlour for the weekend.[23]

Although the front room was not purpose-built for business, it was generic enough in its configuration so that a business could be interchangeable with use as a parlor.

The myriad of different shop/house arrangements represent two kinds of flexibility, cyclic and lineal.[24] Cyclic flexibility is flexibility of use, in which spaces take on different functions at different times, over regular cycles that happen on a daily, weekly or other repetitive basis.

In lineal flexibility, the building use is changed permanently, or the building fabric itself is readily transformed, with renovations, additions or new construction – which, in the case of shop/houses, is often undertaken in order to better allow cyclic flexibility.

Shops may be combined with dwellings in ways that include both the makeshift and the permanent, ranging from the cyclic use of existing rooms for business,

[20] Florida, *Rise of the Creative Class*, 121, 153.
[21] Florida, *Rise of the Creative Class*, 182, 183.
[22] Pyatok, "Design of Affordable Housing."
[23] Brown and Ward, *Village Shop*, 23.
[24] I am grateful to Arijit Sen for putting this idea into such a clear formulation.

PLATES

This color section, mostly consisting of original versions of images that appear elsewhere in the text, is organized so that shop/houses of different cultures are intermingled, to emphasize their ordinariness and their shared features. The sequence of examples, from the informal and makeshift to the designed and permanent, also helps illustrate the ideas in this chapter, into which these plates are inserted.

1 A seventeenth-century cobbler. Drawing by Adriaen van Ostade.
The Metropolitan Museum of Art, Bequest of Edward C. Post, 1930 (30.58.23). Image © The Metropolitan Museum of Art.

2 A stall in Mylapore, Madras (now Chennai), India.
Photograph by author.

3 House and shop in Santiago, Chile. This is the first building one encounters on a road leading into a squatter settlement – everyone passes it on the way in.
Photograph by author.

4 **Shophouse in Siem Reap, Cambodia. In southeast Asia, many houses are raised above the ground, allowing for the ground level to be used for storage or for a shop.**
Photograph by author.

5 **Shophouse in Luang Prabang, Laos.**
Photograph by author.

6 House with shop outside Amsterdam. *Rembrandt, Two Cottages, ca. 1636.*
The Metropolitan Museum of Art, Robert Lehman Collection, 1975.

7 Buildings in the small town of Oudewater, shown on the right and painted by Willem Koekkoek in about 1867, have similar organizational and stylistic features as larger houses in Amsterdam.
© The National Gallery, London.

8 Corner shop with dwelling in Vancouver, British Columbia.
Photograph by Stephen Duff.

9 Corner shop with dwelling in Valaparaiso, Chile.
Photograph by author.

10 Chinese shophouses in Batavia, now Jakarta, in the nineteenth century.
Tropenmuseum, Amsterdam (H-3368).

11 Shophouses in Singapore.
Photograph by author.

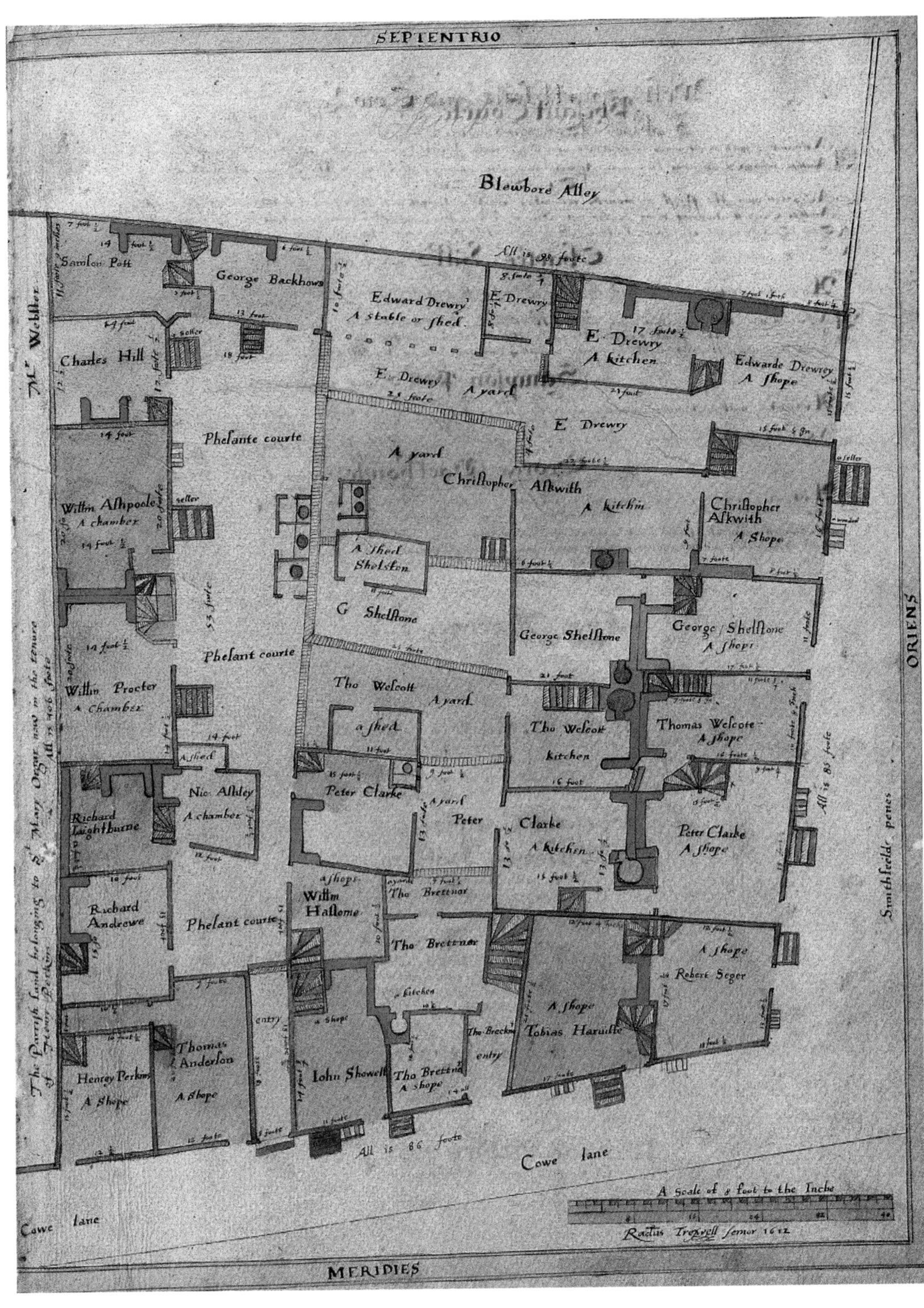

12 **Map of London houses in the late sixteenth century by Ralph Treswell. Most of these buildings have shops in their front rooms and share party walls with neighboring houses.**

Reproduced by kind permission of Christ's Hospital.

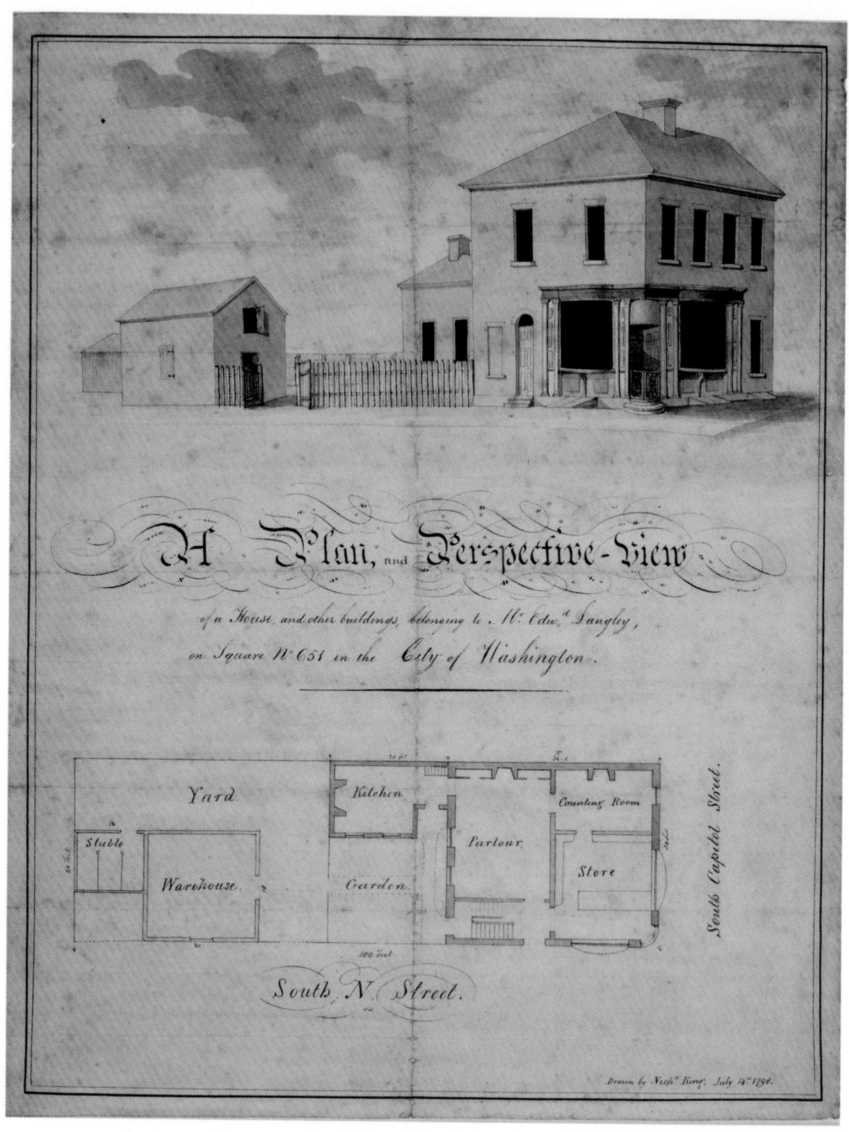

13 **A subtlety of arrangement. In this Washington, D.C. house, the downstairs parlor and kitchen were readily available to the family, through either the stair hall or the counting room. Those intermediate spaces removed the parlor from direct adjacency to the public in the shop.**
Courtesy, The Winterthur Library: Joseph Downs Collection of Manuscripts and Printed Ephemera.

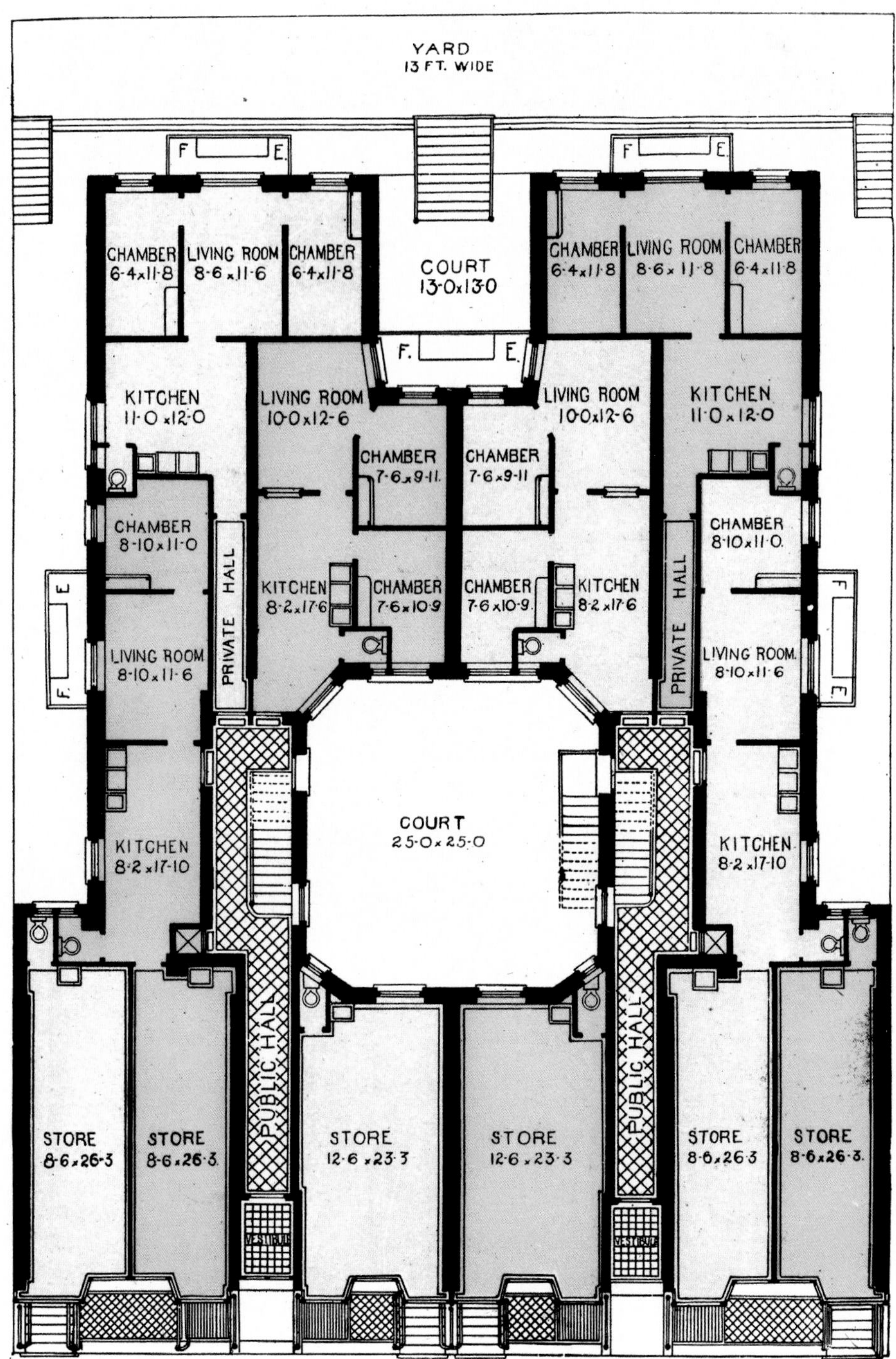

PLAN OF FIRST FLOOR

14 **Plan of two adjacent early twentieth-century tenement buildings in New York. Each has a shop directly connected to the apartment behind, through the kitchen.**

Hesselgren, *Apartment Houses of the Metropolis*.

15 View of a street in Kyoto in the early nineteenth century.
Courtesy Kyoto Municipal Archive.

16 *Machiya* in Kyoto.
Photograph by author.

17 Living over the fishing in Ine-cho, Kyoto Prefecture, on the Sea of Japan. On the land side, the upper floors of these houses are at street level.
Photograph by author.

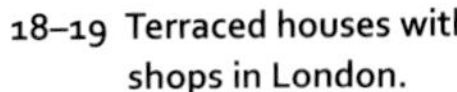

18–19 Terraced houses with shops in London.
Photograph by author.

20 Houses in London with shop extensions.
Photograph by Matthew M. Brown.

21 Shop/houses in piazzetta off the Via dei Giubbonari in Rome.
Photograph by author.

22 Corner house in Amsterdam.
Photograph by author.

23–24 Project with houses and shops in Amsterdam designed by Aldo van Eyck and Theo Bosch.

Photographs by Marc Holt.

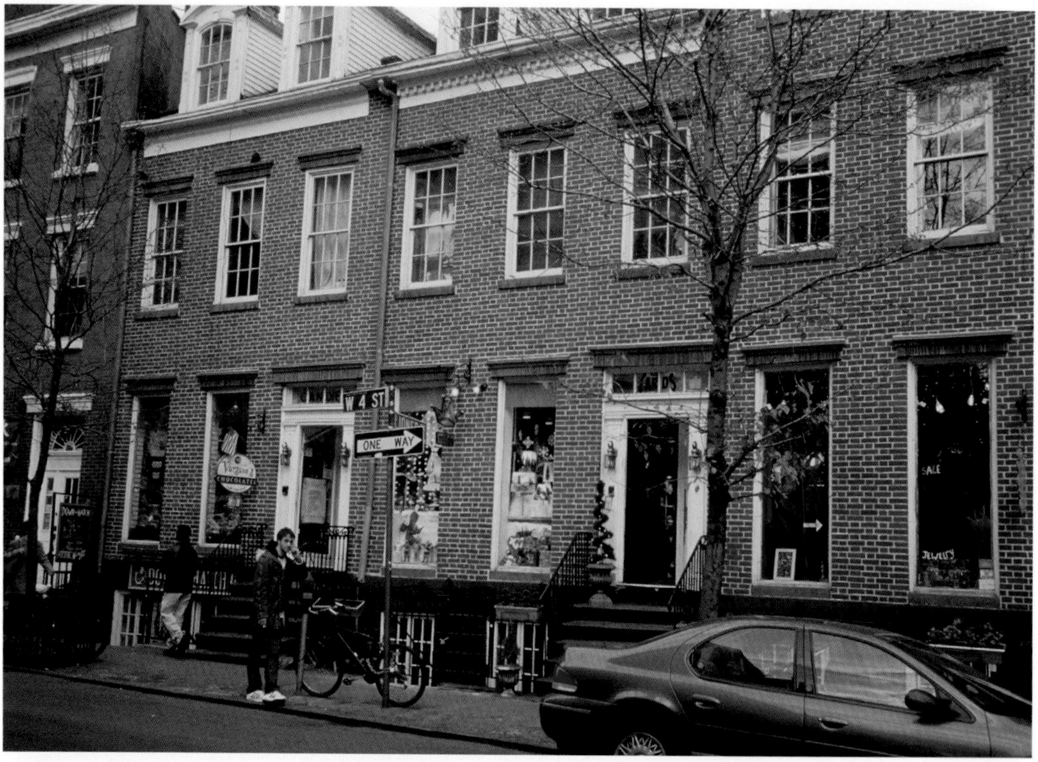
W 4 ST
ONE WAY

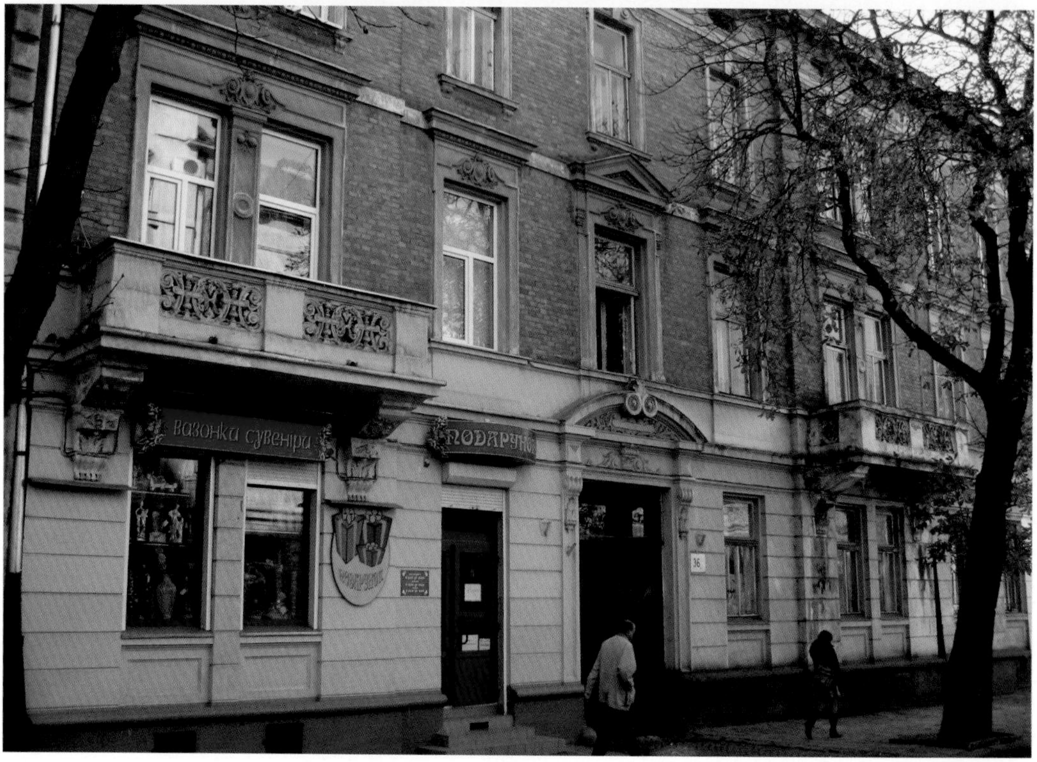
вазонки сувеніри
36

25 (opposite page, top) Houses in Greenwich Village, Manhattan, showing commercial activity at ground floor.
Photograph by author.

26 (opposite page, bottom) Houses in L'viv, Ukraine, showing commercial activity at ground floor.
Photograph by author.

27 House near Berwick-upon-Tweed, England.
Photograph by author.

28 Shop/houses in Brooklyn, New York.
Photograph by author.

29 Shop/houses in Manhattan.
Photograph by author.

30 Merchants' houses in Lübeck.
Photograph by author.

31 Interior of a Lübeck merchant's house looking toward the entrance. The glass-enclosed kitchen is on the left.
Photograph by author.

32 The *braudiele*, or brew hall, in a Lübeck house.
Painting by Hermann Linde.

33 Tailor's shop in Bangkok including dining table and television set.
Photograph by author.

34 Rear of photo-finishing shop in Bangkok showing dining table and shrine.
Photograph by author.

35 Dinner in Taiwan shophouse.
Photograph by Stephen Coffin reproduced with permission of Sophie Chen and family.

36 Shophouses in new development in Bangkok.
Photograph by Thomas A. Kerr.

37 Arcaded street in Guangzhou.
Photograph by Matthew M. Brown.

HOTEL
OSPEDALE H
SS.Giov. e Paolo
PER S.MAR
RAMO
S.ZULI

38 **Venice.**
Photograph by author.

39 **Hudson Street, New York. Jane Jacobs lived on this block when she was writing *The Death and Life of Great American Cities*, first published in 1961.**
Photograph by author in 2009.

40 Belmont Street, Portland, Oregon.
Photograph by author.

41 (opposite page, top) Shophouses in Bangkok's Chinatown, showing area above canopies that shade commercial street below.
Photograph by author.

42 (opposite page, bottom) Shophouses in Bangkok's Chinatown, showing commercial street shaded by canopies.
Photograph by author.

43 Ruins of ground floor and part of second floor of ancient apartment buildings in Ostia Antica, showing shopfronts with built-in counter.
Photograph by author.

44 The Jewish ghetto in Rome in the nineteenth century.
Watercolor by Ettore Roesler Franz. Roma, Museo di Roma, Archivio Fotografico Communale.

45 Shophouses in Ahmedabad, India.
Photograph by author.

46 Shophouses in Chandigarh, designed in the 1950s.
Photograph by Jonathan Alex Jensen.

47 Shop/house in San Francisco, designed by Ned White.
Photograph by Wyatt Hammer.

48 New building with architect's office and residence, left, on commercial street in Toronto.
Superkul Architects.

49–50 Paris.
Photograph by Alvin Comiter.

51 Paris.
Photograph by author.

IKBEISL
BANK
REDITANSTALT · BANKVEREIN

52 (opposite page) Apartment building designed by Otto Wagner in Vienna.
Photograph by author.

53 Hong Kong.
Photograph by author.

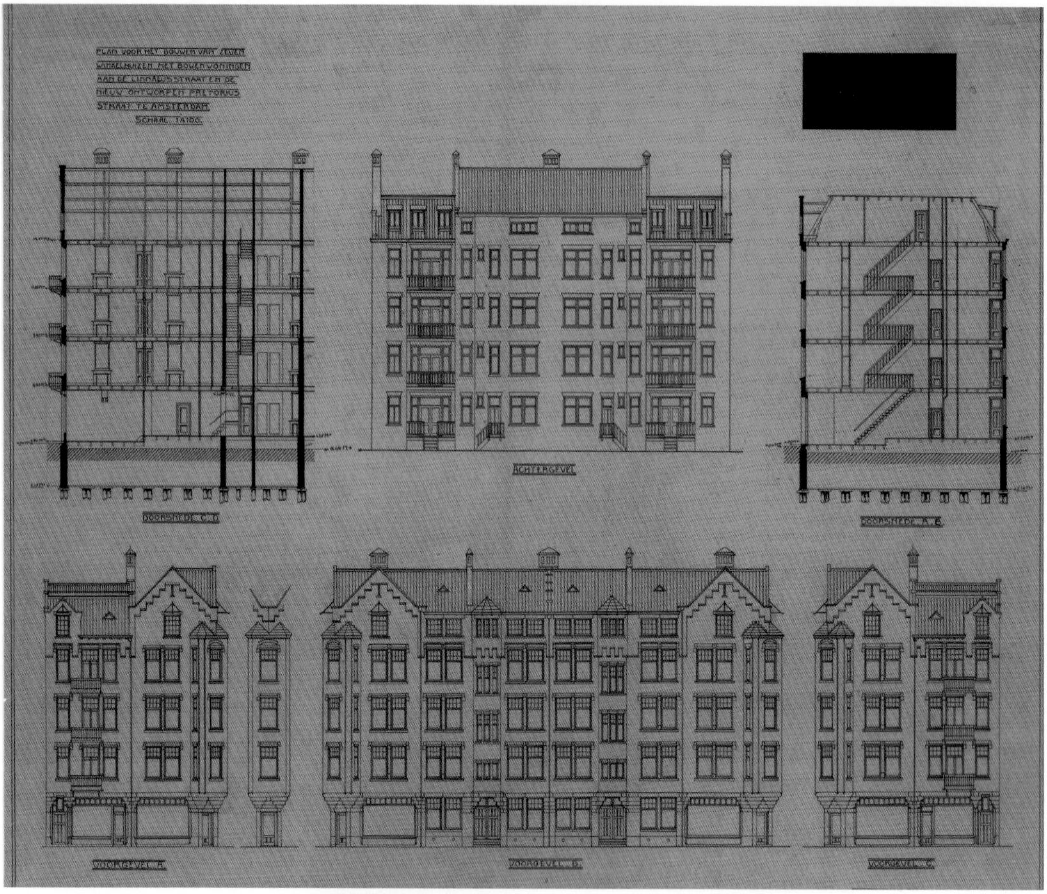

54 Twin apartment buildings with stores at Linnaeusstraat, Amsterdam, 1905: elevations and sections.
Netherlands Architecture Institute.

55 Public housing block in Vienna.
Photograph by author.

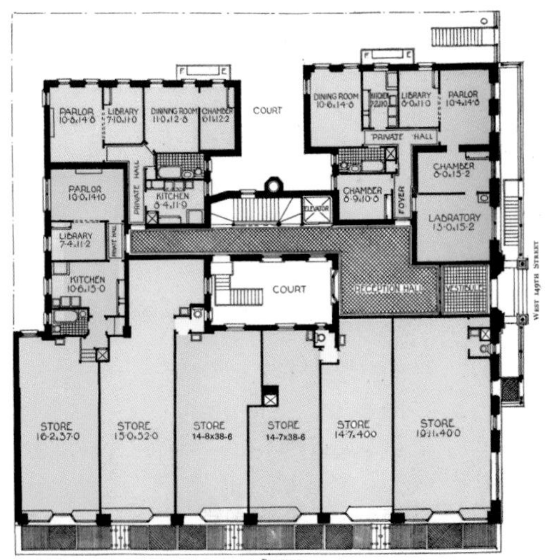

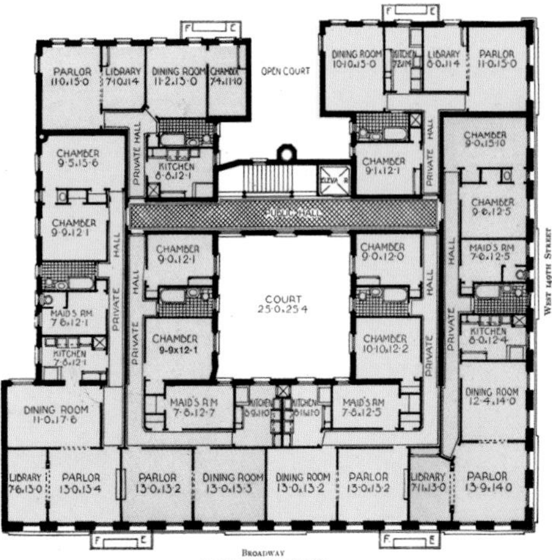

56 Plans of early twentieth-century apartment building in New York.
Hesselgren, *Apartment Houses of the Metropolis*.

57 New York apartment houses with shops, of different eras.
Photograph by author.

58–59 (top and middle) Sketch and rendering of Crescent Village, Eugene, Oregon.
Rowell Brokaw Architects.

60 Front Street Redevelopment, New York.
Cook+Fox Architects.

7.05 A seventeenth-century cobbler.
Drawing by Adriaen van Ostade. The Metropolitan Museum of Art, Bequest of Edward C. Post, 1930 (30.58.23). Image © the Metropolitan Museum of Art.

to the permanent use of existing rooms for business; from the conversion of existing rooms, to specific additions to the house, to the initial construction of the house to include specific spaces for commercial use.

The garage sale, the farm stand and the makeshift or temporary stall are at one end of the spectrum (Fig. 7.05 and Plate 1). Requiring little or no physical change, they exist on property already owned by the family, and allow for additional income, whether regular or intermittent. Similarly, cooking the family meal may turn into a business if the institutional and architectural constraints are minor. In Palermo, small unmarked and illegal trattoria began as simple lunch counters attached to houses, in which wives made food for their husbands and their co-workers. In one place ". . . this used to be a taverna – a hall where men drank grappa until sunrise. Then, one summer about 40 years ago, [Mr. Balestreri] rolled a barbecue grill onto the driveway and started cooking meat. Next thing he knew, he had a trattoria." In these places the police may look the other way – because they like eating there, too.[25] In the United States, there is a movement toward "rogue restaurants," with gourmet chefs, in which meals are cooked and served in houses.[26]

In Brooklyn, New York during the 1950s, Fanny and Eddie Jacob occupied a hardware-and-housewares store. They lived in two crowded rooms behind the store – a combined kitchen/living room and a small bedroom. To help make ends meet, they also rented out an alcove adjacent to the kitchen/living room, to an electrician who was building a small business. He put the Jacobs' address on his business cards, and used the space to store coils of wire and electrical parts (Fig. 7.06). The Jacobs made maximum economic use of the space they rented, and the electrician, who was by then slightly better off than the Jacobs,

[25] Pergament, "Their House is Your Trattoria," 10.
[26] Garbee, *Secret Suppers.*

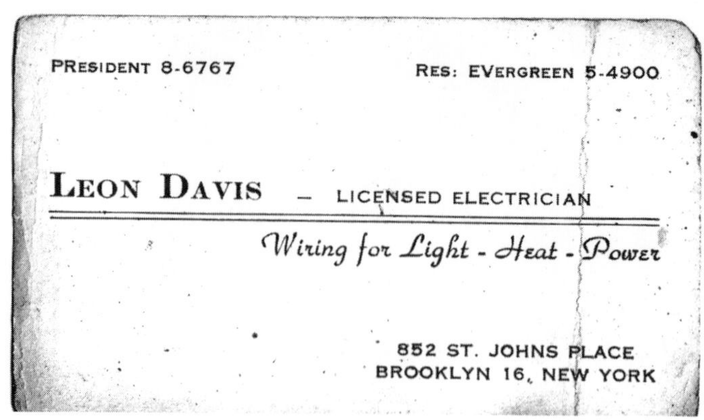
PRESIDENT 8-6767

RES: EVERGREEN 5-4900

LEON DAVIS – LICENSED ELECTRICIAN

Wiring for Light - Heat - Power

852 ST. JOHNS PLACE
BROOKLYN 16, NEW YORK

7.06 The shop/house at 852 St. Johns Place served the economic lives of two families.
Howard Davis collection.

was able to maintain an apartment for his family that was free of the business (except for the monthly accounts that his wife did on the kitchen table) in a more leafy, residential neighborhood of Brooklyn. In this case, a single, combined commercial/residential space was tied to the economic lives of two families.

The importance of contiguous spaces to cyclic flexibility is demonstrated by the words of Elena Cantini, who ran a grocery store while living over it, in Galveston, Texas:

> The store opened at five in the morning. Customers had no refrigeration. They had to buy their meat, their lunch supplies, their milk, their bread before they went to work in the morning. If my husband was 15 minutes late, they would start throwing rocks up at the window. "Cantini, come on down. I got to get my groceries." So he would go down and we would close at 9:30-10:00 at night . . . So, I'd stay in the store. I'd come down about six o'clock and I'd dress my babies downstairs. I'd pile them on my arms and put the blankets on and their clothes on and dress them downstairs where it was warm. We had no heat upstairs. Then they were settled and I'd stay in the grocery store until 10:30 or 11:00 when I'd go upstairs and start my dinner. Then after dinner . . . my husband would take a nap for an hour and I'd stay in the store. Then when he came back from buying his produce or whatever in the afternoon and bought what he had to have, then I went back upstairs and as the children were older and going

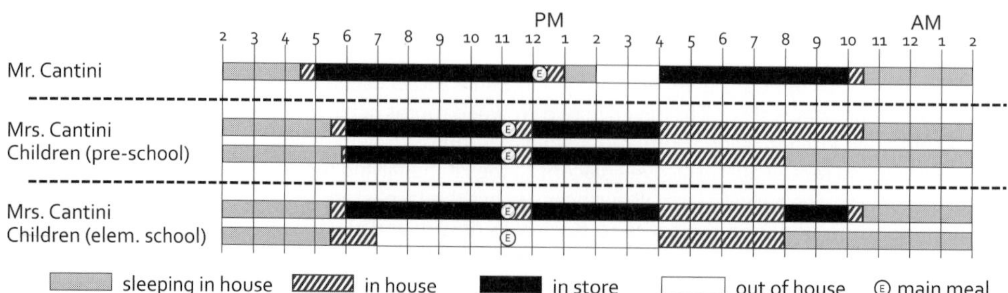

7.07 The interweaving of space and time in the Cantini household over the course of a day.
Chart by Matthew M. Brown and Sam Yerke.

> to school, I didn't come back downstairs in the store after that. I would stay upstairs and take care of them with their homework. Then I went back in the store for a couple of hours and stayed there until bedtime.[27] (Figure 7.07)

The economic benefit of this arrangement was described by Ross Novelli, another Galveston shopkeeper, who said that "[grocers] could always eat and they were going to be buying [food] at cheaper prices to start with . . . and if they lived in conjunction with the business, they would have cheaper rent."[28]

A similar schedule is described in a weaver's shophouse in Kyoto. One woman describes flexibility with her time, the ability to take a slightly longer break, and the ability to take care of the children in the evening.

> When a person works at home, it doesn't matter how long he works. Our schedule is left to our independent judgment. Only factory workers observe the eight-hour day. But those of us who have families can't keep those hours when working at home.[29]

(However, sometimes the conflicts between family and work are strong enough that someone will wish for a separation between the two.[30]) Women were able to weave and also take care of children and the household, and variation in the quantity of work meant that women could vary the amount of time they spent at work.[31]

The nature of the flexible relationship between work and dwelling varies from culture to culture, over history and according to economic class. There was an ambiguity of use of space in houses in Northamptonshire during the seventeenth and eighteenth centuries.[32] Probate inventories indicate the same thing with early New England houses.[33] Although houses in Northamptonshire or New England were built with some understanding of what room uses would be, this was not rigidly followed. Neither the fitting out of rooms nor their positions was so specific as to constrain their dual use, and architectural flexibility served functional flexibility. This is also found in seventeenth-century buildings in London.[34] In early Washington, D.C., a shop/house may have been subtly designed to allow for a close relationship between family and work, by putting living space at the ground floor, but also allowing for more limited access from the shop to the dwelling by strangers, in keeping with the mores of Virginia society (Fig. 7.08 and Plate 13).[35]

In modern Bangkok, a tailor who occupies a modern shop eats most of his meals at a table set up in the middle of the shop, and has a television in the shop window, facing toward the table (Figs. 7.09, 7.11, Plate 34). The proprietor of a photo-finishing shop, in which photo equipment alternates along the walls with fish tanks and a refrigerator for cold drinks, does the same thing (Figs. 7.09, 7.10, Plate 33).

In each shop, there is little distinction between space of business and space used by the shop owners when not engaged in business. In the tailor's shop, customers may easily go deeper into the building than the dining table for purposes of fitting, paying or selecting fabric. The photo-finishing shop has a clearer demarcation for customers at the front and along one side of the counter, but here as well, one is in the same space as the shopkeeper even when he is eating his meal.

27 Beasley, *Corner Store*, 28.
28 National Building Museum, website in connection with 2000 exhibition "The Corner Store," accessed July 4, 2011, www.nbm.org/Exhibits/past/2000_1996/Corner_Store.html.
29 Hareven, *Silk Weavers of Kyoto*, 189.
30 Hareven, *Silk Weavers of Kyoto*, 262.
31 Hareven, *Silk Weavers of Kyoto*, 82–83, 91.
32 Stobart, "Accommodating the Shop," 357–363.
33 Copy of the Inventory of the Estate of Wm. Paine of Boston, Merchant, Appraised by Hen. Shrimpton, Joshua Scottow and John Richards, and Allowed in Court at Boston, Nov. 14, 1660, Upon Oath of Mr. John Paine, His Son. In Dow, *Every Day Life*, 258–261.
34 Brown, "Continuity and Change," 578–582.
35 Martin, "Commercial Space as Consumption Arena," 212–213.

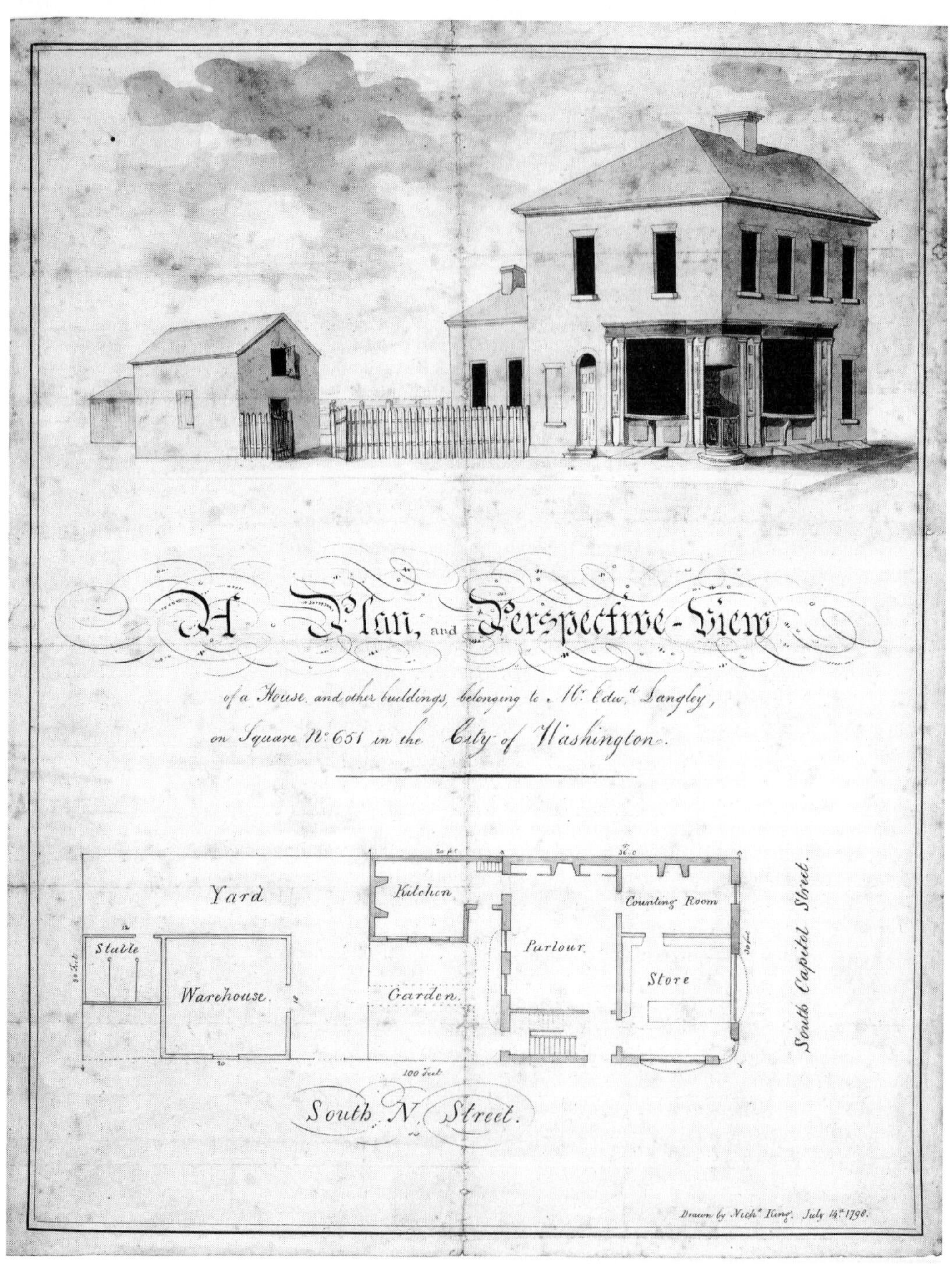

7.08 In this Washington, D.C. house, the downstairs parlor and kitchen were readily available to the family, through either the stair hall or the counting room. Those intermediate spaces removed the parlor from direct adjacency to the public in the shop.

Courtesy The Winterthur Library: Joseph Downs Collection of Manuscripts and Printed Ephemera.

7.09 Plans of Bangkok shophouses with tailor shop (double building, above) and photo shop (below).
Drawings by Will Krzymowski based on measurements by author.

7.10 Photo shop, Bangkok. The combined setting for work and family life.
Photograph by author.

7.11 Dining table and television in tailor shop. Bangkok.
Photograph by author.

7.12 Initial transformations in Greenwich Village houses, with shops in ground-floor rooms.
Photograph by author.

7.13 Initial transformations in house in L'viv, Ukraine with shop in ground-floor room.
Photograph by author.

7.14 Shopfront installed in house in Berwick-upon-Tweed.
Photograph by author.

In smaller Bangkok shophouses the line between shop and family life may be even more ambiguous. In some of these houses, the tables where families eat their regular meals are out on the sidewalk, near the curb, so that passersby – even those who have no business with the shop – walk between the table and the shopfront.

Although the ground floor of shophouses accommodates a mixing of shop and domestic functions, there is always a barrier beyond which the customer is not welcome without invitation. This is at the back of the shop, the wall that leads to the stair and kitchen, and often corresponds to the place where one must remove one's shoes before going further. The kitchen and upstairs rooms are private spaces, reserved for the family and its guests. But even here, goods of the shop may be stored beyond this barrier, in the back or upstairs, with shop functions overlapping with domestic space.

This relationship is different in Japan. In some Kyoto shophouses – other than a restaurant in which the restaurant kitchen was used for family meals and the children did their homework at the restaurant counter – there is a stricter separation. In two *machiya*, with a shoe shop and a clothing store, there were no places to eat in the shop, and children would not spend time there when they were not in school.

The formality of the Japanese shophouse may be accompanied by a special room in between shop and dwelling. In the *machiya* with the shoe shop, during shop hours, the woman was often there alone. She sat at a table in a small room in the residence, just behind but with a view of the shop, able to take care of both shop and household. Her position, away from the public realm but having a glimpse of it, is similar to that described by one writer, who says that even at the Gion Festival (in Kyoto):

> upper-class women couldn't slip outside to watch the floats going past. There was a thin lattice partition between the women's quarters and the shop so, instead of watching the parade like anybody else, the lady of the house would have to sit inside, with a fan in her hand, watching in secret behind the partition.[36]

Likewise, Nakagawa describes a *chanoma*, or small tea room – an informal place for family meals – in between the shop (of a stationer) and the kitchen.[37] Despite the flexibility of Japanese rooms, the activities in them were not necessarily in public view.

If the basic building type allows for it, the front room of a dwelling may be permanently converted into a shop or work space (Figs. 7.12, 7.13, 7.14; Plates 25, 26, 27). In these cases, the position of the front room on the street allows it to be flexibly used as either a room of the dwelling or as a shop. Depending on how that room is connected to rooms behind it, the business may be shallow or deep relative to the street, and may change its depth as economic needs warrant.

Housing flexibility has been a recurrent theme in modern architecture. The Diagoon houses in Delft, designed by Herman Hertzberger and built in 1971, incorporated a basic core and structure within which occupants could make choices and transformations, to include a variety of functions including work. The project is one of a number of Hertzberger's buildings, including the Centraal Beheer insurance headquarters in Apeldoorn, in which people can personalize

[36] Saga, *Memories of Silk and Straw*, 139.

[37] Nakagawa, *Japanese House*, 115–117.

7.15 Axonometric of Diagoon project by Herman Hertzberger.
Courtesy Office of Herman Hertzberger.

7.16 House plans and section of Diagoon project.
Courtesy Office of Herman Hertzberger.

7.17 Variations of house uses within basic house design in Diagoon project.
Courtesy Office of Herman Hertzberger.

7.18 Grocery-store addition to house in Albany, Oregon.
From Albany Regional Museum *Robert Potts' Photo Collection*.

[38] Conversation with Jo Noero, March 22, 2009.
[39] Communication with Thomas Kerr, Asian Coalition for Housing Rights, Bangkok, April 2009.

spaces, within a permanent structural framework, with non-structural partitions and elements. (Figs. 7.15, 7.16, 7.17)

Within a concrete frame, the houses have two fixed elements: a stair and a stacked plumbing core serving a kitchen and a bath. Room configurations and adjacencies are changeable: non-structural infill walls can be easily inserted or removed. A staggered section allows adjacent levels to communicate with each other, or – if walls are built – to be separate. Hertzberger's diagrams show some lower-level spaces, including the garage, being used for work functions – similarly to Michael Pyatok's Gateway Commons project, illustrated in Chapter 11.

If the site is large enough, a room may be added to the house for the purpose of a business (Fig. 7.18). This has traditionally happened in American towns, often in residential neighborhoods, where there is available land on residential lots, and on London streets that turned out to be busy enough so that shops could be built replacing front gardens, and in many other places.

In Bangkok, several shophouse owners reported that they had made considerable changes to their buildings over the years, almost always to improve the business – and sometimes at the expense of the dwelling. The owner of the tailor shop described above bought an adjacent building to expand the shop, and now there is a well-appointed shop double the size of the original, but vacant rooms as part of the expanded residence upstairs.

An entry in a United Nations-sponsored competition for low-cost housing in the slums of Lima was developed from patterns that were the result of careful observation of daily life. The party-wall houses are each organized around three courtyards that become increasingly private farther back from the street. The houses are organized in a site plan with a hierarchy of public spaces, ranging from large marketplaces to very small squares. Houses on the marketplace allow any householder the option to have a shop built in at the outset, and the house designs themselves were flexible enough for small shops to be added later. Houses also had options for a room for rental to be included, in a place where it would not disturb the privacy of the family (Figs. 7.19, 7.20, 7.21, 7.22).

Contemporary projects in South Africa and in Bangkok do similar things. Designed by the Cape Town firm Noero-Wolff, the Pelip Housing project in Port Elizabeth allows for an initial repetitive unit design to be transformed over time by incremental improvements initiated by residents. The position of the unit on the site allows for extensions, and the stair location permits separate use of different floors and additions that may be connected to, or independent of, the original unit. The building can accommodate an extension of the original dwelling unit, an additional dwelling unit, or a space for a home business (Fig. 7.23).[38]

Numerous projects in Thailand are financed and built by the Community Organizations Development Institute, with community participation in design and management. Houses are arranged in simple site plans, and designed so the ground floor can easily become a shop. Concrete-frame construction allows the front wall to be quickly replaced with a rolling metal shutter, for a retail shop or workshop. Local steel fabricators can make shutters in a day or two, and the investment for the conversion is relatively small. Soon after completion, these projects become busy neighborhoods with shops throughout them, even on lanes that are away from principal streets.[39] (Figs. 7.24, 7.25, 7.26).

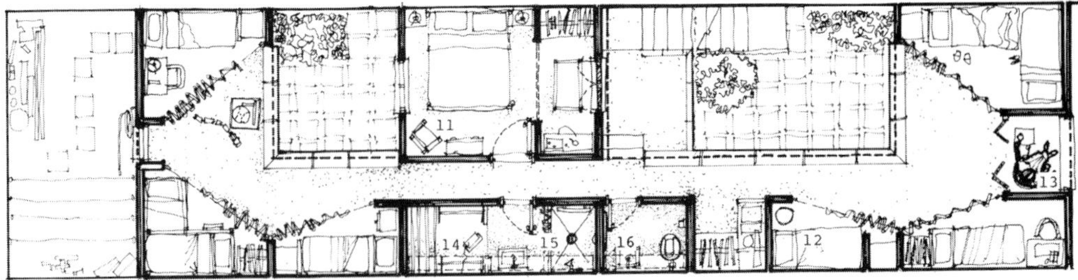

second floor

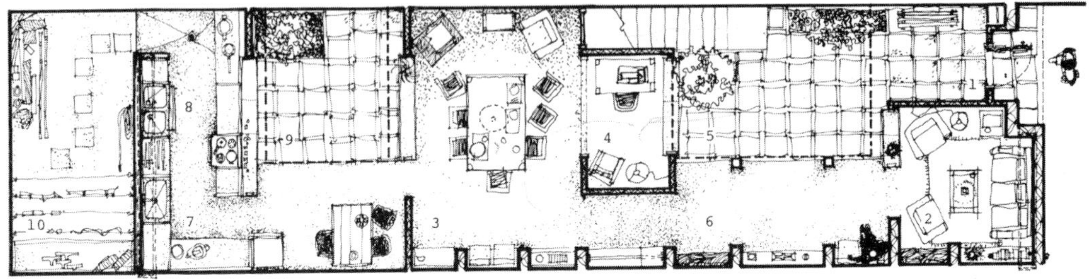

first floor

7.19 Generic house plan in Lima project, designed by Christopher Alexander and the Center for Environmental Structure.
Printed with permission of Christopher Alexander.

7.20 Possible positions of shops in houses in Lima project.
Printed with permission of Christopher Alexander.

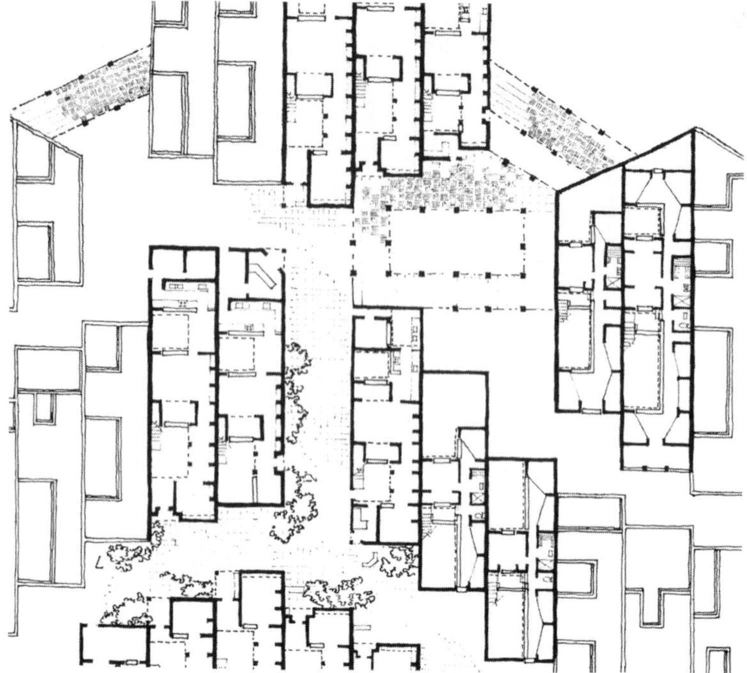

7.21 Portion of site plan showing houses with shops forming public space in Lima project.
Printed with permission of Christopher Alexander.

7.22 Shop/house in Lima project.
Printed with permission of Christopher Alexander.

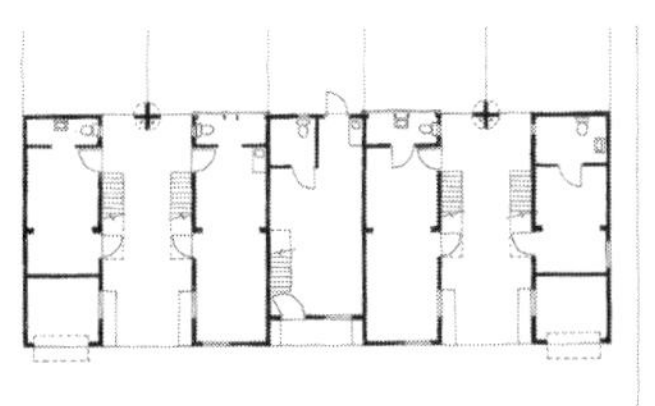

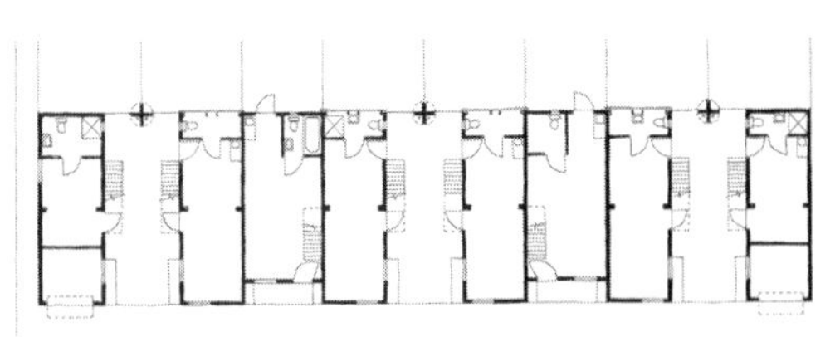

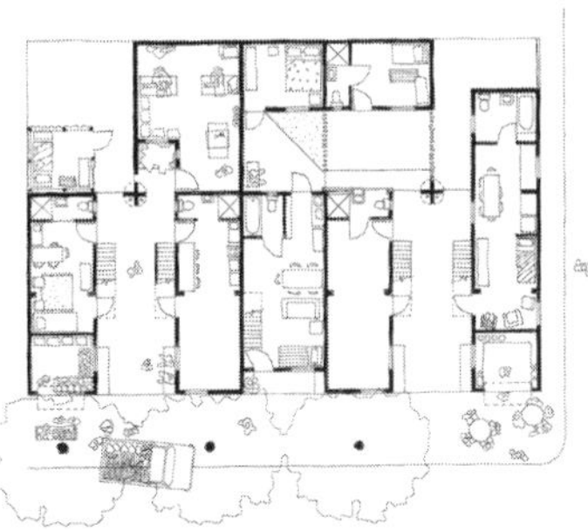

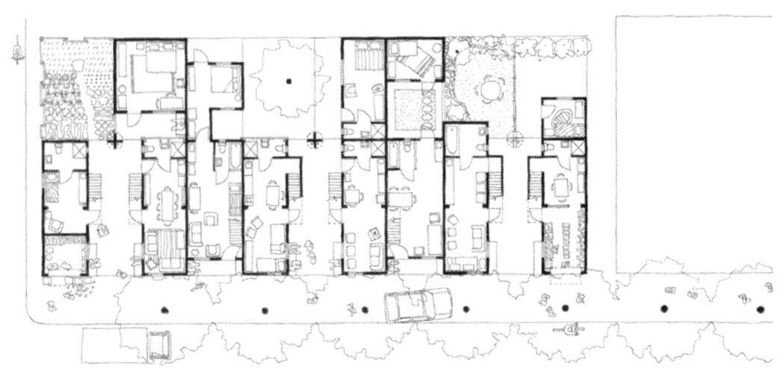

7.23 Before-and-after plan of Pelip housing project in Port Elizabeth, by Noero-Wolff Architects designed so that houses can easily expand. This is similar to more recent projects of Elemental/ Alejandro Arevena in Chile.

Drawing courtesy of Noero-Wolff Architects, Cape Town.

7.24 Row of new Bangkok shophouses with restaurants and shops.

Photograph by Thomas A. Kerr.

7.25 Plans of new Bangkok shophouses showing how ground floors are used flexibly.
Drawn by Will Krzymowski from information supplied by Thomas A. Kerr.

7.26 New Bangkok shophouse with grocery at ground floor.
Photography by Thomas A. Kerr.

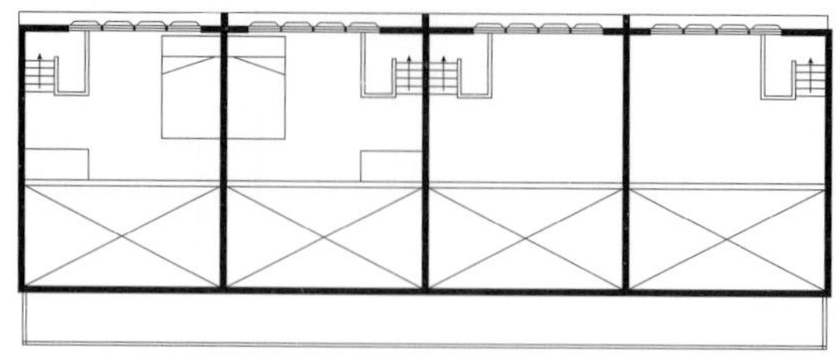

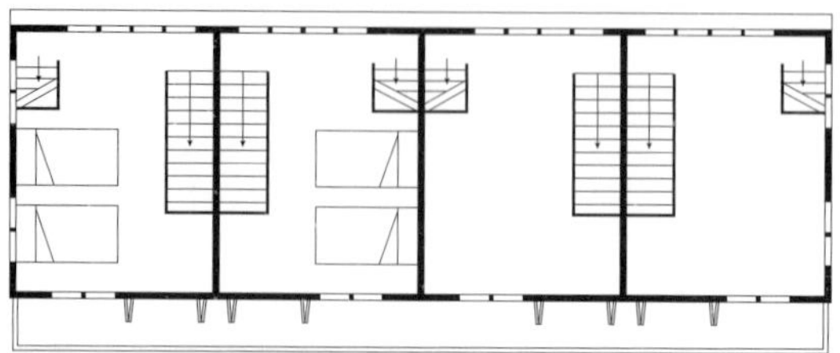

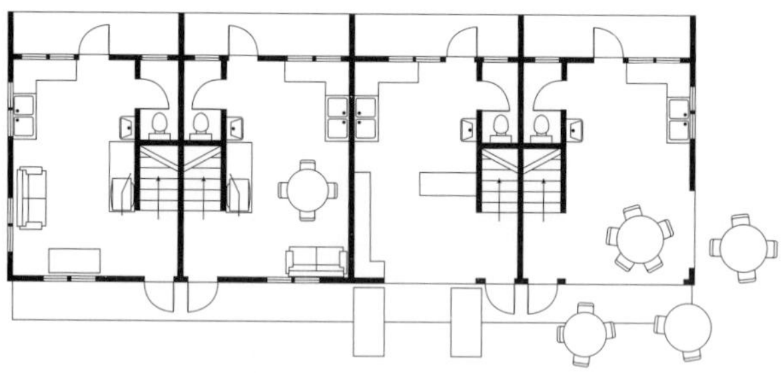

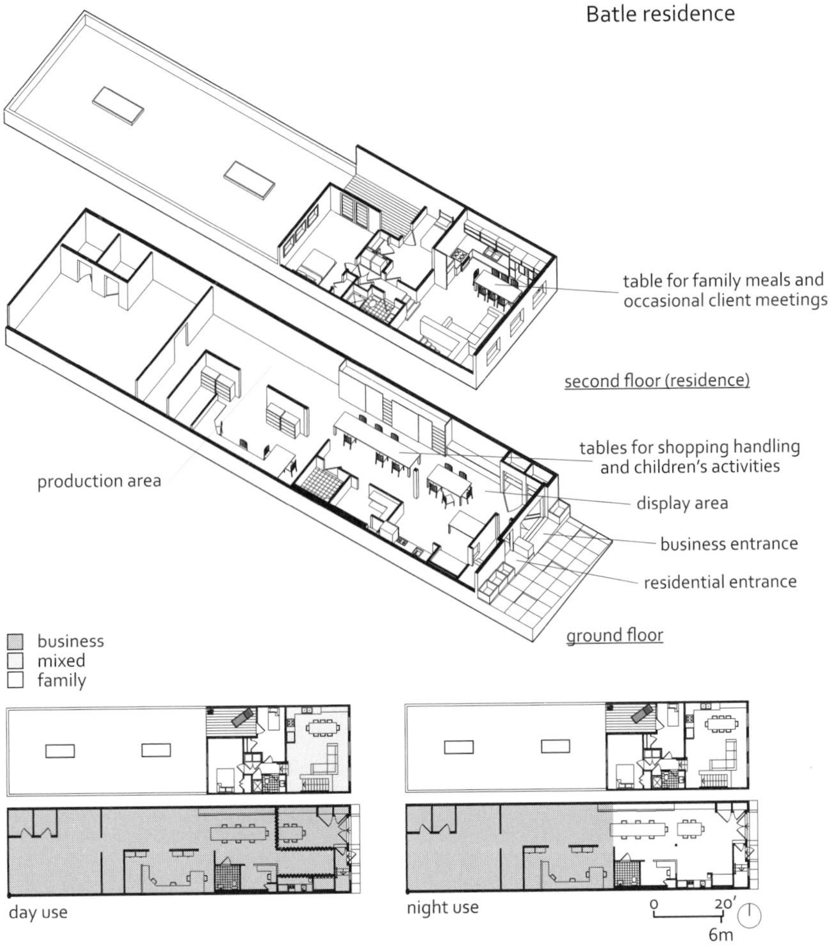

Batle residence

table for family meals and occasional client meetings

second floor (residence)

tables for shopping handling and children's activities

production area

display area

business entrance

residential entrance

ground floor

business
mixed
family

day use

night use

0 20′
6m

7.27 (top) San Francisco shop/house, showing how functions change from day to night/weekends.
Designed by Ned White/McCoppin Studios. Drawings by Wyatt Hammer and Sam Yerke from originals by Ned White/McCobbin Studios, San Francisco.

7.28 (bottom left) San Francisco shop/house on the edge between houses and light industrial buildings.
Photograph by Wyatt Hammer.

7.29 (bottom right) Ground-floor tables in San Francisco shop/house, used for client meetings, art display and children's games and homework.
Photograph by Wyatt Hammer.

[40] Conversation with Agelio Batle, December 2008, with thanks to Ned White.

New family shop/houses

On the boundary between a residential and light industrial neighborhood in San Francisco, a two-story building was originally a Victorian house and had been renovated numerous times. When the present owners bought it, the building had a long extension to the rear, filling the 25′ × 110′ site. It had been the home of a failed dot-com business, with a 900-square-foot apartment upstairs (Figs. 7.27, 7.28, 7.29).

The new owners are an artist who designs and manufactures graphite objects that are sold to museum shops, and conducts art classes; his wife, a partner in the business; and their two sons, aged 12 and 10 in December 2008.

The renovation was designed to maintain a strong interaction between the two floors. The front of the ground floor is used for client meetings and as a gallery, by the children for homework and to play with friends, and for family meals when there are many guests. Curtains are pulled between the front and the back work space to help the front act as a family space in the evening. The boys do homework on large tables that are used for the business during the day, and a piano is sometimes moved to the front. The upstairs is sometimes used for meetings, for design work, and to get away when downstairs activity is too intense.

Although each floor has its own street entrance, there is also a door to the stair from the downstairs space, allowing the two floors to be used closely together. During the day, the family may eat downstairs, where a small kitchen is also used by the staff of seven.

This is a multiply-hybrid building. When the renovation was being designed, the owners decided not to extend the 900-square-foot apartment (although the architect, Ned White, did redesign it) because domestic activities could also take place downstairs. The artist says, "We thought of it as live-work, but it's really seamless."[40] A similar project is in Toronto (Figs 7.30 and 7.31).

Resilient urban districts

Finally, districts with resilient buildings are themselves resilient: the flexibility of many traditional shop/houses helps their urban district remain flexible, allowing the district's economy to readily respond to economic changes and opportunities.

The addition of shops to terraced houses set back from the street is found on commercial streets all over London (Figs. 7.32, 7.33, Plate 20). In each place, it happened when foot and vehicular traffic increased to the point that business became viable, and the income from the business became more valuable than the increased value of the house that came from the garden alone. The changing urban context drives the transformation, and allows the building to be used to take advantage of local economic opportunity.

The Upper West Side of New York has had a stable spatial structure for over a hundred years, even as individual buildings have shifted back and forth between residential and commercial uses (Fig. 7.34). The London neighborhood of Spitalfields, first built in the eighteenth century for Huguenot silkweavers, has had generations of different immigrants and businesses, and still maintains its structure of terraced houses with what is now a gentrifying population.

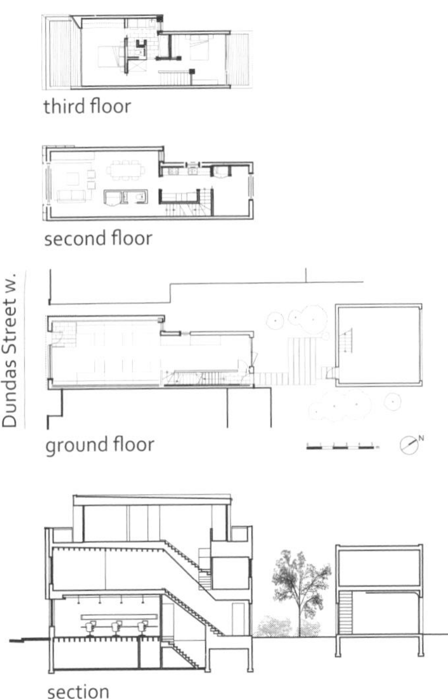

7.30 **Plans and section. In this Toronto project by Superkul Architects, a husband-and-wife architectural team designed the building for use as their office and their residence. The second floor, which is initially designed as the main living floor for the couple, can be divided into a conference room for the business, and the first floor of a smaller residential unit that will be rented and separately accessed from a new stair to be built in the passage alongside the house.**
Courtesy Superkul Architects.

7.31 **Night view of Toronto building.**
Courtesy Superkul Architects.

(a)

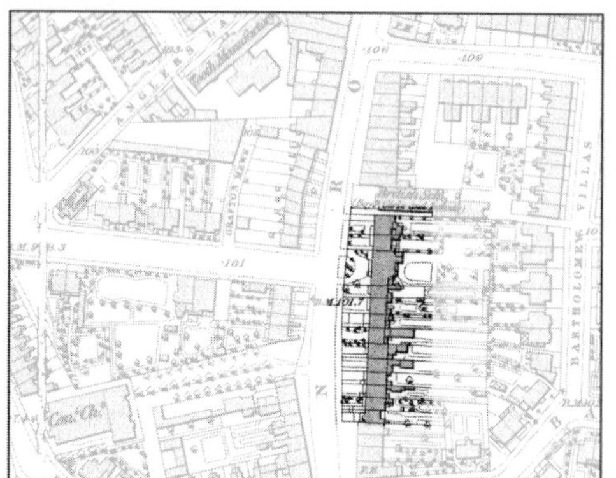

(b)

7.32 (top) Two stages, 1870 (a) and 1916 (b), in the growth of Kentish Town, London. The 1916 map, on the right, shows how commercial extensions filled in the gardens in front of the houses.

Ordnance survey maps courtesy of Alan Godfrey/Godfrey Editions.

7.33 (bottom) Commercial extensions to houses in Kentish Town, London.

Photograph by Matthew M. Brown.

7.34 The Upper West Side in 1929, 1959 and 1993, showing the resilience of its urban fabric. Buildings shown in black are shop/houses.
Maps by Matthew M. Brown and Sam Yerke based on research and initial maps by Howard Davis and Steven Miller.

The kind of economic flexibility described here applies not only to the single-family shop/house but also to the multiple-unit building, in which the owner-family may or may not occupy the shop. In such a building, the family may expand or contract its own dwelling, may occupy the shop or not, may rent more or less of the dwelling space or shop space to others – and thereby use the building to optimize its own financial situation. This is the case in one of the buildings in Guangzhou described earlier in this chapter, in brownstones and terraced houses in New York and London, and larger buildings where apartments may be combined, shops expanded, second floors converted from apartments to shops and back again to apartments when the market changes. In all cases, the building's configuration, along with the conditions of rental and occupancy, allow for continual adjustment of use.

* * *

This chapter has dealt with architectural flexibility largely from the point of view of economic need, which is a critical but not exclusive component of people's motivations to build. People take advantage of the adaptability of buildings in order to serve their changing family lives, changing desires for status, as well as changing economic lives. And buildings take on a myriad of particular configurations as a result of what is often an ad hoc inventiveness, in response to these needs.

But this wide variety of solutions embodies a few common configurational ideas that form the basis of many of the types presented in Part I, and that will be specifically described in the next chapter.

8.01 Shop/house in Brooklyn showing separate door to stair hall and strong division between commercial and residential parts of the façade.

Photograph by author.

8

THE ARCHITECTURE OF HYBRID TYPES

> *The same pragmatism that imparts such clarity to the façades of the buildings also makes the disposition of their internal spaces – shops below, four floors of apartments above, served by elevators and therefore equivalent in scale and status – clearly legible from the street.*[1]
>
> (Eve Blau, on the Vienna buildings of Otto Wagner)

Architects designing contemporary shop/houses almost always incorporate attributes that are similar to those in the historic examples in this book, allowing commercial/work functions and dwelling functions to co-exist. These attributes are used differently in different cultures, and among different people. The boundary between the more public realm of the shop or workplace and the more private realm of the family quarters may be different in different places. Some individuals may want to be able to remove themselves from their work in different ways than others. Because of this diversity, it is difficult to develop a broadly applicable set of explicit guidelines or patterns. But describing these attributes is helpful both for understanding cross-cultural commonalities as well as for laying out critical issues for new projects – for which project-specific guidelines may be developed.

The attributes are as follows:

1 Housing is more specifically designed than commercial space – sometimes resulting in challenges with respect to building configuration and structure.
2 Buildings or building units have narrow frontages, with direct connection to the street or public realm.
3 On the commercial street, the shopfront takes precedence over the residential door and circulation – although there is a need for a balance between dwelling and commercial activity.
4 There are varying and fluid relationships between shops and dwellings – relationships that often need to balance the desire for work and dwelling to be intertwined, and the desire to be able to "get away from the work."
5 The kitchen is often located in between the shop and the dwelling, or in a place that is easily accessible to both.
6 The façade expresses both the openness of the shop and the privacy of the dwelling – while also being unified as an architectural composition.

In a research report on the inclusion of home businesses in urban neighborhoods, Sherry Ahrentzen describes the need for such features as vertical and horizontal distancing, to allow people to get away from their work; multiple ground-floor entries; visual access between one functional area and the other; and the ability for adaptability or flexibility.[2] These features help reconcile the potentially conflicting functions of dwelling and work, and are particularly

[1] Blau, *Architecture of Red Vienna*, 244.
[2] Ahrentzen, "Housing Home Businesses," 5–6.

8.02 Shophouses in Bangkok's Chinatown: relative peace and quiet above the canopies.
Photograph by author.

8.03 Shophouses in Bangkok's Chinatown: the busy market below the canopies.
Photograph by author.

applicable to contemporary situations where a balance is wanted between work and family life. The discussion that follows incorporates several of these ideas.

1 *Specificity of housing vs. generality of commercial space*
Considered separately, buildings intended for housing and buildings intended for production or retail purposes have different requirements for daylight, internal organization and entrance location.

Dwellings generally require a high level of spatial articulation, constraining architectural configurations. To provide daylight, most rooms are a maximum distance from an outside wall, increasing the length of the building's perimeter. This results in courtyard buildings, "slab blocks," buildings with indentations that increase the length of the perimeter, and various hybrids. It also means that public, vertical circulation must be located in places that allow circulation paths within units to move from a central location to the building perimeter, the location of major rooms.

On the other hand, contemporary retail spaces and spaces for production are designed for internal flexibility. Their design often stops with the shell, allowing the individual tenant to control the design of the shop's interior space. With many work spaces, although visibility from the street is not necessarily important, flexibility that allows for the company to rearrange its space may be critical. Daylight may be provided with higher floor-to-ceiling dimensions than residential space, allowing lighting from the side, or with skylights.

With large buildings, the complex and often imbricated formal arrangement of housing may be in a potential conflict with the required simplicity of commercial space. Commercial space becomes less flexible if exit stairs come down into the middle. Structural loads from narrow building wings above must be transferred in ways that put load-bearing columns and walls in places that leave commercial space open. The need to have shear walls that can take care of lateral loads, made greater by the mass of building above, may be in conflict with the need to have internal openness of commercial space, and openness of commercial space to the street (Fig. 8.04).

Large modern buildings with reinforced concrete column-and-slab systems allow for more flexibility. In these buildings, apartment layouts are coordinated

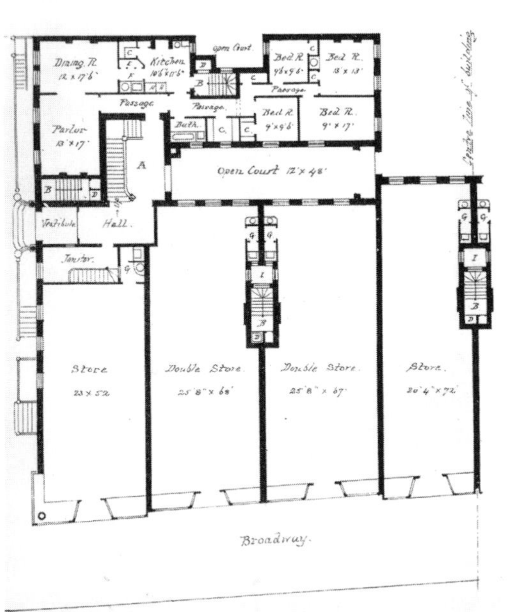

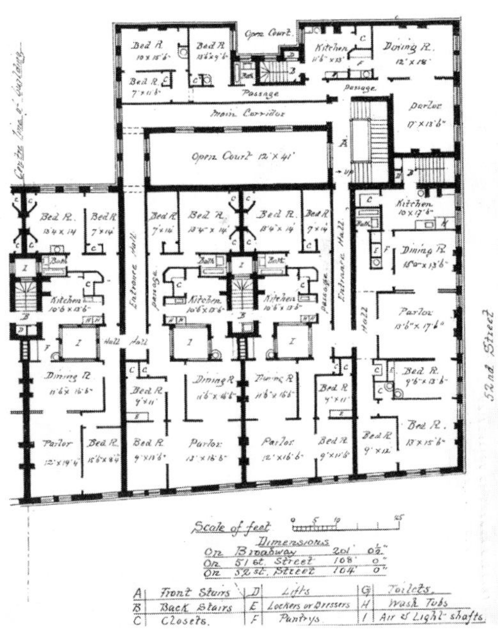

8.04 Plans of "Albany" apartment house, New York. In this 1876 New York building, the primary structure consists of a series of parallel walls. These define distinct shops, separate the apartments, and provide locations for service stairs that connect the apartments to the basement. This allows for flexibility within the shops, but does not easily allow shop spaces to be combined into larger units. The apartments themselves have light wells that do not continue to the ground-floor level, allowing maximum space for shops.

From *American Architect and Building News* I, 1876.

with primary positions of vertical structure that are far enough apart to allow for flexibility of the ground-floor shop space. With another system, used in buildings up to four or five stories high, lighter steel or wood frames come down onto concrete slabs (which provide fireproofing between the commercial and residential floors) allowing the concrete slab to distribute the loads, and reducing the structural need to coordinate apartment layout with commercial layout. Exit stairs come down to the ground floor in positions that are associated with service spaces, so they do not interfere with the flexibility of the shop space.

2 *Small units with narrow frontages, with direct connection to the street or public realm that is strongly connected to the street*

Many of the specific building types discussed in the first four chapters have narrow frontages, and are relatively small units (Fig. 8.05). This allows for economic independence of the unit or building, for many buildings to be together on the same street, permitting competition and helping to create an active street. It allows businesses to each have a connection to the streets. And it also facilitates transformation over time, so that two or more buildings can be easily combined or connected, or for buildings that had been combined in the past to be easily separated.

The need for a street connection varies according to the type of business, and has changed over history. Adjacency to a busy pedestrian street is most important for retail shops but, as will be described in the next chapter, even

8.05 Narrow shophouses in Luang Prabang, Laos. Photograph by author.

this need increased during the eighteenth and nineteenth centuries, as the importance of marketing grew. But this adjacency may be also important for workshops with frequent deliveries and shipping, or where walk-in trade may be a factor.

At the same time, many older apartment buildings in Paris, Vienna, and other Continental cities have businesses of one kind or another distributed among the upper-floor apartments – one has only to look at the name plates at the front entrance to understand this – and there are many "unmarked" businesses in apartments all over. Businesses range from the historic piecework in the needle trades, to professionals such as lawyers and doctors, to artists and writers, to firms of all kinds that do not have large stock or require constant walk-in trade. Loft buildings have small businesses of different kinds on upper floors.

Despite these exceptions, the connection between the public realm of the street and the most public parts of businesses often needs to be strong, particularly for retail businesses and others that depend on visibility or easy access. Multi-floor signage in places like Hong Kong is a way of providing visibility, if not access. The low-rise sections of older cities, such as Greenwich Village in New York, are often admired because of their "human scale" – i.e., low building heights. But the frequency of connections between buildings and streets – or more precisely, between different buildings and streets – is as important, leading to choice, diversity and socially active streets.[3]

The apartment-building and loft examples suggest new higher-building prototypes that extend the public realm up from the street, onto upper floors. A conjectural hybrid of two modernist projects – Le Corbusier's Unité d'Habitation in Marseilles and Michiel Brinckman's Spangen Quarter project in Rotterdam – might do this. One floor of the Unité included shops – but this floor is like others with apartments, and not well connected to the public realm outside the building. The Spangen Quarter building includes an upper level that is better connected to the public realm below (and was made partly so that street vendors could access it, with freight elevators) – but does not itself include shops. A hybrid between these two projects would allow shop/houses to be well connected to a public walkway that is itself well connected to the street.

3 Shopfront takes precedence over the residential door and circulation
Historically, the need for retail frontage along the commercial street often trumped the position of the residential entrance and the location of the residential stair (Figs. 8.06, 8.07). To maximize commercial frontage, the width of the residential entrance is minimized or moved to a side street, and vertical circulation is pushed away from the street. In contemporary situations, however, people may be more interested in maintaining a balance between dwelling and work, and indicating that balance with the building. Having a separate residential entrance – and putting it on a different street – may help give the dwelling its own identity.

When the residential entrance is on the side street, it may be wider and more elaborate than on the commercial street. Since the residential frontage may not be as valuable in terms of commercial rent more space can be given to this function. This is the case with corner apartment buildings in New York, which may be more prominent than the lower row houses along the residential street. The visible and elaborate entrance allows the building to have a strong

[3] Hillier and Hanson, *Social Logic of Space*, 126–132. The work of Bill Hillier and his research group on space syntax helps give mathematical precision to such intuitions.

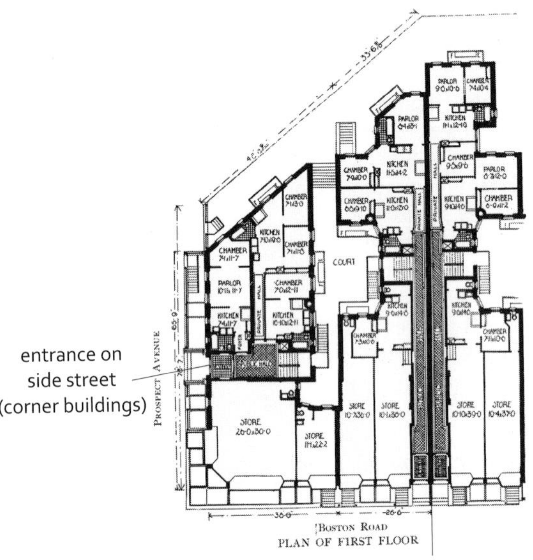

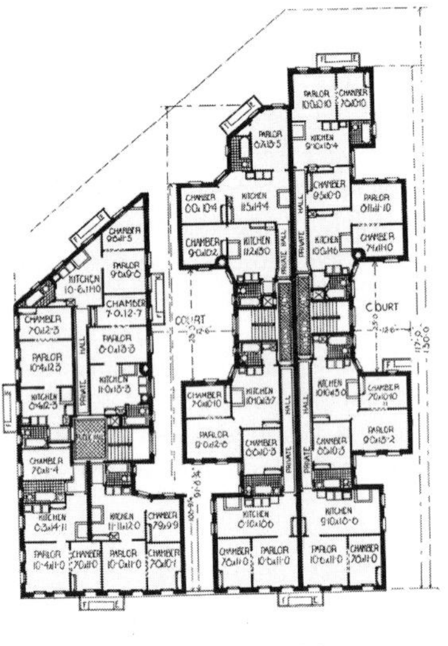

8.06 New York buildings photographed by Walker Evans. The corner building has its residential entrance on the cross street, and in the building next to it the residential entrance is narrow.

Library of Congress.

8.07 Adjacent New York apartment buildings. In the mid-block buildings, on the right, the residential frontage is minimized, and hallways lead back to the stair and ground-floor apartments. The corner building has its residential entrance on the side street, and that entrance is wider.

From Hesselgren, *Apartment Houses of the Metropolis.*

residential identity – and command higher residential rents – even though many of the apartment windows are actually over stores on the commercial street.

The circulation system is also affected by the need to maximize commercial frontage. In family shop/houses, such as those in Asia, there is not necessarily a separate corridor leading to the private quarters, as the shop itself acts as the entrance room. But when there is a separate stair, it may either be very narrow, or pulled back into the building.

A tightly designed plan is that of an apartment building in Vienna designed by Otto Wagner. In this building and similar ones, the apartments were arranged to put major rooms on the exterior and minor rooms off a courtyard. At the ground floor, the commercial street has only shops, and the residential entrance is placed as far from the commercial street as possible. On entering the building, one sees the light of the courtyard, and the principal stair also benefits from that light.[4] The commercial space and residential entrance are each in a place where it makes the most economic sense. New buildings follow similar principles (Figs. 8.08, 8.09).

4 *Fluid relationship between shop and dwelling*

In single-family shop/houses there is often an ambiguous boundary between the space occupied by the shop and that occupied by the dwelling. Shop functions, such as storage or meeting with important clients, may move into the dwelling; and dwelling functions, such as meals or visiting with neighbors, may take place in the shop. Activities may not respect a physical boundary between the two zones. This may be particularly true for children, who behave according to different rules than adults, and for whom the shop or workspace is just another part of their natural realm (Fig. 8.10).

Today, people have different ideas about the relationship between the dwelling and the workplace. These words are being written in a studio from which I can see my living/dining room through an interior window in front of me, and easily access different rooms of the house. Other people want more separation – sometimes to the extent of having the workplace as an entirely separate building.

Different preferences may be supported by the position of a second entrance, in addition to the one into the shop, that allows direct access to the dwelling, or by having the stair to the dwelling just inside the single entrance. This may easily occur in corner buildings, where a side entrance can lead directly to the foot of a stair that is also accessed from the shop.

In some cases, as with the Japanese *chanoma*, there is a special room that is part of both realms, and in others, as with the San Francisco building described at the end of Chapter 7, the overlap is more a matter of social convention, supported by adjacent rooms that are flexible enough to take on two different functions.

Three shop/house types in Chandigarh, the capital of India's Punjab, for which the master plan was designed by Le Corbusier, have varying relationships between shops and dwellings. They were generally located along "V4" roads – thoroughfares of medium width that served commercial areas near the centers of sectors. All three types provided for access to the flats from the side of the building facing away from the commercial street. One important difference

[4] Wagner, *Modern Architecture*, 5; Geretsegger and Peintner, *Otto Wagner*, 106; Blau, *Architecture of Red Vienna*, 218, 354–357. One of Wagner's specialties in his early career was apartment houses. Harry Mallgrave writes that "Wagner's . . . early practice was centered on the design of urban apartment houses, almost all of which he lived in before building the next one." Working in a city where such buildings were the norm, he asked his first-year architecture students at the Academy of Fine Arts to design "an apartment house of the most ordinary kind." He encouraged students to study the modern urban vernacular – not as an investigation intended to lead toward nostalgic design, but as a means to uncover more lasting fundamentals about architecture. A number of his students went on to participate in the Viennese public housing program of the 1920s and 1930s .

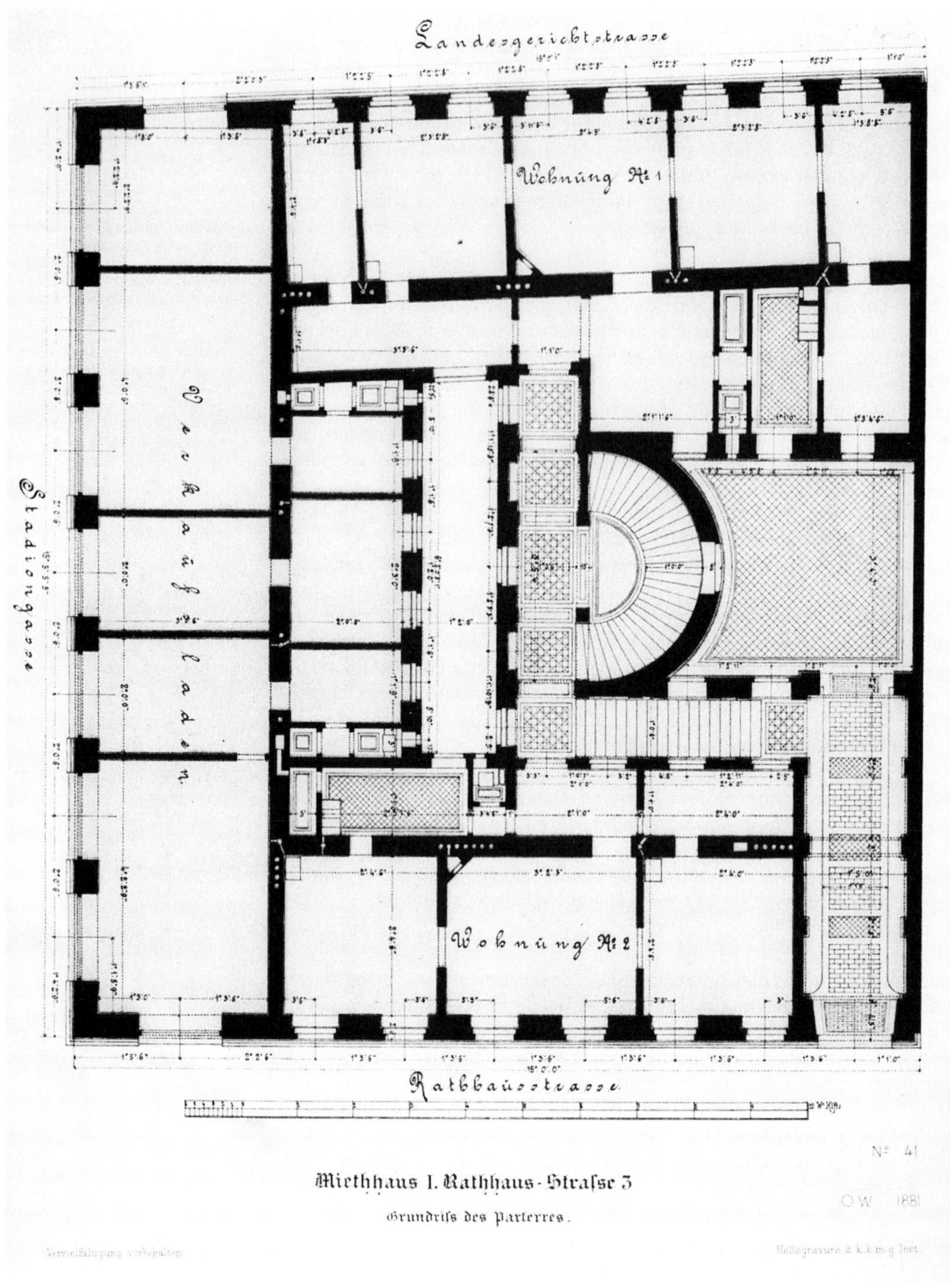

8.08 Plan of ground floor of apartment building by Otto Wagner. The shops are along the left, and the residential entrance at lower right.

Österreichische Nationalbibliothek Bildarchiv, Vienna.

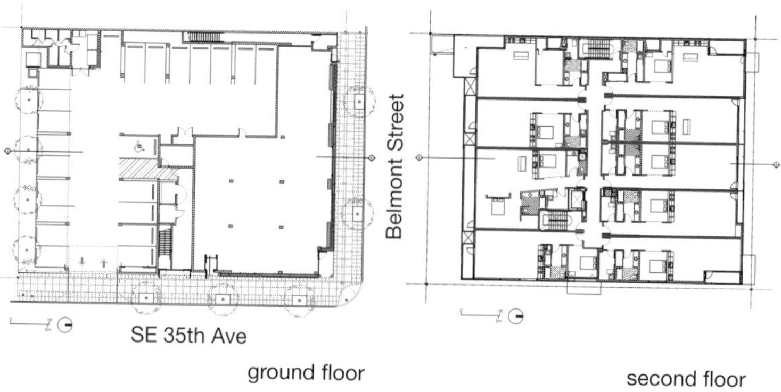

8.09 Ground- and second-floor plans of Belmont Lofts designed by Holst Architecture. In this new building in Portland, Oregon (see also Chapter 11), the commercial space occupies almost the entire frontage on the commercial street, with only a narrow door for the fire stair, and the residential entrance is around the corner on the residential street.
Plan courtesy of HOLST Architecture, Portland.

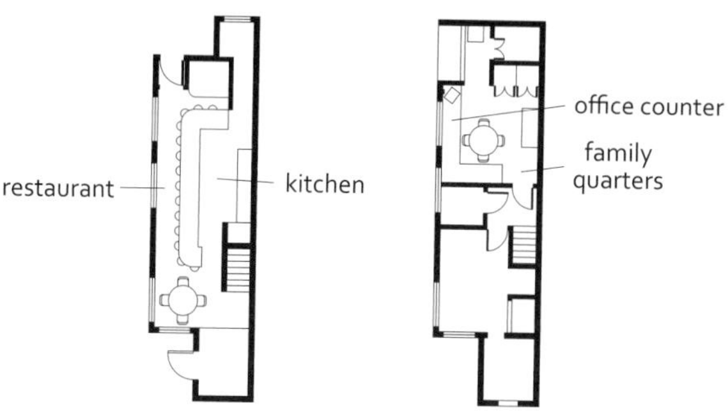

8.10 Plans of Raku Raku restaurant in Kyoto, where the restaurant kitchen is also used to prepare family meals.
Drawn by Will Krzymowski based on measurements by author.

between the buildings, however, was in the internal relationship between shops and flats (Figs. 8.11, 8.12, Plate 46).

The only one of the three types that clearly mixes residential and commercial uses *on the street itself* is SH-2, in which the family seems as likely to enter through the shop as through the narrow rear courtyard. With the other two types, the building type turns residential entrances away from the commercial street onto a small residential lane.

5 *Position of the kitchen*

The overlap between functions and their spatial realms may be supported by the position of the kitchen, which often straddles the boundary between shop and dwelling (Figs. 8.13, 8.14). This allows for a blurring of roles as the person preparing meals may be tending the shop. There is sometimes a second kitchen upstairs, for use on Sundays and holidays, or in cases where the person cooking never works in the shop.[5] In businesses where food is prepared, the kitchen may not only be adjacent to the shop, but acts as the shop itself.[6]

An analysis of the Treswell plans of early London houses shows the centrality of both the shop and the kitchen in the morphology of the building, when the stair comes down close to the street. In one house, typical of London houses before the development of the side passage, the shop – although it is at the front of the house – is central to the plan (Fig. 8.15). It is at the intersection of two lines of rooms – to the back and upstairs – so everyone needs to pass

[5] This was the case for example, in one shophouse in Guangzhou, where an elderly woman was brought from the family's hometown to cook and take care of the children. Here, the kitchen was on the third floor and there was no kitchen in the shop.

[6] Thanks to Akira Mizobuchi, virtuoso chef-cum-musician at Raku Raku restaurant in Kyoto, for his insights into life in a house/restaurant.

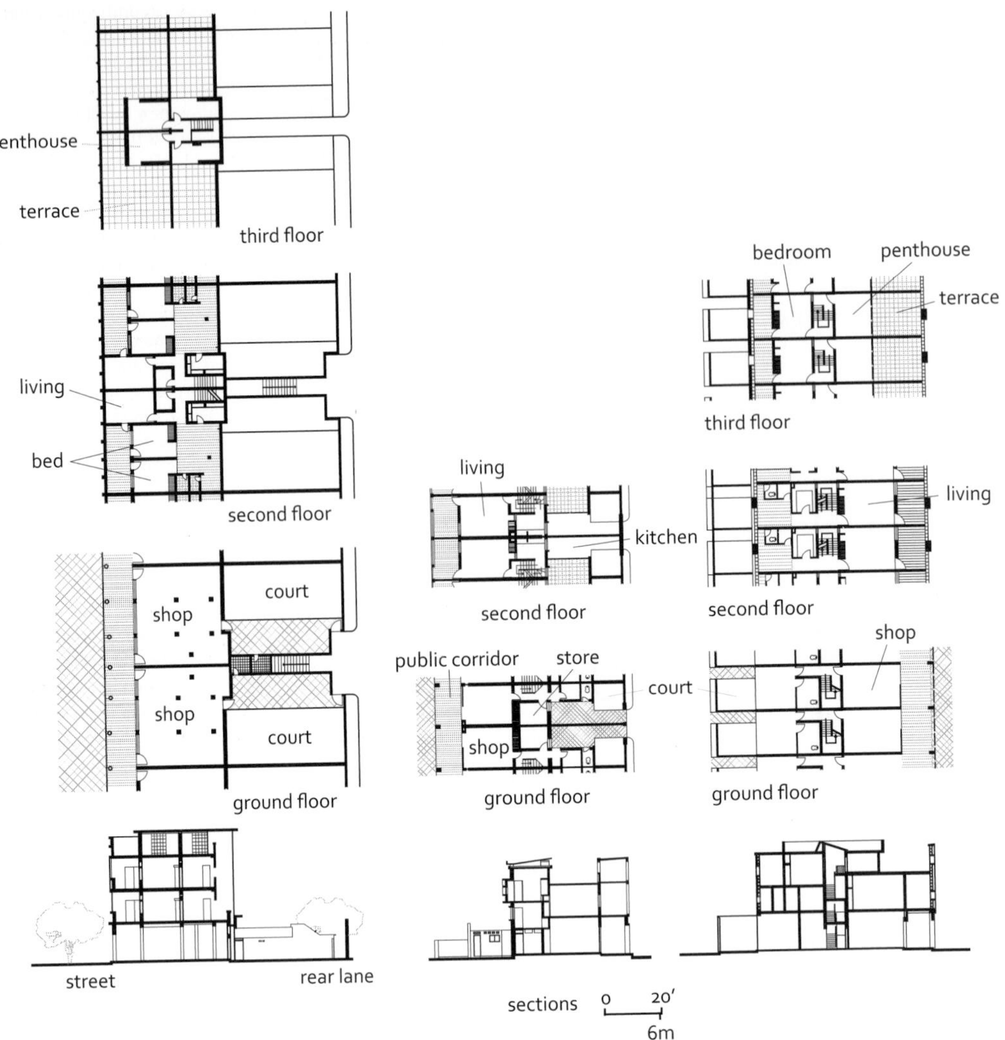

8.11 **Three shop/house types at Chandigarh. Shop/house SH-1 (left), designed by Maxwell Fry, was designed so that the flats were completely independent of the retail space below. The staircase leading to the flats, entered from the rear, bypassed the shops, so that the two sets of occupants might never come in contact with each other. Presumably this allowed for the flat-dwellers to have the benefits of a central location along with choice as to when they would associate with shopkeepers and tradespeople.**

Shop/house SH-2 (middle), designed by Jane Drew, was smaller than SH-1, and designed so that the shopkeeper had easy access to the single dwelling above, through an internal stair. These buildings were meant for the shopkeeper's family alone, but the existence of a secondary entrance from the back, and a door between the shop and the stair hall, might have allowed the shop to be rented separately (even though the toilet would have been shared).

Shop/house SH-3 (right), designed by Pierre Jeanneret, allowed the shopkeeper to have a direct connection with the dwelling above, or for the shop to be closed off and the dwelling above to be accessed only from the non-commercial street in the rear. SH-3 buildings in one sector face private houses on the residential street, allowing for the two sides of the building to relate to the city in different ways.

Drawn by Paola Beatriz Ludueña and Sam Yerke from originals in Joshi, *Documenting Chandigarh*.

through the shop when going to any room from the street. Since the kitchen is immediately adjacent to the shop it is adjacent to these two lines of movement. In some old New York tenements, shops were connected to ground-floor apartments through doors that led directly into the kitchen.

8.12 View of Chandigarh shop/houses.
Photograph by Jonathan Alex Jensen.

Apart from the economic benefit, the adjacent kitchen helps make the shop a social place. This may have been particularly true in general stores in small American towns in the nineteenth century, which served as social centers.[7] In cultures where tea or coffee is routinely served to customers, or where shop workers have a meal in the shop, the kitchen may be an essential part of the business. And it is still the case in Bangkok where, although the kitchen is typically located at the back of the ground floor, meals may be brought through the shop to be served at a table on the sidewalk, in front of the building.

6 The building façade

Shop/houses with an important commercial street presence need a façade that reconciles the openness and flexibility of the ground floor with the enclosure of upper floors that is often desired for privacy, and for the building to be seen as having an important residential component (Fig. 8.16, Plate 50).

The distinction between the open, commercial ground floor and the more closed, residential upper floors is a transformation of classical ordering systems of façades. In traditional Renaissance *palazzi* the base was solid, and often

[7] See, for example, Sutherland, *Expansion of Everyday Life*, 188.

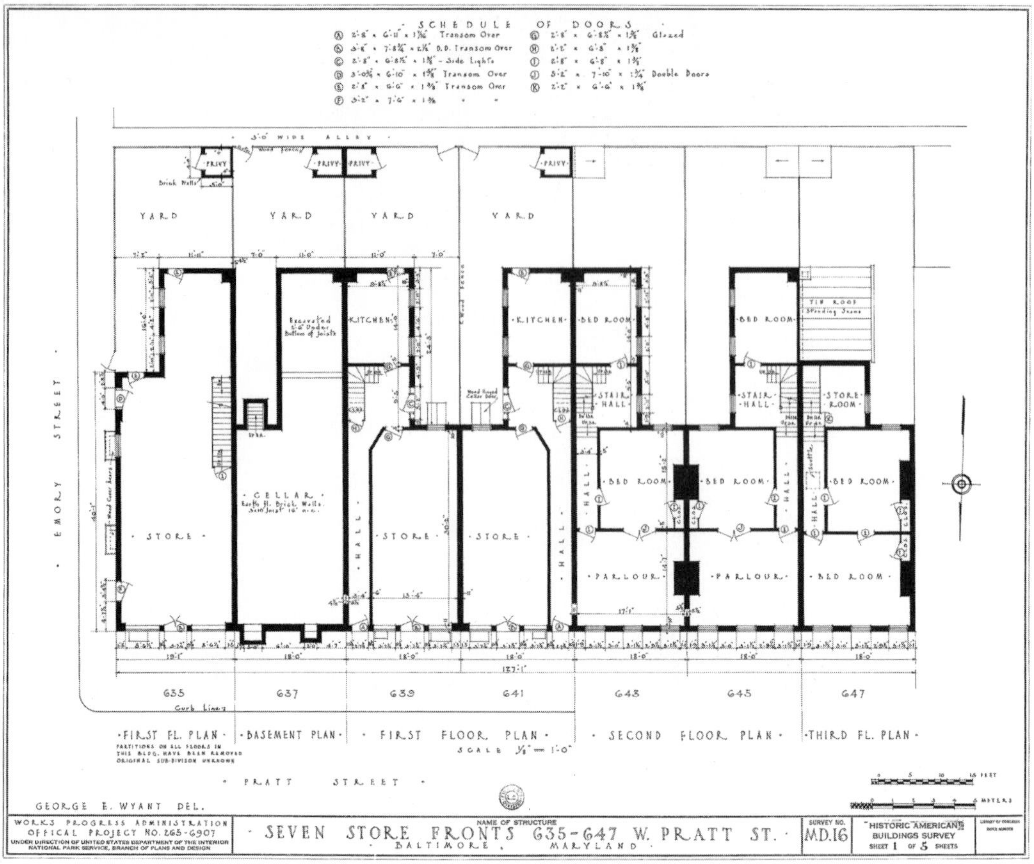

8.13 In these shop/houses in Baltimore, the kitchens are at the back of the ground floors, allowing easy access from the shop and from the dwelling.
Library of Congress/Historic American Buildings Survey.

8.14 Yolanda's soap and cleaning products shop, under the family dwelling, Valparaiso, Chile. The downstairs kitchen (there is also one upstairs) is at the back of the shop, on the right.
Photograph by author with thanks to Michael Bier and Paz Undurraga.

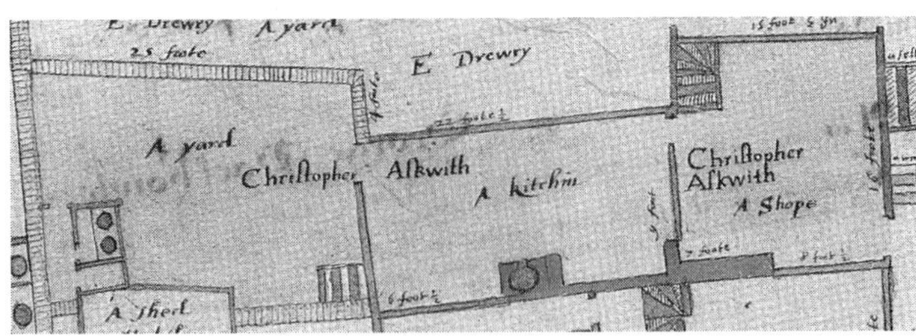

8.15 Detail of a London house in the Treswell map.
Reproduced by kind permission of Christ's Hospital.

rusticated, with the *piano nobile* and its large windows above. The ground floor contained service functions – and shops – when the building had them. Although the open ground floor of the modern façade is an inversion of the closed ground floor of the *palazzo*, it remains part of the same classical idea.

Typical nineteenth-century Parisian buildings have seven stories, including a mezzanine above the ground floor and rooms in the roof. In the façade, the mezzanine is separated from the first floor by a continuous or nearly continuous balcony. Other balconies above the third floor, and a principal cornice near the top of the building, help unify the façade. The lower balcony helps separate the shop-and-mezzanine unit from the main body of the façade. It also allows visual variety in the commercial base, without disturbing the regular order of what is above. At the same time, the vertical lines of the façade formed by the positions of windows and wall segments are continuous from bottom to top, helping to tie together the two parts of the composition (Fig 8.17).

The contrast between the open shopfront and the more solid wall above may be a structural issue in buildings with load-bearing front walls. Traditional Venetian buildings that were purpose-built with shops at their base had a continuous timber beam, resting on columns of Istrian stone, to support the plaster-covered brick above.[8] Many early twentieth-century American shop/houses are of brick construction above the ground floor. For the shopfront to be open, a steel beam transfers the load of the brick wall to the outer corners of the façade. Contemporary American buildings are usually of frame rather than load-bearing wall construction, and structural modules of steel or reinforced concrete are wide enough to allow sufficient areas of glazing in the shopfronts (Fig. 8.18).

Early twentieth-century apartment buildings designed by architects such as Auguste Perret in Paris, Hendrik Petrus Berlage in Amsterdam, and Otto Wagner and Adolf Loos in Vienna, are particularly effective in the integration of commercial and residential elements in their façades (Figs 8.19–8.22, Plate 54). Regarding two adjacent buildings by Wagner, Eve Blau writes:

> At close range both buildings rigorously maintain a pedestrian scale, and their surfaces dissolve into a transparent wall of shop windows at street level along the Wienzeile. The continuous glazing stops at the corner of the Kostlergasse, a secondary, less-trafficked street than the Wienzeile, where business is mostly local and conducted in small shops and workshops. Here the more modest scale of trade is accommodated by modestly scaled doors and shop windows. The same pragmatism that imparts such clarity to the façades of the buildings also makes the

[8] Goy, *Venetian Vernacular Architecture*, 84.

8.16 Paris building, showing contrast between open shopfronts and more private residential floor above.
Photograph by Alvin Comiter.

8.17 Paris apartment building.
Photograph by author.

8.18 Elevation study for Crescent Village (see Chapter 11) by John Rowell. Although the apartments have large windows, the buildings maintain a distinction between the housing and the commercial base.
Rowell Brokaw Architects.

8.19 Apartment building on Linke Wienzeile, Vienna, designed by Otto Wagner.
Photograph by author.

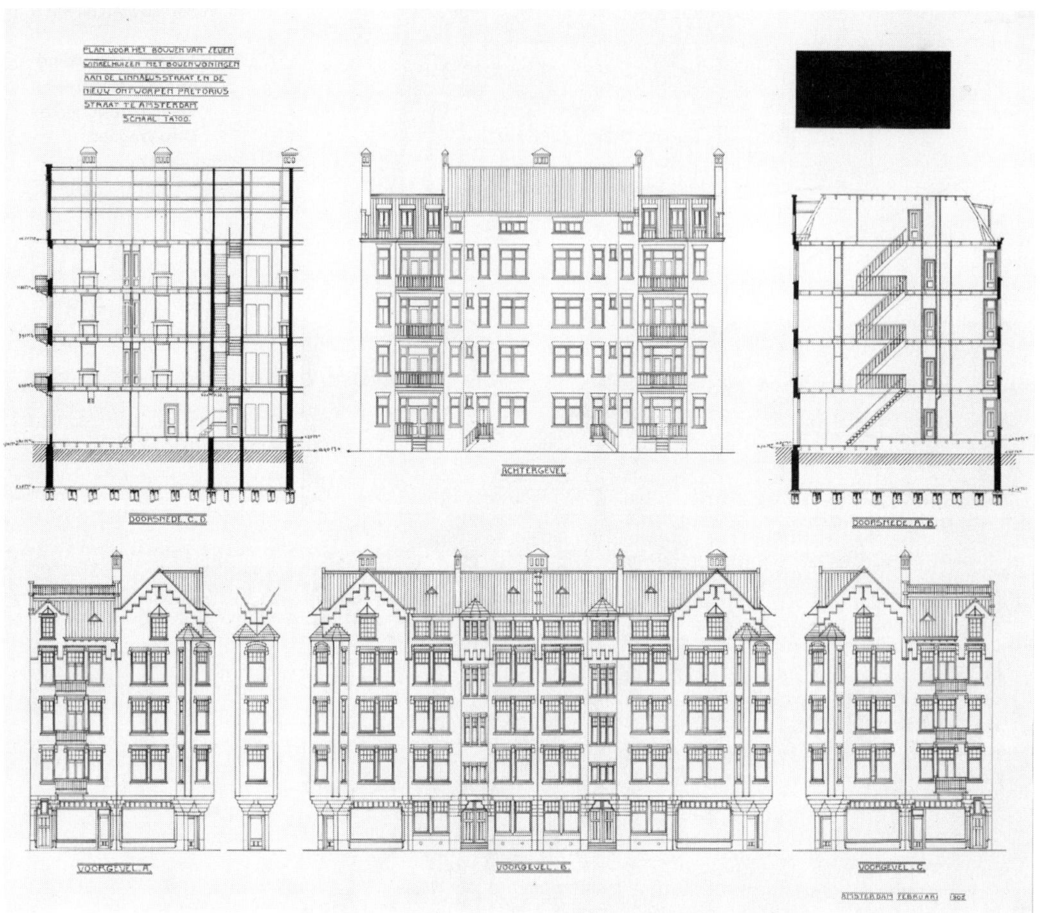

8.20 Twin apartment buildings with stores at Linnaeusstraat, Amsterdam, 1905 designed by Hendrik Petrus Berlage: elevations and sections.

Netherlands Architecture Institute.

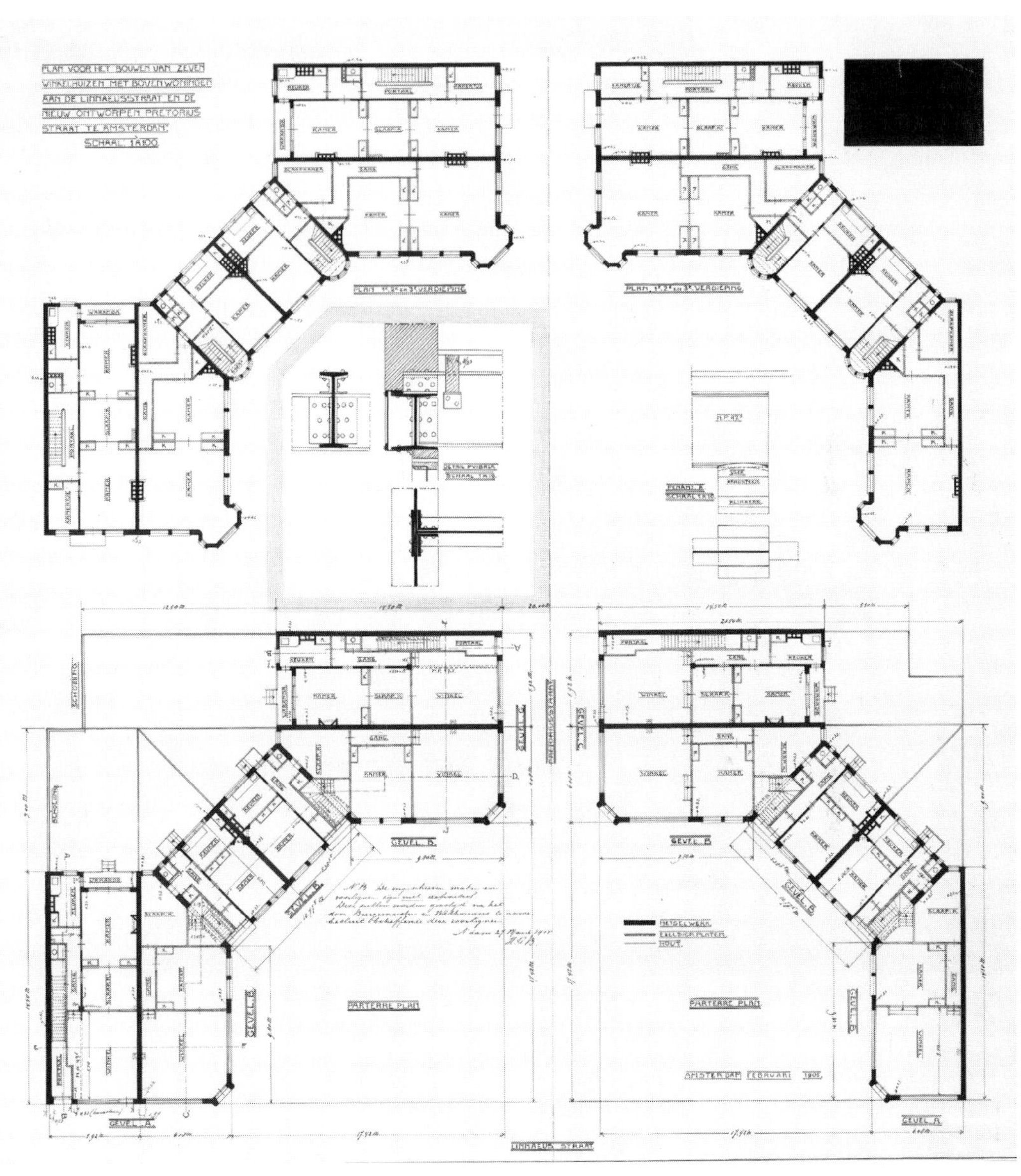

8.21 Twin apartment buildings with stores at Linnaeusstraat, Amsterdam, 1905 designed by Hendrik Petrus Berlage: plans.
Designed by H.P. Berlage. Netherlands Architecture Institute.

8.22 Building for Goldman-Salatsch firm (Looshaus), designed by Adolf Loos.
Photograph by Simon Kates.

disposition of their internal spaces – shops below, four floors of apartments above, served by elevators and therefore equivalent in scale and status – clearly legible from the street.[9]

Wagner's apartment buildings, which visually express a strong integration between commercial and residential function, may be contrasted to the Goldman-Salatsch building, by Adolf Loos, a mixed-use building for a firm of tailors. In the façade, Loos developed a strong contrast between the openness of the commercial base and the tight enclosure of the residential upper floors, and detailed the commercial base to draw more attention to it. In Loos' words, "In order to separate the commercial and living sections of the house . . . the design of the façade was differentiated"[10] – perhaps presaging future, more explicit doctrines about the separation of urban functions (Fig. 8.22).

[9] Blau, *Architecture of Red Vienna*, 244.
[10] Heynen, *Architecture and Modernity*, 93.

Case study: the row house

In the row house, with its myriad individual types, the essential attributes of shop/houses are often straightforwardly resolved. The row house is a party-wall building, often narrow parallel to the street and deep perpendicular to the street, with a chain of rooms from front to back served by a circulation spine along one edge. Although in the simplest row-house form daylight can only come through the front and back walls, there are variations with back extensions (Lübeck and London), interior courtyards (Japan, China and Italy) or stepbacks of the rooms (San Francisco) to provide daylight while maintaining the basic organization.

The party-wall row house allows a maximum number of buildings to occupy a given length of street frontage, making it suitable for commercial streets. Because it may be narrow (and tall) it easily allows for a gradient of privacy from the shop back into the dwelling, allowing for a combination of commercial activity and family life, and providing privacy within the family realm. Because of its organization with two parallel lines of spaces – one for rooms and one for circulation – it allows for flexibility over time. Together, these geometric attributes appear in many different row-house types (Fig. 8.23).

In traditional row houses, the front room and adjacent main entrance hall share the street frontage so the front room can be accessed directly from the street or from inside the house. Likewise, the ability to access the basement directly from the street as well as with the internal stair allows the basement to be an independent business, an apartment independent of the main residence, or part of the main residence. Finally, because the main entrance hall leads to a circulation system that is tangential to a series of rooms that are arranged in a continuous linear fashion, all rooms or contiguous groups of rooms may be accessed independently, allowing for a diversity of independent uses in the building (Fig. 8.23).

The vertical nature of the building permits clusters of rooms on one floor to be separate from similar clusters of rooms on other floors, allowing relative isolation of uses. Secondary paths of circulation are possible directly from room to room, bypassing the primary path and allowing for organizational complexity and gradients of privacy within individual uses.

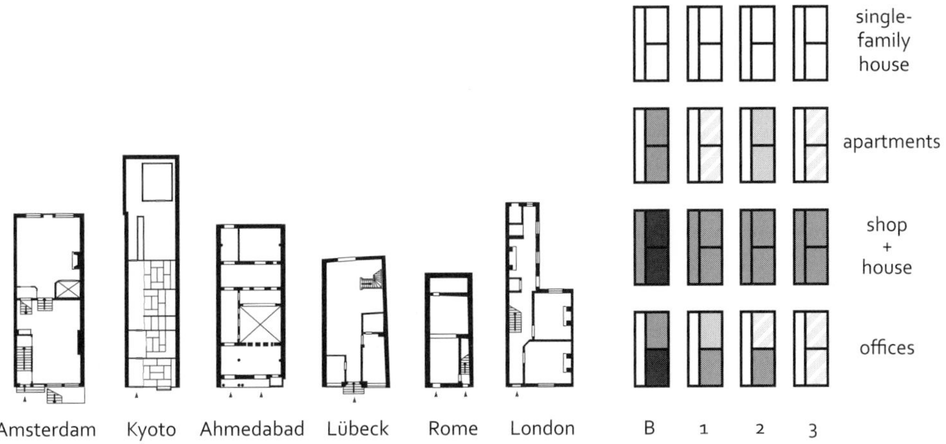

8.23 Comparative organization among row houses in different traditions. The circulation paths through or along one edge of the buildings allow for flexibility of use and for the shops to be bypassed while accessing the dwellings. The diagrams on the right show how the row house may take on a variety of different configurations.

Plans and diagrams by Matthew M. Brown and Sam Yerke.

8.24 Housing with shops in Jordaan district of Amsterdam designed by Aldo van Eyck and Theo Bosch, shown in historic context.
Photograph by Marc Holt.

8.25 View of Amsterdam project showing curved roofs.
Photograph by Marc Holt.

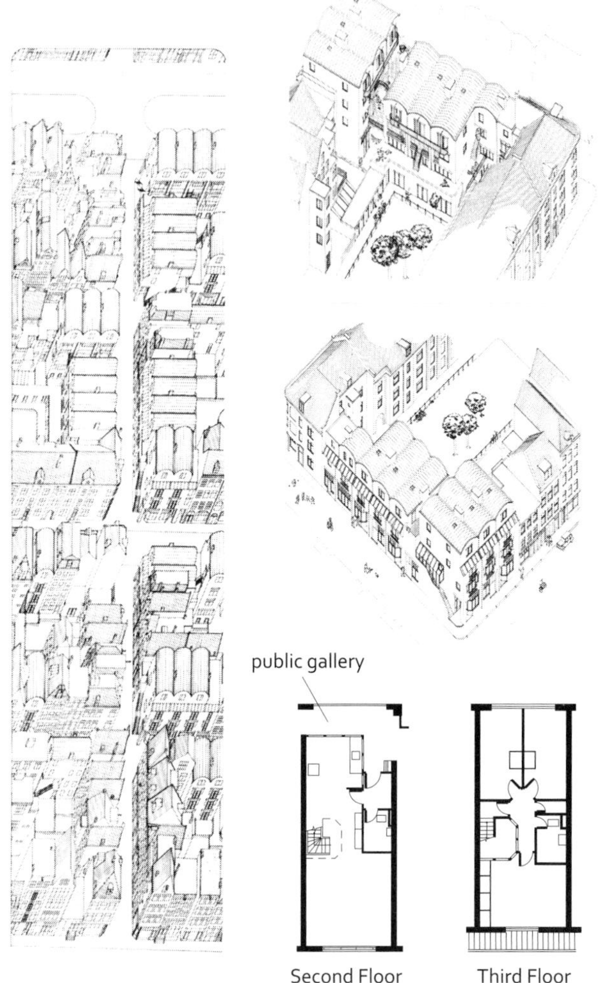

8.26 Amsterdam project. Plans of housing unit at second and third floors, and axonometric view of buildings.

Drawings by Will Krzymowski and Sam Yerke; axonometric from Ligtelijn, *Aldo Van Eyck, Werken*.

A modern transformation of the traditional Amsterdam row house is in the Jordaan neighborhood, which was one of the first extensions outside the medieval core, built in the early seventeenth century to house working-class people and their businesses. The 1970s project, designed by Aldo van Eyck and Theo Bosch, is a group of three-story infill buildings, consisting of fifty dwellings and twenty-two shops, that preserved the streetscape and interior garden spaces (Figs. 8.24, 8.25, 8.26; Plates 23, 24).

The shops occupy almost the entire ground-floor frontage. A common stair leads to a second-story gallery, at the back and along the garden, from which the individual housing units are entered. The housing units are each two-stories, with an internal stair. The kitchen looks out onto the entrance gallery and the living room looks down to the street. The exterior wall of the master bedroom is pulled back from the street wall allowing the master bedroom to have some increased privacy.

This scheme allows for maximum commercial frontage and for the entrances and kitchens to help contribute to life in the block interior. Although the housing and shops are completely separate and accessed separately from the public realm, it would be easy to imagine a variation in which the separate exterior entrances are maintained, but where there would also be the option of direct connections between the shops and the dwellings.

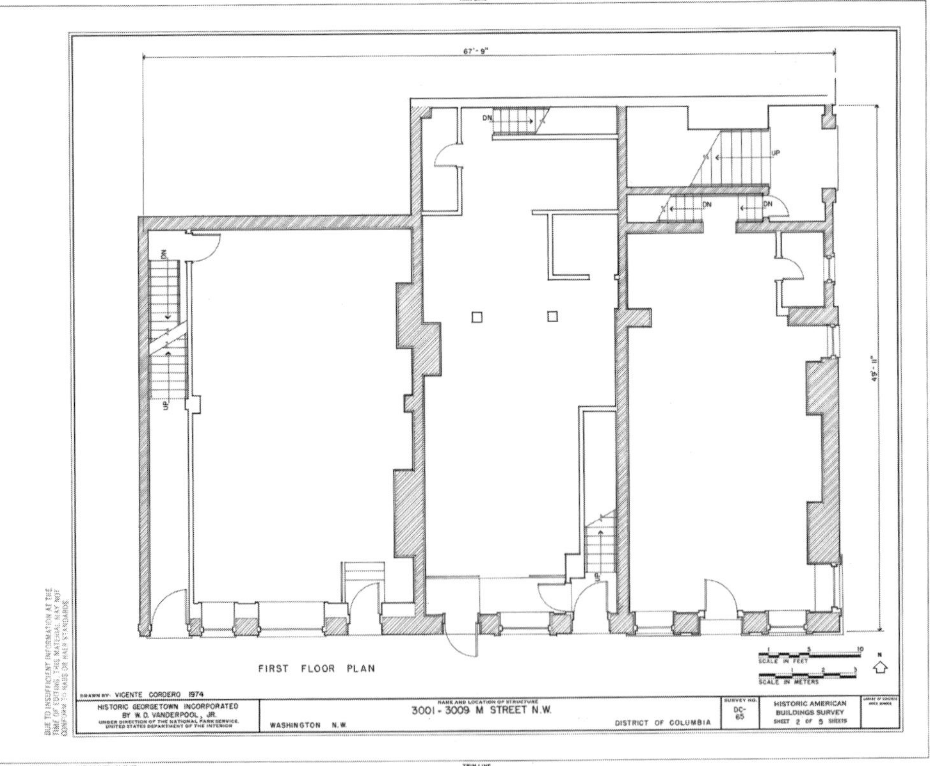

8.27 In these row houses in Washington, the shopfront dominates the residential entrances. In the two mid-block buildings, the residential entrance is very narrow, and in the corner building on the right, the residential entrance is on the secondary street.
Library of Congress/Historic American Buildings Survey.

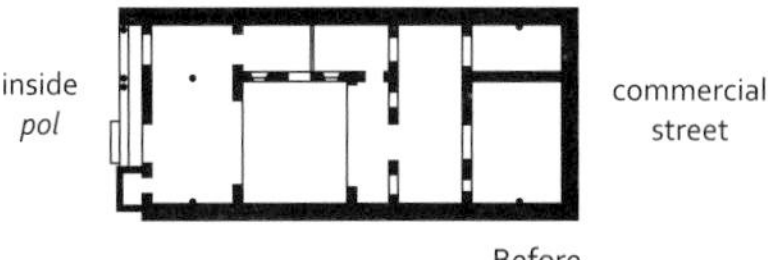

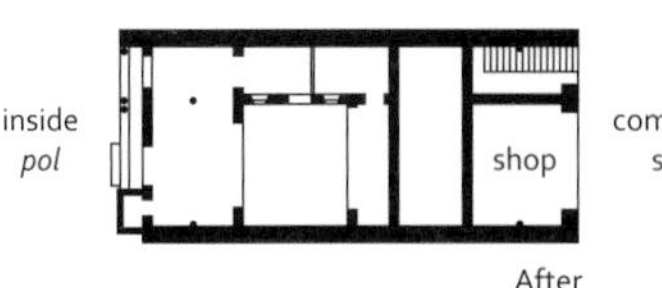

8.28 In this traditional Ahmedabad house, described in Chapter 2, the major-minor organization allows not only a transformation that includes commercial uses, but also a second entrance to a stair that faces away from the common residential courtyard onto the commercial street.
Drawing by Will Krzymowski from material provided by Akbar Nazim Modan.

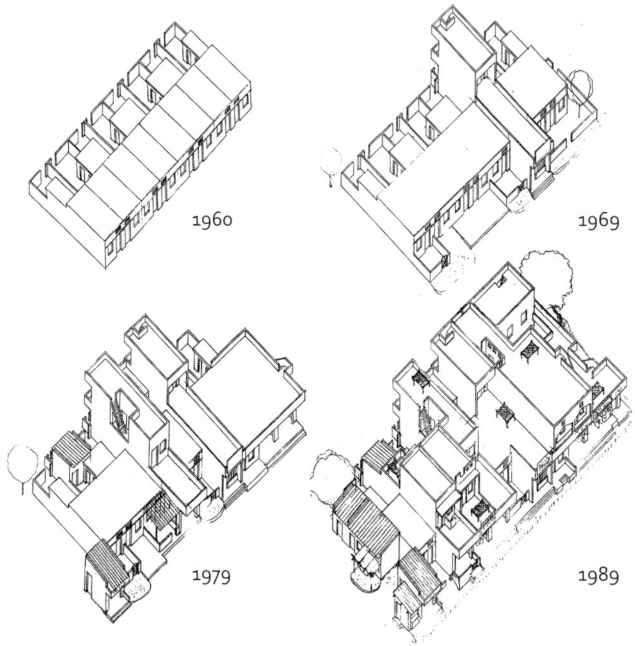

1960

1969

1979

1989

8.29 Sequential additions to modern row houses in Bapunagar, Ahmedabad, India. The drawings show original buildings from 1960, then additions from 1969, 1979 and 1989.
Research and drawings by Thomas A. Kerr.

8.30 (bottom) Additions to row houses in Bapunagar, Ahmedabad, India.
Photograph by Thomas A. Kerr.

8.31 The flexibility of row houses. Harlem Street II, 1938.
Photograph by Berenice Abbott. Museum of the City of New York, Gift of the Federal Arts Project, Works Progress Administration.

8.32 Row-house flexibility on West 79th St, Manhattan.
Photograph by author.

The flexibility of the row house is an almost universal phenomenon. In India, where most publicly built housing is user-owned rather than rented, people can make changes to their own houses. The Ahmedabad house, illustrated in Chapter 2 and in Fig. 8.28, is flexible partly because of its row-house configuration, with the circulation space continuing from front to back. Also in Ahmedabad, Bapunagar is a government-financed housing project, consisting of row houses and four-story apartment buildings arranged on a hierarchy of streets including main roads and smaller lanes. The project was built in 1960, and since then has undergone considerable change (Figs. 8.29 and 8.30). Virtually all of the row houses have had additions built. Where the row houses are on the main roads, their additions include shops in the space in front.

Case study: the early twentieth-century New York apartment building

New York apartment houses with ground-floor commercial space built early in the twentieth century demonstrate organizational principles that are related to those of smaller, family shop/houses.[11] In an intensely mercantile city, these buildings optimized the balance between dwellings, retail shops and professional offices, yielding a maximum of rent while providing accommodation for a variety of tenants.

Advertising for these buildings was directed largely at the middle class. But the plans suggest that they housed a much wider mixture of people – ranging from the building's superintendent occupying an apartment in the back of the ground floor, to a shopkeeper occupying an apartment behind his shop, to a variety of families occupying the apartments themselves.

Although these are multiple-unit buildings, they exhibit similar attributes to small shop/houses:

1 They maximize commercial frontage on the commercial street, very often by putting the residential entrance onto the side/residential street, leading to public circulation that allows maximum floor area to the shops.
2 They give the residential entrance some architectural distinction on a street that was often characterized by individual row houses and leafy calm. The entrance seemed to be part of a building that appeared not as a commercial building but as a stately version of the smaller row houses (Fig. 8.34).
3 When shops are directly connected to apartments the kitchen was at the threshold (Fig. 8.33).
4 The façades incorporate an effective balance between an open and public ground floor, and upper floors that are more closed and private (Fig. 8.35).

In these buildings, the upper floors are arranged to maximize residential rents, and the area given to public hallways is minimized. Apartment plans locate important rooms, like parlors and dining rooms, in prominent positions – even if this means long internal hallways to reach them from the apartment door. The building's organization allowed apartments and shops to co-exist easily. External fire escapes meant that there were fewer needs for vertical coordination between different floors, and the internal courtyard necessary to provide light to the apartments could become narrower at the ground floor to allow maximum area for commercial rental.

[11] Hesselgren, *Apartment Houses of the Metropolis*.

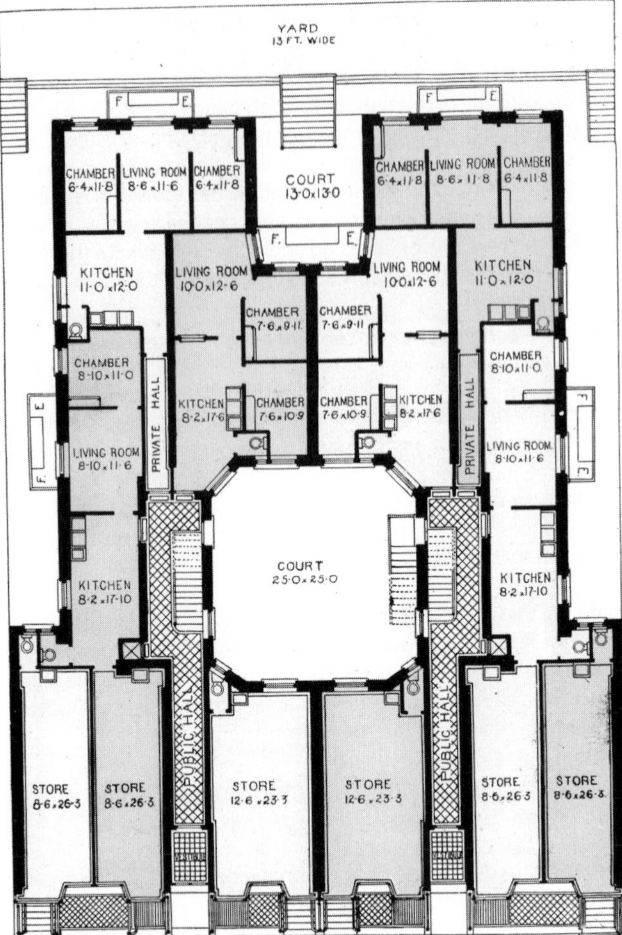

8.33 Tenement buildings on Houston Street, Manhattan. In each building, one shop connects to an apartment, through the kitchen.

Hesselgren, *Apartment Houses of the Metropolis*.

The buildings allowed rental potential to be maximized from a particular piece of avenue real estate, while at the same time allowing upwardly mobile tenants to feel that they were *not* living over the store. The Lower East Side tenement dwellers were fine with living over the store – they had relationships with people in the store, may have worked in a similar store, may have been of the same background as people in the store. But when these people entered the middle class, they wanted to be among other middle-class people. The configuration fostered a class separation at the building and city scale, while at the same time providing maximum profit for the landlord.

8.34 **Ground-floor plan and upper-floor plan of "The Mansfield," Broadway and West 149th Street. Even on the ground floor, the building contains: an apartment/office for a doctor, an apartment attached to a shop, but also accessible from the public hall, a store with a back room and window, suggesting a bedroom, and an independent apartment, not associated with a business. To maximize commercial area, the courtyard narrows at the ground floor.**
Hesselgren, *Apartment Houses of the Metropolis*.

8.35 **Artist's rendering of "The Mansfield."**
Hesselgren, *Apartment Houses of the Metropolis*.

Case study: the contemporary tall, mixed-use building

Finally, the large contemporary mixed-use urban building also exhibits the principles described here, within contexts of contemporary planning, construction and development economics.[12]

The interaction between dwelling units, retail space and parking is largely resolved with the placement of the vertical elevator/stair cores and the parking layout. Building wings are shallow enough to allow light into dwelling units, and the upper floors come down onto a base that allows maximum space for retail and/or appropriate dimensions for parking bays. Usually, the residential entrance is not on the busiest commercial street, allowing for maximum retail frontage, and the parking entry, services and loading dock are at the least valuable frontage (Figs. 8.36, 8.37, 8.38).

These ideas are interpreted differently in different urban contexts. Sacramento has blocks that are roughly square but with east–west alleys bounded by important east–west streets and less important north–south streets. This leads to configurations in which residential entrances share frontage with stores on the east–west streets, and where north–south streets are used for less valuable retail frontage and for parking entrances. San Francisco's South of Market

[12] Much of the information in this section comes from conversations with Kevin Sauser of Ankrom-Moisan Architects in Portland, Oregon, who also draw the diagrams.

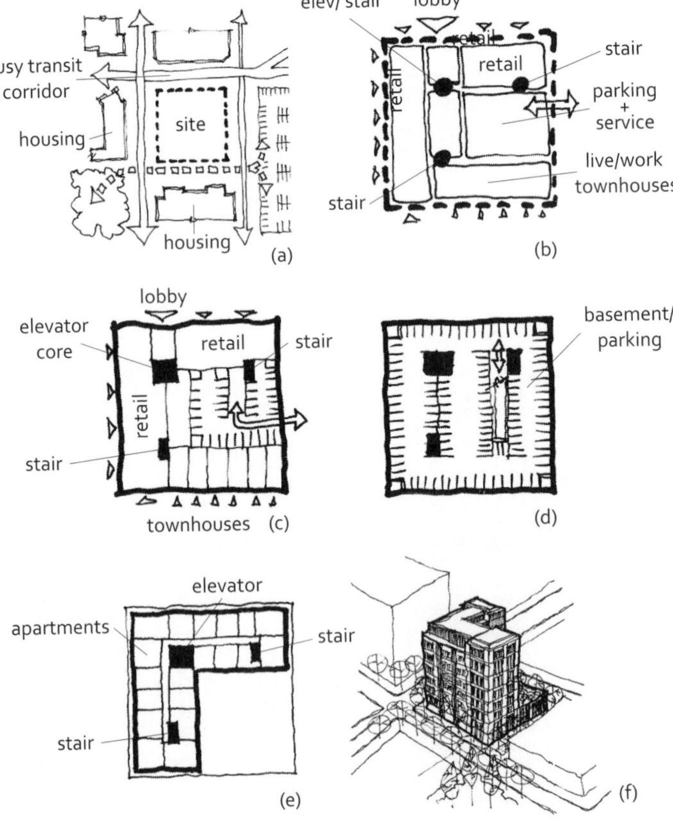

8.36 Diagrams, (a)–(f), describing design sequence of a contemporary mixed-use building with "L"-shaped residential block on a square base of retail and parking. The location of the vertical cores allows retail space to be maximized and for efficiency of the residential floors above and parking below.
Diagrams by Kevin Sauser, Ankrom-Moisan Associated Architects, Portland.

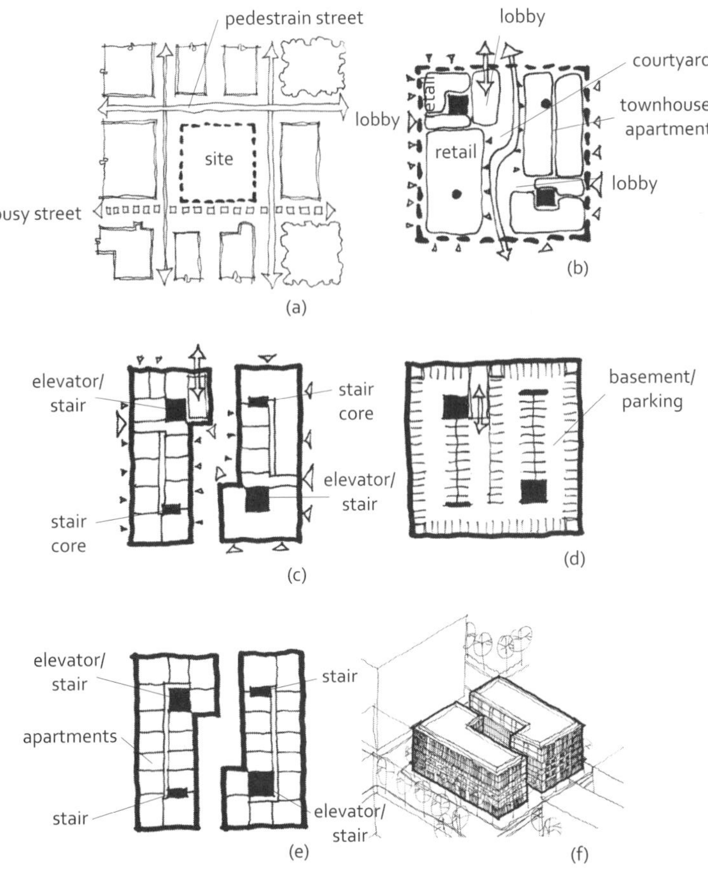

8.37 Diagrams, (a)–(f), describing design sequence of a contemporary mixed-use building with two residential bars on a square base of parking. Two vertical cores are necessary for each residential bar. The main lobby serves the courtyard as well as the street.

Diagrams by Kevin Sauser, Ankrom-Moisan Associated Architects, Portland.

8.38 "The Burlington," mixed-use building designed by Ankrom-Moisan Associated Architects, Portland.

Photograph by Kirsten Force, Ankrom-Moisan Associated Architects, Portland.

district has long east–west streets, with alley-like parallel streets between them. When possible, the minor streets are used for residential entrances, which may also share frontage with stores on the major east–west streets.

Downtown Portland, and Portland's newly redeveloped Pearl District with numerous new mixed-use buildings, have square blocks making the street hierarchy less clear than in cities with rectangular blocks. Nevertheless, different uses tend to gather on different streets, affecting the relative positions of the residential entrance and commercial frontage. But since retail is less important to the financial pro-forma in higher buildings, the position of the residential entrance may be determined by factors other than the value of retail frontage – such as perceived prestige or access to open space.

* * *

The common attributes of architectural organization described in this chapter are not specific enough to be guidelines for actual projects, which need to be carefully based on local conditions of culture, client and building purpose. But they do help to set the framework for such guidelines, while pointing up the commonalities of shop/houses across different cultures.

Part III

THE DEATH AND LIFE OF THE MODEST SHOP/HOUSE

Part III: THE DEATH AND LIFE OF THE MODEST SHOP/HOUSE

The pervasive effect of modernism on the shape of cities all over the world did not happen all at once. The functional separation of the Western city began even before new retailing practices, the rise of industry and the separation of classes accelerated during the nineteenth century. And by the beginning of the twentieth century, even before zoning was generally instituted in the United States, the trend toward a divided city was clear, and cultural ideals combined with financial realities to point the way toward a situation in which the shop/house became a typological outcast.

But at the same time, change happened in the context of cities that were being built as they always had been. Zoning did not automatically result in cities with monofunctional districts. Modernist ideas did not automatically change the practice of thousands of practicing architects and builders. And even well-known architects did not suddenly abandon their knowledge of how to make urban buildings. The building culture changed more slowly.

Within this slow change there were exceptions to the modernist ideas of functional separation, and transitional figures – including architects such as Otto Wagner in Vienna and Hendrik Petrus Berlage in Amsterdam – adopted some modernist tenets but retained historical ideas at the same time. And by the 1960s – only thirty years after modern architecture was given legitimacy through a now-famous exhibition at the Museum of Modern Art – there was beginning to be serious critical disquiet, and the beginnings of resistance to modernism in urban design. Jane Jacobs' *The Death and Life of Great American Cities* was published in 1961; the first American historic preservation act was passed in 1966; the Pruitt-Igoe housing project was destroyed in 1972; Robert Venturi's *Complexity and Contradiction in Architecture* was first published in 1966. Modernist urban design as a widely accepted philosophy represented a relatively brief interlude – however destructive – in the long history of the connected city.

During this time, practice and the persistence of traditional urban fabric helped ensure that valuable aspects of the pre-modern city remained. Even zoning often stipulated that existing uses could remain in place, so that many cities maintained districts that continued to have a fine grain of different uses. But through these decades the forces of zoning applied to new projects, rules of development finance, urban redevelopment and class-exclusive attitudes toward the city were taking their toll.

The contemporary city is not monolithic in its origin, its form or the processes that make it. The persistence of older urban forms and buildings is helping to form a basis for the reintroduction of the shop/house. But the building culture of contemporary America still operates with a particular set of assumptions about the idea of the mixed-use building, its role on the street and its role in the local urban economy. Simply put, the shop/house is largely excluded from the intentions of builders, from what is acceptable in zoning and from people's understandings of what is normal. This exclusion emerged gradually, beginning at least as early as the eighteenth century, and culminating in the zoning ordinances and lending practices that impede or prevent the construction of what were once among the most common urban buildings.

In the American context, the demise of the shop/house was not simply the result of laws and procedures preventing the construction of buildings that people wanted built. Institutional change and popular sentiment emerged simultaneously. Yet, popular sentiment was never monolithic, and the institutions of government and finance were responding to popular will in ways that did not always reflect the diversity of the population and its desired ways of living in – or out of – cities. Today, it is the increasing interest in shop/houses among people of different income levels, and among developers, that will cause change in institutional constraints, just as those constraints were themselves at least partly formed by the desire for a functionally separated city.

9.01 15 Elm Street, Boston, photographed in 1962.
From Library of Congress/Historic American Buildings Survey.

9

THE GRADUAL SEPARATION OF FAMILY AND BUSINESS

Rising straight up from [the street] are walls of houses, which . . . present a grotesquely jagged silhouette of gables, attics, and zinc chimneys. At the very bottom of this scenic railway lies the street, plunged in eternal twilight. The sky is a remote hope far, far above it. The street is no more than a trench, a deep cleft, a narrow passage. And although we have been accustomed to it for more than a thousand years, our hearts are always oppressed by the constriction of its enclosing walls . . . The street consists of a thousand different buildings, but we have got used to the beauty of ugliness for that has meant making the best of our misfortune. Those thousand houses are dingy and utterly discordant one with another. It is appalling, but we pass on our way.[1]

(Le Corbusier, *Oeuvre Complète*)

[1] Le Corbusier, *Oeuvre Complète 1910–1929*, 118.
[2] Alonso, "The Economics of Consumption," 11–14.

While typical households once harbored many activities that had monetary exchange value, contemporary households do so much less. Rural farmhouses, large houses in which functions such as laundry, cheese- and butter-making, and even the education of children, happened, and urban shop/houses all contained functions with monetary exchange value (Fig. 9.02). Even though cash might not have changed hands, the economic value of those functions can be understood when such factors as the cost of washing machines, prepared foods and formal education are taken into account – all connected to functions that people used to do themselves, but are now willing to pay for. The shift of unpaid labor to the use of money in the modern household corresponds to the externalizing of functions that used to happen at home. For most people, the preparation of food has been replaced by buying pre-prepared food; the time-consuming procurement of food has been replaced by the use of the automobile to reach all-purpose supermarkets; and crafts that once took place at home have been replaced by the purchase of mass-produced goods.[2]

In the seventeenth century, public life took place outside the house, in the life of the street, festivals, church . . .

. . . while in the twentieth century, public life moved inside the house, in entertainment systems, internet, TV.

In the seventeenth century, productive functions took place inside the house, in processing food, making clothes, educating children . . .

. . . while in the twentieth century, productive functions moved outside the house, in making clothes, the manufacture of washing machines, dry cleaning, educating children, manufacturing, processing food.

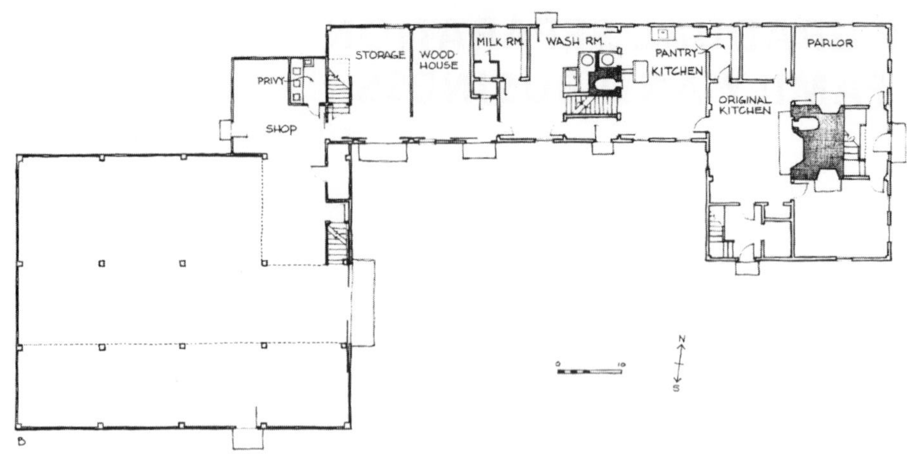

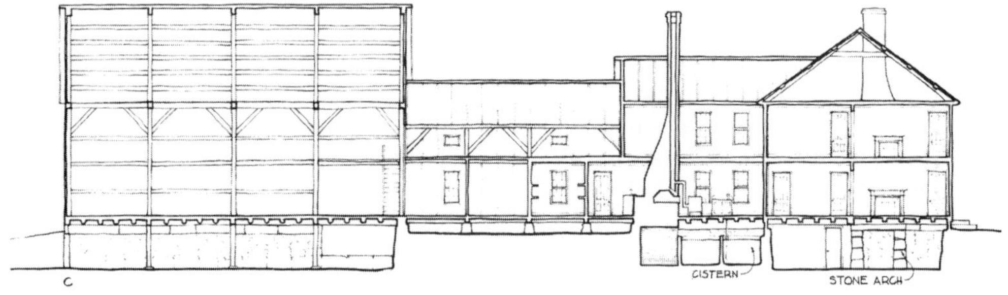

9.02 Connected farmhouse in North Yarmouth, Maine, showing integration of productive functions in the household.
Courtesy of Thomas Hubka, from Hubka, *Big House, Little House, Back House, Barn.*

In summary (recognizing the approximation of this generalization):

- *Public functions have moved from outside to inside.*
- *Productive functions have moved from inside to outside.*[3]

Beginning in about the seventeenth century, this inversion of functions was accompanied by more specific nomenclature and more specific use of architectural space, as the Enlightenment's emphasis on classification changed how architectural space was understood.

In pre-seventeenth-century houses, for example, circulation was through rooms themselves, and most rooms were not assigned specific functions. "Chambers," rather than bedrooms, housed a varied set of activities, including sleeping, writing letters and even the receiving of business guests.[4] Social convention, rather than architecture, was the mediator of social relations.

In the shop/house, the shop was at the beginning of a sequence of movement from street to dwelling, and commercial activity was very much part of the household. During the seventeenth and eighteenth centuries, rooms took on

[3] Shammas, "The Domestic Environment." The equivalence of rural houses to aristocratic ones in which the processing of food was important is mentioned in Sarti, *Europe at Home*, 77.
[4] See for example Ajmar-Wollheim and Dennis, *At Home in Renaissance Italy*, 58–63.

increasingly specific functions.[5] Social separations within the household became stronger, so servants and children increasingly had their own place, with human interactions regulated more and more through architectural means rather than social convention. The advent of the corridor, parallel to what was often an *enfilade* arrangement of rooms, allowed the separation of servants from the family (the members of which still enjoyed a vista from room to room and the ability to move directly between them). This furthered the use of architecture to reinforce class separations between people,[6] and this idea spread to city planning as well.[7]

The separation of functions within the home was one manifestation of a general fragmentation of the city in which public life was separated from private life, and private life separated from production. By the twentieth century, Walter Benjamin could write about Paris, "Ever since the time of Louis Philippe, the bourgeois has shown a tendency to compensate for the absence of any trace of private life in the big city. He tries to do this within the four walls of his apartment."[8] This separation from the public realm was true not only for the bourgeoisie but also for the working class, for whom a higher value was being placed on domestic life.[9]

Along with urban space, people's time became fragmented, bounded by the punching of time clocks and new time periods required for "commuting." The demise of the shop/house – to be guaranteed by coming changes in zoning, building codes and methods of building finance – was a manifestation of a larger change in attitudes toward architectural and urban space and the time of day.

Transformations of commerce and daily life

These transformations fundamentally altered, and nearly destroyed, the shop/house. The evolution of English shops over several hundred years helps explain its fate.

In northern and western Europe, during medieval and post-medieval times, there were few fixed shops and retail trade in foodstuffs and ordinary household goods took place at temporary stalls, in market squares and streets. As the importance of the periodic market declined, first by extending itself throughout the week, and then by becoming more and more permanent, the fixed shop took over. Norman J.G. Pounds points out that in northern Europe this simply restored what had never disappeared in southern Europe – the fixed shops or *tabernae* that were present in the cities of ancient Rome.[10]

The transformation of houses to accommodate shops was initially makeshift, as shops themselves may not have been open on a regular basis. Buying and selling sometimes happened directly through the front window of the house, with an extended sill set up below the window, or a flap that allowed the window to be converted into a counter space. Such arrangements allowed for commerce to take place without the customer entering the house. Before the eighteenth century, few windows were glazed, allowing for a direct exchange when the window shutters were open, but preventing the use of the window for permanent display. This supported what Cox calls "the concept of an open market," in which buyer and seller could come to an agreement about price and where the transaction was open to public scrutiny.[11]

5 Some of this is known from probate inventories, which by describing the items to be found in each room after a person's death also described the number of rooms. By the sixteenth century, in England, even the houses of modest people, had multiple rooms, indicating an increasing separation of functions. See, for example, Shammas, "The Domestic Environment," 138–139. See also Eleb and Debarre, *Architectures de la Vie Privée*.

6 Evans, *Translations from Drawing to Building*, 55–92.

7 See also Markus, particularly *Buildings and Power*, throughout.

8 Benjamin, *Arcades Project*, 20. This is also discussed in Rice, *Emergence of the Interior*, 11–36.

9 Daunton, *House and Home*, 37.

10 Pounds, *Hearth and Home*, 348–349.

11 Cox, *Complete Tradesman*, 77–85.

In medieval cities, shops of particular kinds were often clustered together, a pattern that was maintained into more recent times. This was partly the result of social restrictions that put certain kinds of objectionable activities away from the center, and sometimes the result of guild organization that put people following the same trade together for mutual benefit. As people were living above and behind their own shops, business ties were also ties among families. Nancy Cox quotes Defoe:

> Some, especially retailers, ruin themselves by fixing their shops in such places as are improper for their business. In most towns, but particularly in the city of London, there are places as it were appropriated to particular trades, and where the trades which are placed there succeed very well . . . as the orange-merchants and wet-salters about Billingsgate, and in Thames Street; the costermongers at the Three Cranes; the wholesale cheesemongers in Thames Street; the mercers and drapers in the high streets, such as Cheapside, Ludgate Hill, Cornhill, Round Court, and Grace-Church Street, &c.[12]

This sort of concentration, especially perhaps of the mercers and drapers on main streets, was the antecedent of today's shopping street. The eventual emergence of "shopping" as a unique activity, and often to be engaged in by the middle and upper classes, abetted the eventual emergence of exclusively retail and exclusively residential districts. But this separation took place gradually.

In the eighteenth century, the economy was still characterized by small entrepreneurs. These were retailers and craftsmen, who together formed up to half the recorded population in some towns.[13] Apart from the implications for the physical environment of cities, these numbers are striking in the picture they offer of economic life: many people were involved in the production or sales of tangible things; and because that activity was largely in small shops, it was visible to all (Fig. 9.03). The nineteenth century brought a strong separation between places of production and places of consumption, but in eighteenth-century towns there was a fine mixture between the two. The lack of social distinction between family life and business life that Philippe Aries described extended into the economic realm as well. Many shops incorporated craft manufacture, wholesaling and retailing – and the history of commerce is partly an account of how these functions became separated from each other, and how specialization increased.[14]

Data about the Lancashire town of Chorley indicates the transitional nature of the location of manufacture in 1851 (Table 9.1).[15] Certain kinds of manufacture still largely happened at home, but others had been moved to factories away from the home.

Even from these few numbers, one gets a picture in which "heavy industry", or processes where large-scale mechanization was cost effective, had already been moved out of the home, but functions that could remain in the home did so. This included most retail and wholesale trade. As the century progressed, more and more manufacturing moved out of the home, and as sales outlets grew, they also moved to functionally specific quarters.[16]

[12] Cox, *Complete Tradesman*, 66.
[13] Everitt, "Country, County and Town," 105. See also Warnes, "Early Separation of Homes," 105–135.
[14] For a general account of this process, see Hower, *Macy's*, 70–85.
[15] Warnes, "Early Separation of Homes," 135.
[16] Kathleen Conzen writes explicitly of "the close relationship between the Industrial Revolution and the functional segregation of cities into discrete areas of work and residence. Only when production was transferred from the workshop to the factory could large-scale purely residential areas emerge." In Conzen, "Patterns of Residence," and Schnore, *New Urban History*, 149.

9.03 In the evolution of shops, some were typologically between the simple open window and the glazed shop in which buyer and seller were both inside. This view of Bishopsgate in 1736 shows a shop on the left with an open front, but with an inside counter. It also shows a fully glazed shop, and a butcher shop in which business took place on the street.
City of London, London Metropolitan Archives.

Table 9.1 Domestic workplaces in Chorley

Industry	Percentage of workers working domestically
Cotton: spinning	0
Cotton: weaving	66.8
Cotton: bleaching and dyeing	0
Other textiles and clothing	89.0
Iron founding and manufacture	0
Other metal manufacture	60.5
Other manufacture	71.7
Retailing and wholesaling	89.0
Personal and office workers	41.8

Source: Warnes, "Early separation of homes from workplaces," 135.

Changes to shops

At the same time the city was being reorganized, the shop itself was also changing. Even when houses and shops were still located in the same building, some shops got larger, occupying several rooms and maintaining a distribution of goods within them that allowed frequently traded goods to be located toward the front. In buildings where living quarters were located behind shops, this allowed sales of less frequently sold goods – including those over which longer deliberation or negotiation was needed – to happen closer to the living quarters. So shops themselves developed gradients of privacy, but in which there was still not necessarily a sharp distinction between commercial and residential functions. A frequent and trusted customer might enter into the residential portion of the house or rooms that had a residential character.

9.04 Tradecard of Benjamin Cole, showing room with hearth beyond the shop.
Heal collection, Prints and Drawings, British Museum, no. 70.39. Copyright © The British Museum.

The calling-card of Benjamin Cole's shop at St. Paul's shows, at the end of the shop, an open door leading to a room behind that has a fire burning in the hearth. There are windows in the wall between the shop and that room. This physical arrangement was emblematic of a social order in which shopkeepers and shop customers had varying relationships with each other – and the advertisement suggests that the possibility of a close social relationship between the customer and shopkeeper was itself something to aspire to (Fig. 9.04).

But even within the shop/house, the smooth gradient between commerce and dwelling began to give way to a clear separation. A London shop/house designed by George Dance the Younger in the eighteenth century had a parlor on the ground floor, immediately behind the shop, beyond which was a warehouse (Fig. 9.05). This building had a separate external stair leading to the upstairs residence, so it is highly unlikely that the parlor would have been exclusively for family use. Most likely it was used to receive clients and make them comfortable with the sale.[17] The side passage, connected to the entrance, is more accessible to the upstairs rooms than is the shop, indicating the importance of privacy of the upstairs rooms from the shop.

The eighteenth-century shop was gradually transformed from a business that existed to serve customers' wants to one that existed, at least partly, to encourage those wants. Although the specially designed shop window was not yet common – it would not become so until the nineteenth century[18] – the interior of the shop was designed with a view toward the attractive display of goods and the creation of an environment intended to set a particular mood and make the buyer feel that their comfort or status would increase if a purchase were made. Entering the shop, rather than conducting business only through an opening, became necessary to appreciate the display. Josiah Wedgwood laid out his shops with complete table settings of his dinnerware, evoking a mood of refinement and distinction. He required that these displays be changed frequently, to lure people back to the shop and remind them that they were again "behind the times."[19] His shop allowed for a variety of selling situations, including self-service.[20] The advent of cheaper glass meant that potential customers on the street could see goods without the need for human intercourse, and shops developed fancy show windows, sometimes as bow windows that projected out from the façade.[21] These different strategies for the advertising, display and marketing of goods all helped to dissolve the human links that existed before advertising and marketing became important.[22]

[17] Kalman, "Architecture of Mercantilism," 74.
[18] See, for example, Sawtelle, "Commercial Landscape of Boston," 208, and referring to Kalman, "Architecture of Mercantilism."
[19] Cox, *Complete Tradesman*, 93.
[20] Cox, *Complete Tradesman*, 99.
[21] Kalman, "Architecture of Mercantilism," 70–82.
[22] Alexander, D., *Retailing in England*, 11.

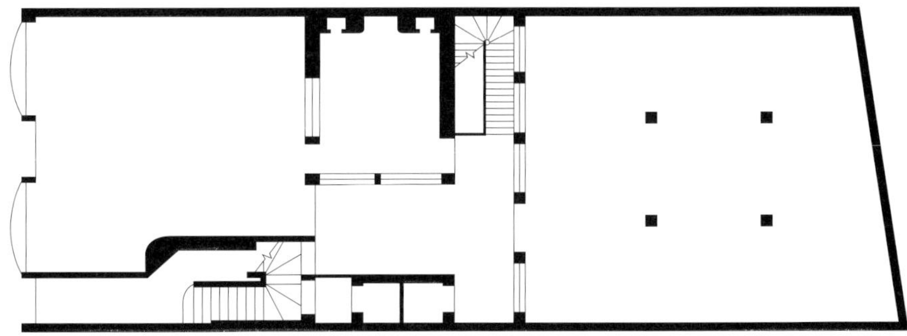

9.05 Building designed by George Dance the Younger in the eighteenth century. The room at the left with the bow windows is the shop, and the adjacent room with the fireplace is the ground-floor parlor.
Drawing by Will Krzymowski.

As merchants aspired to more upscale and elaborate shops, they also wanted more upscale locations for their dwellings. Beginning in the seventeenth century, it became more unfashionable for merchants to live in the same building as their shop. This separation was realized first for the wealthy and upper classes, and only later for ordinary artisans and shopkeepers. (Indeed, at the middle of the twentieth century, there was still a considerable number of English shop owners who lived above their shop. As with many phenomena in the world of building, transformations are not sudden, quantum jumps, and it is often the wealthier who lead the way with respect to building type and location.)

So the transformation of functional areas in cities that was occasioned by the Industrial Revolution did not happen all at once. Production in houses remained even as factory production increased.[23] The process differed from city to city, and differed also according to the predominant industry or presence of certain classes in particular places. In eighteenth-century London, shop/houses remained prevalent in wealthier areas as there was a greater market for shopkeepers' goods among people with more money.[24] Into the nineteenth century in Birmingham, for example, the jewelry trades maintained a distribution among many small shops, in or near which workers also dwelled, whereas other industries such as the brass trades, in which factories began earlier, occasioned the development of all-residential districts near the factories.[25] And as the scale of manufacturing increased and the factory model took hold, the apprenticeship model, which helped to organize the retail trade as well as the crafts,[26] was disappearing. Along with this, the tradition of apprentices living in the same house as their masters and their masters' businesses also fell away.[27]

By the end of the eighteenth century, social class was an important consideration in the location of shops. Quoted from the *Autobiography of Francis Place*:

> The new customers I had before we came to Charing Cross had all left us, and our new customers were gentlemen who would not deal with a man in a garrett, and even if any of them shold [sic] be disposed to do so, the having left a good shop and gone into poverty would be conclusive evidence that he was a rogue.[28]

The perceived status of the shopkeeper was a factor in marketing. As merchants began to move away from their own businesses to show their status, some customers saw them more favorably than shopkeepers who continued to live over their own shops. This provided more economic incentive for merchants to turn their businesses into "lock-up shops" and move to strictly residential districts.

The emerging urban pattern supported this separation. Beginning in the seventeenth century and picking up steam in the "Georgian" eighteenth, developers were building an urban structure characterized by leafy residential squares from which shops and visible commerce were excluded.[29] This exclusion was sometimes required through the use of lease covenants that specified long lists of trades that were not allowed to be established in houses, and certain things that could not even be done any longer in shops.[30]

Although upscale merchants may have appreciated these restrictions, as they helped to reinforce the exclusivity of their street, this gentrification was not

[23] Daunton, *House and Home*, 271. See also Muthesius, *English Terraced House*, 39.
[24] Schwarz, "Social Class and Social Geography." In Borsay, *Eighteenth Century Town*, 319.
[25] Vance, "Housing the Worker," 101–108.
[26] Many retailers were also craftsmen of a sort, and learned their work through apprenticeship. Grocers, for example, had to know how to roast coffee, blend tea and spices and prepare various foodstuffs. This was in addition to knowing the "business" side of the operation. They had their hands on the preparation of the various things they were selling. This is described in detailed in a chapter entitled "Shop Tradesmen and Their Craft Skills" in Alexander, D., *Retailing in England*, 110–158.
[27] The apprenticeship system had been declining even before the nineteenth century as the industrial system required wage labor. A final blow came with an Act of Parliament in 1814, striking down the Elizabethan law requiring seven years of apprenticeship. See Derry, "Repeal of the Apprenticeship Clauses."
[28] Cox, *Complete Tradesman*, 70.
[29] Muthesius, *English Terraced House*, 15–16, 38. For a description of the processes of London development see Olsen, *Town Planning in London*.
[30] Olsen, *Town Planning in London*, 101. See also Alexander, D., *Retailing in England*, 10.

necessarily well received by all tradesmen. An article in the *Sunday Times* in the later nineteenth century, complained about its effect on butchers:

> It might be expected that . . . there would be no hard covenants to hamper a man in the conduct of his business. Butchers in Mount Street, however . . . have been compelled in their leases to sign away the right to hang carcasses outside their shop-windows on a rail. The current of air thus obtained does the meat no harm, and in the morning, when the butcher is busy, it gives him more room inside to move about and attend to his customers. He and his confreres have a profound faith in the trade benefits to be derived from what is known as a good display . . . [but] the powers that be do not see the thing in this light, and frown sternly upon the very suggestion to bring "a slovenly, unhandsome corpse between the wind and their nobility." A butcher remarked feelingly on this subject: "A row of clean, white carcasses is rather a taking and pretty object," and Mount Street would, perhaps, have been none the worse if the monotony of its southern façade had been broken by the raw material of the roast beef of Old England swaying in the breeze.[31]

The growth in the size of shops was first handled by the expansion of businesses outward into the ground-floor premises of adjoining buildings, from their initial positions on the ground floor of a single party-wall building, and then upward, adding to the pressure for upstairs dwellers to move elsewhere. This expansion may be seen, for example, on some of the late nineteenth-century Goad's insurance maps of London, showing businesses straddling party walls that had openings cut into them (Fig. 9.06). Many of these incrementally formed large shops were then replaced by large purpose-built shops, without dwellings being part of the buildings, to which shop owners and shop workers came to work from different parts of the city. "By mid [nineteenth] century, the central area shop was much less a house from which its inhabitants traded than a commercial building in which its workers, in many cases, still happened to live."[32] In some places in the United States, this process happened earlier, where shop/houses were replaced by exclusively business buildings that could begin to accommodate larger firms.[33] But even Abiel T. LaForge, one of the early partners of Macy's department store, continued to live over the store with his wife and young family until 1875, "and they often worked nights long after the employees had gone home, marking special lots of merchandise or figuring inventories and profits of the season."[34]

Shop/houses became expressions of failure, even if it was the more "modern" form that failed economically. In Spitalfields, London, in 1905, an entrepreneur named Abraham Davis erected the Fashion Street Arcade, a shopping arcade with sixty-nine shops. The venture – a combination of the nineteenth-century urban shopping arcade and precursor of the twentieth-century shopping mall – failed, "and the dream building turned into workshops with living accommodation above."[35] Whoever built the shop/house apparently had a better sense of the local market than Mr. Davis did.

The rise of the middle class included new symbols of status in both the well-fitted shop and the residence located in a purely residential neighborhood. People who lived in new middle-class neighborhoods did not want to shop at street stalls or general stores in houses, but at fancier shops on the high street, and did not want to do manual labor themselves. Lower-class people now

[31] Banfield, *Great Landlords of London*, 60–61, quoted in Olsen, *Town Planning in London*, 101–102.
[32] Alexander, D., *Retailing in England*, 202.
[33] For example, see Shaw, *City Building*, 78.
[34] Hower, *Macy's*, 127.
[35] Kershen, *Strangers, Aliens and Asians*, 63.

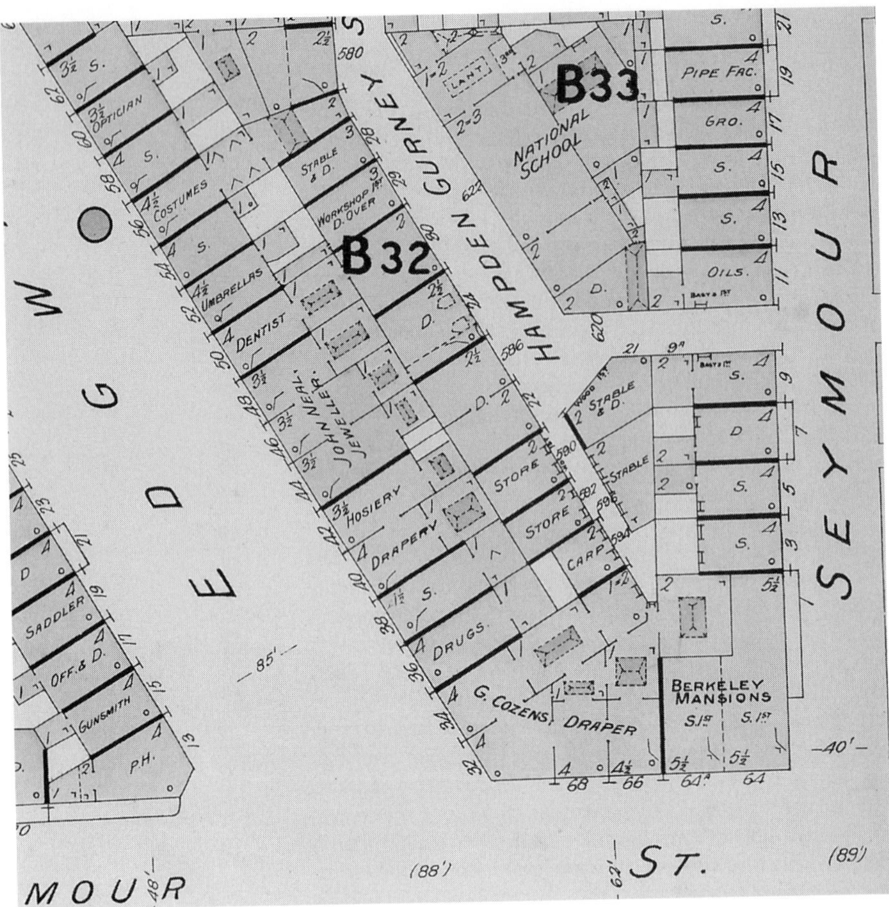

9.06 Goad's insurance map of buildings on Edgware Road, north of Oxford Street, London, about 1899. This shows three instances in which standard 7- or 8-meter wide terraced buildings are being combined. These buildings have since been replaced with much larger ones.
Map © The British Museum Board Maps 145.b.24, f.B8.

worked in factories away from their houses. Daily life and the people who made it up were now segregated by class and function.[36]

And the disappearance of the small shop/house diminished the character of their streets by eliminating active, family-based commerce. Gillian Tindall writes about Kentish Town in London in the twentieth century:

> The corn-and-seed merchants now sells second-hand office equipment, as does its neighbour (same firm). The corner shop where the gentlemanly grocer lived is a Neighbourhood Aid Centre, its window decorated with cartoon posters about tenants' rights. The coffee and dining rooms used to be a junk furniture dealer's but has in recent years gradually elevated itself into a true antique shop. The bacon shop is the headquarters of a Task Force, another of those benevolent enterprises which now cluster as thickly in west Kentish Town as the old "slum mission" and soup kitchens ever did. Then come two shuttered shops – also a feature of Kentish Town today – and then a "Centre for Recycling" which . . . soon degenerated into a dumping ground for rusting broken pushchairs, dismantled water-heaters of an obsolete pattern and sodden sofas with the stuffing sprouting

[36] Tindall, *Fields Beneath*, 145.

> like fungus. The oil-and-colour shop where lived the "two pretty and vivacious daughters" is now a cheap clothes-boutique called "Route 24" – the number of the bus that has replaced the Malden Road trams.[37]

This kind of urban landscape is a familiar one in England and the United States. It consists of places that have become undesirable for most commerce, with lowered land values and rents, often overlooked as new development becomes attractive elsewhere. Eventually, these places themselves became candidates for "slum clearance" and redevelopment, as the vitality of the former neighborhood faded from memory.

The shop/house in the American city

In the American city before the Revolution, there was considerable mixing, not only of dwelling and commercial functions in the same building, but also of different kinds of businesses, manufacturing and retail, fancy shops and ordinary ones, on the same street.[38] This mixing did not imply a lower social status – prominent merchants lived on the same streets as less prominent ones and often lived in shop/houses.[39] In Philadelphia, more valuable buildings, and businesses typically associated with them, were on major streets, with less valuable buildings on nearby alleys – but all in the same neighborhood.[40] In late eighteenth-century Portsmouth, New Hampshire, Market Street had buildings in which merchants lived over their own cellar and ground-floor shops. These were wooden buildings, replaced with brick after a series of fires.[41]

This mixing persisted in some places through the nineteenth century and into the twentieth. Even after the Civil War, a fine-grained mixing still existed. In Charlotte in 1877, "business proprietors, office employees and manual laborers [were] living side-by-side on nearly every block."[42]

Although through the nineteenth century significant numbers of people still maintained dwellings over shops, the separation of dwelling from shop was already under way in many places, particularly on the principal streets of large cities, at the beginning of the century. By the last third of the eighteenth century, at least, New York neighborhoods began to distinguish themselves according to class and economic level.[43] In Boston in 1800, it became fashionable for merchants and aspiring merchants to move to all-residential houses away from principal streets. But in many cases, they did not replace the shop/house with a structure that had an exclusively commercial use. Instead, they rented the dwellings to other people, meaning that the street retained its mixed-use character, although with a very different kind of mixture.[44] This separation occurred later in cities first established during the nineteenth century.[45]

In early nineteenth-century New York, local, craft-based production co-existed with large manufacturing and marketing.[46] This period marked the beginning of the factory system, which occasioned the need for larger factories and stores that were free of dwellings. Like commercial districts, manufacturing districts were increasingly distinct within the city. And corresponding with the formation of all-commercial and all-manufacturing districts, journeymen tended to no longer live with their masters, as they did during the eighteenth century, but rented dwelling spaces, sometimes in enormously crowded buildings.[47] The separation of businesses from dwellings was accompanied by

[37] Tindall, *Fields Beneath*, 196.
[38] For Philadelphia, for example, this is described in Upton, *Another City*, 28.
[39] Harrington, *New York Merchant*, 22.
[40] Blumin, *Emergence of the Middle Class*, 48.
[41] Candee, *Building Portsmouth*, 90–91.
[42] Hanchett, *Sorting Out*, 39.
[43] Abbott, "Neighborhoods of New York," 42–43.
[44] Sawtelle, "Commercial Landscape of Boston," 164, 202.
[45] Shaw, *City Building*, 3–4.
[46] Rock, *Artisans of the New Republic*, 151.
[47] Rock, *Artisans of the New Republic*, 254.

the separation of different aspects of businesses – particularly manufacturing and sales – from each other.[48]

The class differentiation that had accelerated in the nineteenth century now began to turn into a separation within people's own lives. During the nineteenth century, there was a lot of attention paid to the ordering of the public sphere, and the encouragement of commerce into particular places.[49] Within and around this evolution, residential districts – and class distinctions between them – were beginning to be established through private initiative. When it finally arrived, zoning simply turned what was a growing, implicit practice of use separation into a rigid set of legal requirements.

The separation of functions, which began to happen long before it was mandated through zoning ordinances, was one aspect of an urban vision that had long captured people's imagination. This vision, that in Europe was manifested in places such as the Edinburgh New Town and Haussmann's Paris, and in plans such as Christopher Wren's for London after the 1666 fire, was of geometric order, visual uniformity, and the spatial sorting of different classes of people. The rectangular or square grid, and the development of major visual axes, facilitated this kind of rational organization, within which it was conceptually easy to develop an understanding of buildings that were also visually uniform.[50]

Although, even at the middle of the twentieth century, many dwellings remained over shops, the trend toward separation was clear much earlier and, in retrospect, we can see the forces that created the separation acting as early as the eighteenth century. In summary, those forces included:

1 the "domestic ideal," and desire of the rising middle class to live in exclusively residential districts;
2 the decline of the apprenticeship system, which made shop apprentices into shop workers, and put them out of the houses of their masters. (The formal, guild-based apprenticeship system as it existed in England did not take hold in the American colonies.)
3 the increase in size of shops;
4 the growing idea of the shop as a specially designed environment to promote the most effective marketing and display of goods, replacing the generic front room of the house;
5 the need for marketing that was occasioned by the apprenticeship system;
6 the rise of "shopping" as a leisure activity, on the part of the middle and upper classes, that began to demand exclusive districts dedicated to that activity alone.

By the twentieth century, the buildings that maintained the combination of dwelling and shop were often in blue-collar neighborhoods, rather than in white-collar, wealthier ones. The shops in these buildings provided people with their livelihoods or second livelihoods. They also provided everyday goods such as groceries, and convenient service for people who could not travel far to do their shopping because of issues of time or expense.[51] And women, when they had their own businesses, often had them at home, in the house itself or in shops connected to the house. They were supported by local, neighborhood networks, maintaining their ability to fulfill domestic responsibilities while gaining a foothold in the world of paid work.[52] So into the century, shop/houses existed, even if endangered.

48 Blumin, *Emergence of the Middle Class*, 84–95.
49 Shaw, *City Building*, 32–33.
50 For example, see Upton, *Another City*, 3–4. The theme of "sorting" the city is present in a number of books on urban history, including Upton, *Another City*, Shaw, *City Building*, and Hanchett, *Sorting Out*.
51 Hanchett, *Sorting Out*, 105.
52 Deutsch, *Women and the City*, 133–4.

But as the century progressed, architecture, urban theory, the law and public policy worked together to solidify the idea of the divided city. Le Corbusier's rejection of the traditional urban street and his promotion of the functionally zoned city – in accord with the ideas of twentieth-century planners – were supported by new zoning laws and the growing idea of land-use planning. These developments followed a long history of economic, social and urban transformation and culminated in the building culture of the late twentieth and early twenty-first centuries, in which the existence of the shop/house has been discouraged if not altogether outlawed.

10.01 Chicago. In the early twentieth century, the increasing height of urban buildings meant that commercial uses at their ground floors were less important to their economic success.

Photograph by author.

10

THE BUILDING CULTURE OF THE DIVIDED CITY

Any business establishment is likely to be a genuine nuisance in a neighborhood of residences.[1]

(Supreme Court of Louisiana, case quoted in Euclid vs. Ambler, the 1926 Supreme Court case that affirmed the constitutionality of zoning)

The vision of the city that began to emerge in the early nineteenth century ultimately made the construction of shop/houses an extraordinary act – rather than the ordinary act it was through most of history. Monofunctional zoning is often cited as the reason mixed-use buildings are difficult to build. But zoning is only an instrument that transmits a social vision into built form. Since zoning began with reasonable intentions and solved real problems, it was difficult to see, at its inception, how it would contribute to the fragmentation of American cities and provide a legal basis for racial segregation. Today's enlightened citizens and planners want an inclusive city, with mixed uses and walkable neighborhoods. But the rule systems of the building culture support a stubbornly archaic vision.[2]

As zoning was introduced, building codes were specifying stricter requirements for different functional uses within buildings, and more robust fire separations between uses. These changes drove up the cost of building and increased problems of architectural coordination between uses. Simultaneously, development finance became more specialized, making it difficult to borrow for a building that combined different uses. Today, there are different developers for commercial and residential property – each with its own sources of funding.

But over and above the pressures felt by individual institutions, there was a suburban "ethos" within which people genuinely wanted the kind of environment that was being produced. Sam Bass Warner wrote that in the nineteenth century, Americans increasingly aspired to the "divided city."[3] The divided city was realized with opposing attributes: crowded vs. open, city vs. country, poor vs. rich, poor vs. middle class, workplace vs. house – and black vs. white. The city in which opposing attributes were mixed became objectionable, and this controlled marketing and policy. Developers who built suburban transit lines and the framers of zoning ordinances shared the view that the mixed city was a problem and the divided city its solution. The Fifth Avenue Association – a group that promoted the preservation of Fifth Avenue as an exclusive street – was instrumental to the passage of New York's 1916 Zoning Resolution, setting the stage for similar ordinances all over the United States.[4] Zoning went beyond issues associated with the insalubrious and crowded city, and helped solidify the spatial separation of economic classes.

1 State vs. City of New Orleans.
2 For a general discussion of the rule systems of building cultures, see Davis, H. *Culture of Building*, 127–129.
3 Warner, *Streetcar Suburbs*, 1–14, and throughout.
4 Page, *Creative Destruction of Manhattan*, 61–65.

The ethos of the divided city also applied to the place of women. The domestic ideal that emerged in the nineteenth century, in which the home was not to be the place of domestic work as it had been the century before, meant that the home was "not factory, not marketplace, not place of work [and] the factory, the store, and so forth, in turn were not homes."[5] If women were to be paid for their work, it would be away from the home.

In these various contexts, the shop/house took on a persona of insalubriousness and poverty, and became synonymous with the objectionable characteristics of the pre-modern city. It mixed people of different classes. It denied people the domestic peace and quiet of suburban life. And for the commercial activity to be economically viable, there had to be sufficient density – a density that was too high for comfort.

Motivations for zoning

Although zoning began with reasonable intentions, not all the arguments for it were rational. Euclid vs. Ambler,[6] the 1926 U.S. Supreme Court case that affirmed the constitutionality of zoning, quoted a case of the Supreme Court of Louisiana:[7]

> In the first place, the exclusion of business establishments from residence districts might enable the municipal government to give better police protection. Patrolmen's beats are larger, and therefore fewer, in residence neighborhoods than in business neighborhoods. A place of business in a residence neighborhood furnishes an excuse for any criminal to go into the neighborhood, where, otherwise, a stranger would be under the ban of suspicion. Besides, open shops invite loiterers and idlers to congregate; and the places of such congregation need police protection. In the second place, the zoning of the city into residence districts and commercial districts is a matter of economy in street paving. Heavy trucks, hauling freight to and from places of business in residence districts, require the city to maintain the same costly pavement in such districts that is required for business districts; whereas, in the residence districts, where business establishments are excluded, a cheaper pavement serves the purpose . . . any business establishment is likely to be a genuine nuisance in a neighborhood of residences. Places of business are noisy; they are apt to be disturbing at night; some of them are malodorous; some of them unsightly; some are apt to breed rats, mice, roaches, flies, ants, etc. . . .

This argument is striking in the way it paints a picture of insalubriousness and cost, while offering little that is clearly an unambiguous nuisance within the police-power justification for zoning. The logical conclusion to the argument about the cost of police protection is that all city businesses should be highly concentrated, in a Panopticon-like arrangement, allowing surveillance by a small number of policemen. The argument about street paving leads to a similar conclusion.[8] And the conflation of criminals with strangers suggests that by the time of Euclid, any acceptance of the city as a place where one might be comfortable in the presence of strangers had changed substantially. This was likely at least partly a racist attitude.

The end of the nineteenth century brought about efforts to improve public health through laws and city planning. But the poor conditions that had a negative effect on people were often conflated with the people who were affected.[9] This bluntly shaped policy: people who were negatively affected by

[5] Deutsch, *Women and the City*, 74–75.
[6] Euclid vs. Ambler, 272 U.S. 365.
[7] State vs. City of New Orleans, 97 So. 444.
[8] These new attitudes were not confined to the United States, and were not only imposed from above. Daunton points out that in England, "many members of the working class welcomed and accepted the sterilization of public space, and switched to an expenditure pattern which entailed a more inward-looking life style." Daunton, *House and Home in the Victorian City*, 272.
[9] See, for example, Hanchett, *Sorting Out the New South City*, 97–103.

bad conditions were removed from view or interaction with the rest of society, through zoning and public housing.

The urban economist Homer Hoyt included a section titled "The slums, vice areas and workingmen's quarters, 1863–71" in his 1933 dissertation, "One Hundred Years of Land Values in Chicago," a classic study of the relationship between urban form and economics. Hoyt's association of slums with workingmen's quarters is telling. After quoting an observer describing "the vice area" and a place with a "peculiar, intensive stench that arises from pools of thick and inky compound which in many cases is several feet deep . . . [and where] almost at every step a dead dog, cat or rat may be seen," Hoyt writes that "Other families in the lower-income groups lived over stores in the downtown area or along the secondary business streets."[10] Hoyt's text was based on careful data – but there was also a particular interpretation that associated shop/houses with poverty, crime and disease rather than with upwardly mobile classes.[11]

Yet there was not unanimity about zoning and, until 1926, state courts questioned the use of the police power to uniformly regulate land uses. In 1921, the Texas Supreme Court ruled that businesses could not be excluded from residential districts:

> It is idle to talk about the lawful business of an ordinary retail store threatening the public health or endangering the public safety . . . Retail stores are places of trade, it is true, but as ordinarily conducted they are not places of noise or confusion. This is particularly true of small stores . . . The ordinary trading that goes on in them is reputable and honorable, and can hurt nobody.[12]

In Missouri, one ruling questioned the blanket nature of zoning ordinances: "In other words, a business is unlawful, not because it is a nuisance, but because it is prohibited."[13] The appellate ruling that was reversed by Euclid stated that:

> the plain truth is that the true object of the ordinance in question is to place all the property in an undeveloped area of 16 square miles in a strait-jacket. The purpose to be accomplished is really to regulate the mode of living of persons who may hereafter inhabit it. In the last analysis, the result to be accomplished is to classify the population and segregate them according to their income or situation in life.[14]

One case (later cited by Euclid) clearly asserted that flexibility might have to be the victim of a greater good:

> . . . the harmless may sometimes be brought within the regulation or prohibition in order to abate or destroy the harmful . . . The exclusion of places of business from residential districts is not a declaration that such places are nuisances or that they are to be suppressed as such, but it is a part of the general plan by which the city's territory is allotted to different uses in order to prevent, or at least to reduce, the congestion, disorders and dangers which often inhere in unregulated municipal development.[15]

After Euclid,[16] most municipalities eventually adopted zoning ordinances including use regulations. But change was not absolute or sudden. Zoning ordinances in districts that had already been built often incorporated existing

[10] Hoyt, "One Hundred Years", 97.
[11] Row houses often included shops at the ends of the rows, and their construction was itself a cause for protest by wealthier classes. See, for example, Power, "Unwisdom of Allowing City Growth."
[12] John R. Spann vs. City of Dallas et al., 111 Tex 350. For an extended discussion of the pre-Euclid debate over the zoning of residential areas, including issues of class bias and the domestic ideal, see Lees, "Preserving Property Values?".
[13] City of St. Louis vs. Morris Evraiff et al., 301 Mo. 231.
[14] Ambler Realty Co. vs. Village of Euclid et al., 297 F. 307.
[15] City of Aurora vs. Burns, 319 Ill. 84, p. 98.
[16] Village of Euclid vs. Ambler Realty Co., 272 U.S. 365.

patterns of use into the ordinance. In New York, the general pattern of commercial/residential buildings on north–south avenues and residential uses on east–west streets had already been set in many neighborhoods by 1916. By reflecting the uses that were already in place – and extrapolating that pattern to places in the city and the outlying boroughs that were not yet built – the effect of use zoning in New York was perhaps not as great as that in districts of newer cities, that were not platted and zoned after 1916.

So, in 1916, there were still numerous buildings with multiple uses in single-use districts. Often, these were buildings with commercial uses on residential streets. Furthermore, most zoning ordinances allowed for legal non-conforming uses, which allowed the use to remain until the building was sold or a change of use proposed. This meant a gradual, rather than sudden, disappearance of retail and other commercial uses from residential streets. The two Brooklyn buildings to the west of the tenement at 1292 St. Johns Place that was the beginning of the walk described in Chapter 6, were built in 1909, seven years before the 1916 zoning ordinance. In the 1950s, these buildings had three stores, which had disappeared by 2006, several decades later, and the zoning was for exclusively residential uses.[17] In the 1940s and 1950s, living and working in the same place was still "part of the culture" in Portland, Oregon.[18]

Despite Euclid, the control of uses through zoning is not a black-and-white issue. This is dealt with by Stephen Clowney in a response to a previous argument by Andrew Cappel, based on observations in a New Haven neighborhood, that the market and social norms were enough to regulate use, and that zoning was unnecessary.[19] Clowney used the same methodology as the previous author, but looked at several neighborhoods in the city and found a complex picture in which the choice should be not simply between "zoning" and "no zoning," but including a more nuanced approach to regulation.

Using Sanborn insurance maps made before the 1920s – the decade zoning was introduced to New Haven – Clowney found different kinds of evidence. On one hand, there were incompatible uses – "apartments abutting junkyards, schools and churches adjacent to manufacturing plants, and unrestrained backlot construction . . . it was not uncommon for a single-family home to be completely surrounded by shops and stores." But he also found enterprise by lower-income people: "Without usage restrictions, property owners could easily add small stores to the front of their buildings. This happened throughout the [Wooster Square] neighborhood during the 1910s," and residents remember the vitality that was once present in those neighborhoods.

Clowney concludes that "an unzoned system provides significant benefits to city dwellers in the form of increased housing options, lower housing costs and flexibility. However . . . zoning, at its best, protects all residents of a municipality from the encroachment of industrial nuisance and the unwanted effects of overcrowding."[20]

This nuanced view helps point up the several results of zoning – the prevention of nuisances, the protection of land values, and the separation of economic classes from each other. Even if it is recognized that the nuisance justification for zoning is valid, the other justifications may or may not be valid in particular circumstances. The job of those who frame public policy may be to show that mixed uses are possible without introducing nuisances and without a reduction in property values.[21]

17 New York City Zoning Resolution

18 Thanks to Suzanne Vara, who spent thirty years helping residents obtain change-of-use permits, and who describes herself as a "connoisseur of creative uses of buildings and [their] shaky permit histories," for this observation.

19 Clowney, "A Walk Along Willard." This was a response to Cappel, "A Walk Along Willow."

20 Clowney, "A Walk Along Willard," 18.

21 There is a large literature on how zoning prevents housing from changing as family composition changes. Although it does not deal with commercial uses, an important article is Ritzdorf, "Zoning Barriers to Housing Innovation," 177–184.

Building codes

Since the nineteenth century, building codes have evolved to make the construction of simple, mixed-use buildings more expensive or impossible.[22] Codes were often made more stringent after major fires, sometimes responding to pressure from insurance companies. By themselves, codes did not disallow mixed-use buildings. But in coordination with zoning and financing challenges, they helped create an inhospitable climate for such buildings.

The principal ingredients in this included banning certain uses from buildings with dwellings,[23] requirements that different kinds of occupancies or uses have particular kinds of construction or separation from dwellings,[24] requirements for redundant exit systems, fireproof buildings over a certain number of stories, and a limitation on open areas on the ground floor that was stricter with higher buildings.

Buildings with more than one basic construction system are more expensive, so the construction cost is driven up for the use that does not require the more expensive system, mitigating against its inclusion in the building. Instead of different construction systems, different uses may be taken care of by fire-suppression systems – such as sprinklers, throughout the building – but as such systems might not be required in a building with just one use, they also result in a premium paid for a multi-use building.

The outside fire escape began to be questioned at least as early as the Triangle Shirtwaist Company fire in 1911, and was eventually replaced with the requirement for two fire-protected stairs in most multi-story buildings.[25] In New York this meant two stairs for non-fireproof apartment houses with over twenty-six apartments above the entrance story.[26] Still, although the price of mixed-use buildings was rising, and ground-floor shops became less important to the financial bottom line as building heights increased, they continued to be built on streets that had intense commercial activity, on which the zoning remained mixed use.

A 1912 book on fire prevention and protection clearly stated the importance of limiting the area in buildings that should be allowed to be unobstructed, without internal fire separations (Table 10.1). In stores, warehouses and factories of fire-resisting construction, this limit was greater with lower buildings.[27]

[22] Gary Stanton describes the role of fire in clarifying the increasing separation between dwelling and workplace in Fredericksburg, Virginia. Stanton, "Alarmed by the Cry of Fire," 132–133.

[23] Portland Housing Code of 1919, and other codes as well, banned buildings containing apartments from having bakeries or "place[s] of business in which fat is boiled."

[24] U.S. Department of Commerce, Bureau of Standards, Report of the Department of Commerce Building Code Committee. "Recommended Minimum Requirements for Fire Resistance in Buildings," 10. Such standards were included in the *Portland Building Code 1918*, updated to 1924, and were similar in other cities:
Sec. 673: "If the first story of a building is used as a store with a different occupancy on the upper floors, the building shall be graded according to the occupancy of the upper floors."
Sec. 793: "Where a building is occupied on different floors by different grades of occupancy, a division wall shall be required only for those floors occupied as stores, sales rooms, warehouses, workshops and factories, except when the first floor alone is so occupied no division wall be required. If division walls are required in the upper floors of the building, such division walls may be carried on steel or reinforced concrete girders and columns but such girders and columns shall be fireproofed as required for the structural frame of buildings of Classes II or II construction."

[25] For a history of the fire escape and its replacement, see Wermiel, "No Exit," 258–284.

[26] Wermiel, *Fireproof Building*, 201.

[27] Freitag, *Fire Prevention and Fire Protection*, 300.

Table 10.1 Areas allowed with and without fire sprinklers, relative to building height

	Allowed area without sprinkler, when height not exceeding 55 feet, in square feet	Allowed area without sprinkler, when height limited to 100 feet, in square feet	Allowed area with sprinkler, when height not exceeding 55 feet, in square feet	Allowed area with sprinkler, when height limited to 100 feet, in square feet
Fronting on one street only	10,000	5,000	13,333	6,666
Fronting on two streets	12,000	6,000	16,000	8,000
Corner building, two streets	12,000	6,000	12,000	8,000
Fronting on three streets	15,000	7,500	15,000	10,000

Source: Freitag, *Fire Prevention and Fire Protection*, 300.

[28] Freitag, *Fire Prevention and Fire Protection*, 297.
[29] DeForest and Veiller, *Tenement House Problem*, 439–458.
[30] Hoyt, "One Hundred Years", 245.
[31] Hoyt, "One Hundred Years", 246–247.
[32] Hoyt, "One Hundred Years", 331.

Apart from legal requirements, there was a push toward more rationality and clarity in design, in the expectation that this would make fire-resistant buildings easier to design. One fire-protection expert suggested:

> . . . the subdivision of large unobstructed areas; protection against dangerous adjacent risks by means of blank walls or adequately protected openings; provisions for light and air without introducing interior open shafts; the accessible and commodious arrangement of stairways and their protection against fire and smoke, or the introduction of vertical fire walls; the suitable location of elevator shafts so as to render them capable of fire-resisting construction, as well as convenient and serviceable; and the general scheme of construction which will adapt itself to the employment of wholly suitable materials to be used in the right way.[28]

These ideas are consistent with individual code requirements – and indicative of a modernist approach in which good design was characterized by convenience and simplicity.

Land values and development finance

In 1900, a single block on New York's Lower East Side, containing thirty-nine tenement houses, yielded a total of $113,964 in rent per year. Of this, $36,480, or about 32 percent, came from the rental of stores and shops.[29] The buildings on this block were mostly five- and six-story tenements, most of which had stores at their ground floor, but which also included all-residential buildings at the back of lots, without stores.

Most residential buildings in New York at that time were still walk-ups of six stories or less. One reason for the gradual elimination of shop/houses may simply be that as apartment buildings built for investment got taller, the percentage of financial yield that came from the commercial use got smaller, and that from the housing, greater. Homer Hoyt provides clear evidence of the increasing height of buildings and therefore of the decreasing relative value of shopfront space. He observed that, "Apartment buildings containing less than twelve apartments were considered as semi-investments, as the maintenance and building cost per room were higher in buildings where one steam boiler served only two apartments than where it provided heat for forty residential units."[30] The construction of apartment buildings in districts outside the center caused an increase in land values in those districts, but in "blighted areas" where "vice and delinquency" were rising, there was little new construction and little increase in land values.[31]

Taller buildings were becoming more common in Chicago (Table 10.2).[32] Most of the buildings in the table are office buildings, not apartment buildings. But sometime between 1923 and 1933, the number of buildings in the central business district in which it was reasonable to walk up without an elevator became a minority. This reality helped form a worldview in which tall buildings were acceptable, and desired – and this worldview likely extended to apartment buildings as well.

At the same time that taller apartment buildings were making commercial space financially insignificant at their ground floors, larger commercial buildings were making upper-floor residential accommodation financially insignificant in their upper floors. The rent for stores in some districts outside the center of Chicago increased by 1,000 percent between 1915 and 1928, and there was

Table 10.2 Percentage of cubic feet at given heights to total cubic feet (central business district of Chicago)

Building height in stories	1836	1856	1873	1893	1923	1933
Ground–6	100.0	100.0	99.7	84.3	60.2	46.2
7–12	0.0	0.0	0.3	12.5	26.7	28.1
13–16	0.0	0.0	0.0	3.0	8.3	13.7
17–22	0.0	0.0	0.0	0.2	4.8	9.8
23–44	0.0	0.0	0.0	0.0	0.0	2.2
Total	100.0	100.0	100.0	100.0	100.0	100.0

competition among rival stores for location.[33] Downtown Chicago department stores began to build branches in outlying districts. To attract customers who might otherwise have gone downtown, stores became large operations with parking.[34] They were clearly profitable without housing.

As the financial benefit of mixed use declined with taller buildings, the non-financial liabilities became more apparent, and eventually dominated the argument. The zoning argument that mixed-use buildings are "insalubrious" becomes easier to argue when there is less money to be made.

The agendas of slum clearance and public housing

Finally, changes in the rules that guide development were accompanied by government programs that themselves destroyed the traditional mixed-use urban fabric. In the United States, slum-clearance programs were motivated by overt agendas of public health and the alleviation of poverty as well as more hidden racist agendas. Even though home occupations represented a path to economic self-sufficiency for many people, such activities were seen as problems to be eliminated. Indeed, when the promise of zoning was clean cities with everything in its proper place, slums – with the teeming life that comes from people trying to make their own economic way in the world – were aesthetically and socially objectionable. They did not fit the model. And the public health/poverty argument helped justify policies based as much on the wish for idealistic models as on the pragmatic solution to real problems.

The divided city – and the wholesale destruction of large swaths of the mixed city to help produce it, along with the displacement of poor people – was accompanied by the construction of public housing projects. In 1936, New York began a public housing program with the renovation of existing tenement buildings[35] – a program that in 2009 included 338 developments housing over 402,000 people.[36]

New York's program was modeled partly on that in Vienna, which was initiated by a socialist city administration and resulted in the construction of almost 20,000 dwelling units between 1919 and 1926 alone,[37] and tens of thousands more in the 1920s and early 1930s.[38] While the free-standing Karl-Marx Hof is perhaps the most well known, many buildings in the program were infill buildings, occupying only part of an existing block, and incorporating commercial facilities at their base. These had a name: Lückenverbauung, "building to fill in the gaps."[39] Descriptions of these buildings emphasize communal facilities such as child care centers, often located adjacent to internal

[33] Hoyt, "One Hundred Years", 249.
[34] See, for example, Longstreth, "Wieboldt's, Goldblatt's," for a description of the development of department stores in outlying Chicago neighborhoods.
[35] See, for example, Plunz, *History of Housing*.
[36] New York City Housing Authority, 2009, accessed July 4, 2011, www.nyc.gov/html/nycha/html/about/nycha70.shtml.
[37] Blau, *Architecture of Red Vienna*, 155.
[38] Plunz, *History of Housing*, 165, 273,.
[39] Blau, *Architecture of Red Vienna*, 276.

10.02 Public housing block in Vienna.
Photograph by author.

10.03 "First Houses," the first public housing project built by the New York City Housing Authority, first opened in 1935, incorporating stores. Photograph taken in 1936.
La Guardia and Wagner Archives, La Guardia Community College/The City University of New York.

courtyards. But the buildings often also provided continuity at the street by maintaining the pattern of shops, and partly because of this do not have the stigma of housing projects set off from the rest of the city.

Several early New York public housing projects were also infill buildings and included shops, which helped supplement residential rents. But in 1944, the New York City Housing Authority decided that new post-war projects would no longer include stores.[40] One of the reasons was to keep the housing authority "out of competition with private trade."

The site plans of the projects changed over time, to large buildings within green spaces without street frontage, to allow for maximum light and air to apartments. The separation of functions called for by modernist planning ideology was now written into policy, including rules about the expenditure of millions of dollars of public funds, helping to realize the Corbusian ideas of "towers in a park" arrayed in a regular geometric pattern.

So even if it had been allowed, public housing projects could not support the use of apartments for economic enterprise, particularly retail activity and many kinds of services. It might have been possible for someone to bring piecework home from a garment factory. But apartments were small, and they no longer had a strong connection to the street, as projects were now designed without street frontages. Apartments were accessed via inside stairs or elevators that effectively acted as filters cutting off private space from the public realm outside.

Building types and the contemporary divided city

The rapid suburbanization that followed World War II only accelerated the demise of the shop/house.[41] Financial incentives for suburban houses, government support of highway construction, the demise of public transportation, slum clearance and increased class separation in metropolitan areas all helped form the modern urban/suburban landscape. By 1967 it could be confidently stated that although European residential projects may incorporate shops, "most American builders are reluctant to include any sort of shopping in the project for fear that this may detract from the residential character and downgrade the project."[42]

The contemporary American building culture has four interrelated attributes that make it difficult for shop/houses to be built:

1 a reliance on certain known building types that are monofunctional and inflexible;
2 a tendency toward big projects that concentrate developers' risk;
3 the fragmentation of financing into particular known types, and unique levels of risk;
4 the fragmentation of urban space, supported by land-use planning and zoning.

These result in a self-perpetuating system that works against the inclusion of shop/houses. Christopher Leinberger identifies eighteen "standard real estate types" that are understood by developers, city officials, lenders, architects and sales and leasing agents, and that form the vast majority of new buildings. None of these standard types explicitly combines housing with another use.[43]

[40] Cooper, "Post-War Housing," 15.
[41] For an account of the American suburb up to World War II, see Stilgoe, *Borderland*; for accounts that go to the present, see Hayden, *Building Suburbia*, and Jackson, K., *Crabgrass Frontier*.
[42] Paul, *Apartments*, 103.
[43] Leinberger, *Option of Urbanism*, 51.

Standard real estate types

- Office: Build to suit, mixed-use urban, medical
- Industrial: Build to suit, warehouse
- Retail: Neighborhood center, lifestyle center, big-box anchored
- Hotel: Business and luxury hotels
- Apartment: Suburban garden, urban high density
- Miscellaneous: Self-storage, mobile home park
- Housing: Entry level, move-up, luxury, assisted living/retirement, resort/second home

According to Leinberger, these types "have a proven track record of market acceptance and financial performance."[44] There may be a few more: service station, chain restaurant, multiplex theater, sports facility. But this list covers the vast majority of new buildings that form the built environment of modern American cities.

The preference for big projects comes about in several ways: through fixed costs that are greater per square foot with smaller projects; through bureaucratic procedures that can be handled more readily when there are larger projects and therefore larger fees; and through land patterns in which there has been the steady agglomeration of smaller parcels into larger ones.

But larger projects concentrate risk: if a large project fails, a large piece of the built environment is affected, along with the jobs of many people. Hundreds of shopping malls have declared bankruptcy (by 2009),[45] and large numbers of big-box stores have closed. This risk is exacerbated by inflexibility of the building type – it is difficult for many modern buildings to change their use. A big-box store cannot be readily converted into housing; housing is difficult to convert into open-plan office space; and a location that was desirable for one use may be inappropriate for another.

Mixed-use buildings are seen as risky by developers and banks for which monofunctional buildings are the norm. The industry of development finance has developers who specialize in commercial investments, with their own lenders, and other developers who specialize in residential investments, with different lenders. Loans are made on the basis of elaborate business plans that are backed up by "comparables," or reports of how similar buildings with comparable locations and conditions fared in the market. Without mixed-use comparables, mixed-use projects seem risky. Furthermore, the desire for short-term profit rather than long-term commitment means that solidly built buildings that can change and adapt over time are bypassed in favor of buildings of cheap construction, that are understood to have only a short-term usefulness.[46]

But the reverse may also be argued: many monofunctional buildings are actually more risky, since they have less capability for transformation when the market changes. Ideas of flexibility and adaptability are partly economic ideas that have been unevenly applied to decisions about development.[47]

The risk is abetted by the fragmentation of urban space maintained through zoning ordinances, and that restricts potential mixed-use projects to relatively small areas. Zoning ordinances are most restrictive in residential zones, which take up most of the land area of the city and usually do not allow for commercial activity except where the residential density is high.[48] They may be less restrictive in commercial zones, in which residential uses are sometimes

[44] Leinberger, *Option of Urbanism*, 53.

[45] A website, DeadMalls.com, among many other sources, documents the demise of hundreds of shopping malls.

[46] For a discussion of the importance of combining short-term and long-term investment, see Leinberger and Kozloff, "Financing Mixed-Use," 3–4.

[47] The ability for flexibility varies. Modern office buildings are highly flexible, much housing considerably less so. The flexibility of retail space depends largely on its initial configuration – particularly its size – and its location.

[48] This is a feature of so-called "cumulative zoning," which recognizes the single-family house at the top of a "pyramid" of zones that includes, successively below it, higher-density residential uses, commercial uses, and finally industrial uses. In this pyramid, zones can include uses above it, but not below it. Municipalities vary in their use of cumulative zoning and in some cases "higher uses" are no longer permitted in commercial districts. See, for example, Garnett, "Ordering and Order."

permitted – a feature of zoning ordinances that, in some cities, allows for the construction of shop/houses on older neighborhood commercial streets.[49] But by and large, the use separations that are enforced by zoning apply to most new construction, preventing the construction of shop/houses or any commercial activity at all in residential zones. And decades of habit mitigate against the construction of dwellings in commercial zones, even where they might be allowed.

All this makes shop/houses an uncommon "niche market." And there is ample criticism of this culture and the cities it produces, ranging from the work of the journalist James Howard Kunstler[50] to the architect Andres Duany[51] to the legal scholar Gerald Frug.[52] This criticism relates to the shop/house in particular ways:

Land use. Apart from multi-level shopping malls and older downtowns, virtually the entire retail environment of American cities is in the form of one-story buildings. This includes big-box discount stores, supermarkets, strip malls, individual shops and restaurants, convenience stores, auto showrooms, and many other types. Likewise, many office buildings, particularly those in suburbs, are also one story high.

One analysis indicates that there are 14.2 billion square feet of total retail space, including 7 billion square feet of shopping-center space, including strip malls, in the United States.[53] Assuming a total population of 310 million, this yields 26.6 square feet of shopping-center space per capita. Since this is mostly single-story space, a city of 500,000 has 13,300,000 square feet of single-story commercial space which, if developed into housing above the ground floor, could yield tens of thousands of additional housing units. This does not include the potential of parking lots or the considerable area of single-story retail that is not in shopping centers. The situation is similar in Canada. One estimate is that 22 percent of the total area of Vancouver is available for densification. With 60 percent of buildings being mixed use (ground level commercial and three stories of residential above) along a typical corridor's half-block, a density of 55 dwelling units/acre is possible.[54]

Fine grain. Cities need a mix of large and small buildings, with many more small ones than large ones. Such a mix allows for a scale that is comfortable and comprehensible and for changes to be easily achieved. Although this idea does not relate to shop/houses per se – monofunctional buildings can be either large or small – family-owned businesses will tend to be small, particularly when just starting out.

Human health and emotional well-being. There is a growing body of evidence relating sprawl to poor health. The shop/house is a component of a neighborhood that may promote walking rather than driving, and represents a way to increase building densities that in turn brings people closer together.[55] The lack of such a neighborhood is not only a matter of "lifestyle" but may even have pathological effects.[56]

Buildings as process. The shop/house is dynamic, allowing for transformations, accretions, and subtractions over time. But difficult-to-change, static buildings have energy implications, resource implications,[57] financial implications (at the end of their useful lives buildings become tax burdens without income), implications with respect to the life and connectivity of the city (large areas become disused) and social implications (people and businesses are forced to move, severing their neighborhood social ties).

49 The city of Portland, Oregon allows dwellings in all commercial zones.

50 Kunstler, *Home from Nowhere*.

51 Duany, et al., *Suburban Nation*.

52 Frug, *City Making*, a collection of articles that originally appeared in law reviews.

53 This data comes from the website of the International Council on Shopping Centers, accessed July 4, 2011, www.icsc.org/srch/faq_category.php?cat_type=research&cat_id=3. Thanks to Ellen Dunham-Jones for directing me to this source.

54 Condon, "Growing a Greater Vancouver Region."

55 See, for example, Hirschhorn, *Sprawl Kills*, 188–202.

56 See, for example, Morris, D., *It's a Sprawl World*, 77–92 and Jackson, R., "Impact of the Built Environment," 1382–1383 (this is part of an entire issue of the *American Journal of Public Health* devoted to the question of health and urban sprawl).

57 The production of cement, for example, is responsible for 5 percent of all carbon dioxide emissions in the world. Rosenthal, "Cement Industry."

So flexibility of living and working arrangements, along with the longevity of building types, make the shop/house a potentially critical component of urban sustainability. However, such flexibility is not easy to attain within contemporary regulations. Buildings designed so that change of use may be possible must meet the most restrictive use in the building code. But even this does not guarantee that the change of use will be allowed – a new use permit must be obtained when the use changes, further restricting flexibility.[58]

Community life, local economic life and social justice. In monoculture neighborhoods, with building types that only serve a single function, the opportunity for economic and social ties that come out of a diverse community may be missing. Today's cities keep people in their occupational place.[59]

This is particularly the case for immigrants, who often come from places in which home-based businesses are common, and find themselves in situations where they are restricted or even forbidden.[60] Mike Davis writes about neighborhoods of Latinos, the fastest growing ethnic group in the U.S.:

> Latino "micro-entrepreneurship" is applauded in theory but everywhere persecuted in practice. If the primordial zoning division between home and work is annoying for cybercommuters and self-employed professionals, it is truly punitive for Latino households whose incomes are supplemented by home-based car repair, food catering or bridal sewing. Many cities and suburbs have similarly restricted or even outlawed the weekend garage sales and informal street-curb "swap meets" that are such important institutions in barrio economies."[61]

Women and children. The contemporary city was developed with unstated assumptions about the place of women: that they would remain at home, taking care of the house and children, while their husbands were working somewhere else. But as the place of women in the social and economic world has progressed, the city has mostly remained with its physical separations. These make it difficult for parents – women or men – to be in a place where they can take care of children. And despite the social progress that has been made, it still usually falls to women to drive the children from place to place, to take care of the house, and to make the greater sacrifice when both parents are working – as most parents now do.

The typical contemporary house, although it has changed from the time when the kitchen was a service zone and the realm of women, still does not accommodate women in what remains a building of sexual inequality. More men than women still work outside the home, and when home businesses are started, they are started mostly by women.[62] But house designs take little account of space for work or business.[63]

Children are even less mobile and until their teenage years rely on their parents to get them from place to place, if they are to have a wide range of experiences. Some children stay at home all the time. But even those children who have the benefit of being driven from hockey practice to piano lessons to school, do so within a programmed schedule. The idea of a neighborhood outside the house, which is available to children and which they can explore at will, meeting neighbors and learning on their own about the world of adults, is much less common.

* * *

[58] Thanks to Suzanne Vara for insights about this process in Portland.

[59] The separation of social classes from each other in the city is described in literature that is concerned with zoning, land use, sociology, urban studies and urban history. One book dealing with the contemporary condition worldwide and the role of governments in supporting urban fragmentation is Marcuse and van Kempen, *Of States and Cities*. See also Shaw, *City Building*.

[60] Pader, "Sociospatial Relations of Change," 94.

[61] Davis, M. *Magical Urbanism*, 63.

[62] The classic article on the impact of American zoning on contemporary American domestic life is Ritzdorf, "Zoning Barriers to Housing Innovation." See also Ritzdorf's "Gender and Residential Zoning," 270, for a specific discussion of the impact of zoning on home-based work.

[63] For an excellent discussion of the effect of the built environment on women's lives, see Weisman, *Discrimination by Design*.

The late Aditya Prakash, Chandigarh's city architect who worked with Le Corbusier, wrote a stinging critique of the city's planning, years after the construction of the city. This critique might equally apply to American/Western cities that suffer both from functional fragmentation and from a lack of resilience in their potential transformation:

> All planning tends to turn people into classes, into categories. All planning tends to turn places into zones of activities. All planning tends to freeze time . . . Planning propagates specialization, differentiation . . . in spite of the strict zoning laws since the very beginning of Chandigarh its houses have served a variety of functions: offices, rest houses, shops, clubs, health centres, restaurants, schools . . . indeed it is being done in England where large Georgian houses have been converted to contain any activity other than that of living.[64]

The silver lining is that neither building cultures nor cities change overnight. Habits persist, old laws are "grandfathered" into new ones, and most importantly, buildings and neighborhoods persist in memory and reality. All through the beginning decades of the twentieth century, modernist buildings were being constructed in cities that retained their traditional structure, and in which shop/houses were still being built. And by the 1960s and 1970s, when large sections of cities had been destroyed, but the excesses of modernist urbanism were beginning to be recognized, there was still enough connected fabric remaining, and enough people with vivid memories of vital urban places, to help make a bridge to our present efforts at using the shop/house as a critical element in the revived city.

[64] Prakash, *Reflections on Chandigarh*, 1. In a personal communication in about 2005, Mr. Prakash wrote about the importance of the shop/house in urban life.

11.01 Grocery shop in a railroad viaduct in Brixton, south London.
Photograph by author.

11

TOWARD A RESILIENT URBANISM

[Jane Jacobs] believes that in an open city, as in the natural world, social and visual forms mutate through chance variation; people can best absorb, participate and adapt to change if it happens step-by-lived-step.[1]

(Richard Sennett)

Today's building culture favors the pure over the hybrid, the definite over the ambiguous, the monoculture over the polyculture, the static over the dynamic. How can the building of shop/houses, hybrid and changeable buildings that may be ambiguous in use and spatial definition, become ordinary rather than extraordinary practice? Changing the building culture so the shop/house might become a "standard type" requires a wide variety of initiatives, in policy as well as architecture, to provide examples that can support new attitudes toward a more hybrid and resilient city.

The need and market for shop/houses

Chapter 9 began with a description of how the places of public life and productive life were reversed in the twentieth century from where they had been three centuries before. But in the twenty-first century, the house is again taking on a multiplicity of different functions. These new functions are not the same as before industrialization, but are varied enough that the idea of the house for only one function must be seriously questioned.[2]

In the seventeenth century, public life took place outside the house, in the life of the street, festivals, church . . .

. . . while in the twentieth century, public life moved inside the house, in entertainment systems, internet, TV . . .

. . . and in the twenty-first century, more people are once again recognizing the value of streets and public spaces in fostering public life, in addition to the role of advanced communications in bringing the public world into the house.

In the seventeenth century, productive functions took place inside the house, in processing food, making clothes, educating children . . .

. . . while in the twentieth century, productive functions moved outside the house, in making clothes, the manufacture of washing machines, dry cleaning, educating children, manufacturing, processing food . . .

[1] Sennett, "Open City," 293.

[2] Thanks to Esther Hagenlocher for suggesting extending this analysis in this way.

. . . and in the twenty-first century, the house is again becoming the locus of production and economic activity, but not replacing the role of the city-at-large in providing places for work and exchange.

The emerging city needs to accommodate people who are in different economic places. It includes people who have taken advantage of opportunities and have made money, and those who are seeking opportunity; people who are in a position to employ other people, and those who need employment; people who are just starting out, and others who might use their talents.

It will have shop/houses that serve economic players in the "creative economy" – artists, computer programmers, small-scale entrepreneurs. It will also have shop/houses that serve players in the "subsistence-to-middle-class economy" – people who want to open beauty salons, repair businesses, restaurants, at home (Fig. 11.02). In many cases, the distinction between spaces needed for dwelling and spaces needed for work is disappearing so that, for example, companies that can employ home-based workers for computer reservations or different office functions need zoning that does not discriminate against such functions.[3]

This assertion is supported by demographics. Not only is the percentage of people in creative occupations rising, but the "working-class population" has also leveled off after a decline beginning in the 1950s.[4] These two sectors of the employment population, along with the service class, might benefit the most from the availability of shop/houses. Indeed, the global economy is

[3] See, for example, Elliott, *Better Way to Zone*, 68–69.
[4] Florida, *Rise of the Creative Class*, 75.

11.02 A home-based beauty salon in Anaconda, Montana.
Photograph by author.

undergoing fundamental shifts, and the guarantee of steady employment that the industrial economy provided may no longer be assured. This economic uncertainty results in a need for flexibility in the ways the physical environment supports economic life.

Christopher Leinberger argues that cities that do not take "walkable urbanism" seriously are at risk of losing economic development. Shop/houses that serve economic players in the "creative economy" may be helped by market-oriented strategies that ease the ability of developers and lenders to undertake projects. There are developers who can make money from these markets,[5] and in some cases these may be tax breaks, subsidies or relaxation of zoning standards, in the framework of privately funded projects.

But policies intended to help speculative developers will not be enough, as this need also exists for people at the lower end of the economic ladder. The construction of shop/houses that house people in the "subsistence-to-middle-class economy" may be helped by government-guaranteed loans, direct loans from government, grants from government or private foundations and changes to zoning policies that make it easier, for example, for dwellings to be used for commercial purposes. This kind of help is more difficult to come by in a market-driven world but is essential if the small-scale entrepreneur is not to be driven out of the city.

So two distinct sectors of the employment population can each benefit from the availability of the same kind of urban building. The argument is given even more strength by the fact that in the United States, home-based businesses already exist in large numbers, whether legally or "under the radar" (Figs. 11.03 and 11.04). According to the 2000 census, over 4 million workers, out of a total of over 128 million, worked at home. This is 3.3 percent of all workers, and the actual percentage is likely larger.[6] By 2004, the Bureau of Labor Statistics reported a much higher number – 20.7 million persons, or about 15 percent of total non-agricultural employees said that they work at home at least one day per week.[7] The census numbers report a decline in home-based work from 1960 to 1980, but then a rise over the next two census cycles, to 2000.

Such businesses may be the catalyst for the economic development of a community.[8] They can provide local job opportunities, keep money within the community, and provide an alternative to social services and large, low-wage corporate employers.

From the point of view of urban design, shop/houses can promote efficient land use by putting maximum floor area within a given envelope; they may promote a fine grain of uses; they are flexible; they lead to a reduction in automobile use. The environmental benefits of compact and mixed-use development have been extensively written about. But sustainability depends not only on reduction of carbon emissions and efficient land use, but on closer social ties within neighborhoods, and on regenerative local economies, in which productive activities strengthen neighborhoods rather than sending profits out to corporations in other places.[9] There is an emerging understanding that sustainability is a three-legged table, in which social, economic and energy/material sustainability are equally important.

5 Leinberger, *Option of Urbanism*, 91–101.

6 The 2000 U.S. Census questionnaire only asked whether a particular person "works at home." The answer would likely be "no" for a person who had a small home business to supplement a "regular" job outside the home, or for a person with a regular place of employment outside the home who telecommutes part of the time. See also Garnett, "On Castles and Commerce," for numerous other sources about the pervasiveness of home-based work in the United States. For a U.K. estimates, see Holliss, "The Workhome," 35–41.

7 United States Bureau of Labor Statistics, "Work At Home Summary."

8 Ahrentzen, "Housing Home Businesses," 3.

9 For a description of many contemporary efforts to revive local economies, see McKibben, *Deep Economy*.

11.03 A California project by Michael Pyatok. Gateway Commons, is a development of seventeen houses designed partly to allow low-income families to incorporate economic activity into their dwellings. The front room of units, and the garage, are near the entrance, allowing those spaces to be easily used for a home business. Pyatok calls these dwellings "stealth units," because although intended for economic activity, they satisfy residential zoning requirements.
Courtesy of Michael Pyatok.

11.04 Plans and section of dwelling unit in Gateway Commons project.
Drawing by Sam Yerke.

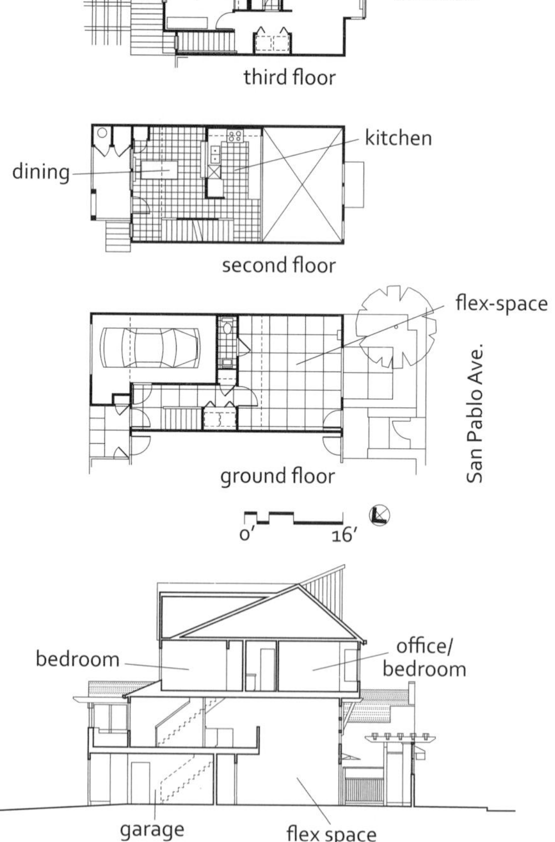

11.05 View of new commercial/residential building in Providence, Rhode Island, designed by Durkee, Brown, Viveiras & Werenfels Architects. The building has four residential units over two ground-floor commercial spaces. The project is part of an ongoing process of neighborhood revitalization, and has followed the restoration of historic and other existing houses, as well as new infill construction on vacant lots. The building provides ample storefront space that turns the corner, with the residential entrance away from the busier street, and a small balcony for each residential unit.

Courtesy Durkee, Brown, Viveiros & Werenfels Architects.

Designing and planning for the resilient city

A resilient city, district or building can accommodate change without changing its essential character.[10] Fixed land-use plans, the definition of zoning districts that resist change, and the design of buildings and building complexes that are for one use only, not only artificially separate functions from each other but also prevent the physical environment from responding to economic and social change.

The sociologist Richard Sennett writes about the problems of the "brittle city," characterized by a building stock that is unchangeable and therefore inflexible over time, and the alternative idea that the city needs to be open, allowing for change.[11] Frank Duffy points out that the new economy may be accompanied by more choice, more individual control over work, and "more connectivity, discourse and respect for others;" and that the environmental consequences of this include "more mixed-use buildings and therefore more opportunities for intensive and interconnected use of spatial resources, and uses that are 'mixable,' i.e., capable of being easily changed over time." He also sees less homogeneous space, with different types and rents in the same place.[12]

The importance of urban resilience was expressed – and acted on – by Jane Jacobs. As "urban renewal" was eliminating whole urban districts during the post-World War II decades, and halting the development of local economies, Jacobs inspired people and community groups to save the fabric of everyday

10 Alexander, C., *Nature of Order*, Book 2, 52–136. In these chapters Alexander outlines the idea of "structure-preserving transformations," providing one theoretical basis for the idea of urban resilience.

11 Sennett, "Open City," 292–293.

12 Duffy, *Work and the City*, 18–19.

13 Flint, *Wrestling with Moses*, 137–180.

life in American cities.[13] Her most famous victory was her contribution to stopping the construction of the Lower Manhattan Expressway, which would have destroyed a wide swath of living neighborhoods in Lower Manhattan.

Around the same time, the artists who had begun to work in SoHo lofts that had been left vacant by the shrinking of wholesale activity in the city – many of which would have been wiped out by the proposed highway – began to live in those lofts in violation of zoning regulations. The regulations were modified, and SoHo is now a vital urban district, too expensive for many artists, but with a strong street life and connections to adjacent neighborhoods. As with many resilient neighborhoods, it has evolved without wholesale demolition and reconstruction. And although the influx of capital and the consequent displacement of lower-income people, including artists, is criticizable, the area will no doubt go through further economic cycles – and that could not happen if it had been wiped out by a major highway. Although many slum areas were replaced by public housing, the historic fabric of mixed-use buildings has been preserved in New York to a larger extent than in other cities.

This success gave impetus to similar fights elsewhere – and there have been successes and failures. Although Portland, Oregon, is well known for its progressive policies in urbanism and transportation, different Portland neighborhoods have fared differently. Just south of downtown, the area now known as Lair Hill was the home of Italian and Jewish immigrants before the urban clearances of the 1950s and 1960s. For several blocks, First Avenue, which had a streetcar line, was lined with two- and three-story shop/houses, with groceries, butchers, hardware stores, drug stores and other businesses of daily life. But large areas of this neighborhood were cleared, and it was cut off from the downtown by the construction of a freeway. The old immigrant population was almost entirely displaced, and the mixed-use fabric disappeared. Now, there are only a few shop/houses left in the neighborhood (Figs. 11.06 and 11.07).

But other districts maintained their mixed-use fabric. Various neighborhoods on the east side of the Willamette River developed around the turn of the twentieth century with the construction of streetcar lines. Two blocks along Belmont Street, among many similar places in the city, still have shop/houses from the early twentieth century, and the street is currently undergoing a revitalization. For several decades in the second half of the twentieth century, the street experienced depressed land values and a deteriorating physical environment. But this provided people with low incomes a place to live, and it also provided low-rent commercial space for cafes, studios and alternative retail. And perhaps most critical is that the neighborhood was not subject to clearance and redevelopment. New building was happening elsewhere: in the suburbs, and closer to downtown (Figs. 11.08, 11.09, 11.10).

11.06 South First Avenue, Portland, Oregon, in the 1920s.
Courtesy Oregon Historical Society.

11.07 South First Avenue, Portland, Oregon, in 2009. The two photographs were taken from the same place.
Photograph by author.

This saved the neighborhood. Although it was not thriving economically, its physical fabric was not destroyed. So now, as it is becoming more desirable, it maintains a context that provides a good framework for new shop/houses; the neighborhood is resilient because its basic structure, including the pattern of lots, has been maintained. And two projects build onto this context with new and renovated mixed-use buildings.

The Belmont Dairy, one of the first new mixed-use projects in old Portland neighborhoods, is on the site of what was a corner grocery in the late nineteenth century, when the area was still mostly rural. For seventy years,

11.08 Conrad Green's grocery store, corner of Belmont and 33rd, Portland, about 1889. This building, without the porch, appears in the street view (Fig. 11.09) and is on the site of what is now the Belmont Dairy (Fig. 11.10).
Courtesy Oregon Historical Society.

11.09 Belmont Street, Portland, in the early twentieth century. The old Conrad Green store remains at the left.
Courtesy Oregon Historical Society.

11.10 The same view of Belmont Street, Portland, in 2009. The building at the left, the Belmont Dairy project, is on the site of the Conrad Green grocery store.
Photograph by author.

11.11 **(left) Belmont Dairy project on left, in context.**
Photograph by author.

11.12 **(right) Belmont Dairy project on left, looking east on Belmont Street. The project was designed by GBD Architects for client The Belmont Limited Partnership.**
Photograph by Dan Childs.

the site subsequently housed a dairy, which finally left its building empty. The new project, including an adaptive reuse of the old building, incorporates retail space at the ground floor and nineteen loft apartments above. Two phases of new housing, supporting the revived commercial activity, are on a parallel street to the north. The project maintains the two-story scale of the commercial street, and has residential lobbies on side streets. The corner market – reprising the use that was first there 120 years ago – strongly contributes to the vitality of the street, helping provide a gateway from the west to these two busy blocks (Figs. 11.11 and 11.12).

The other "anchor" two blocks to the east, the Belmont Lofts building has shop frontage on the main commercial street, a relatively small residential entrance on the secondary street, and parking in the rear (Figs. 11.13 and 8.09). Structurally, the building has post-tensioned concrete slabs above the retail space, allowing for required fire separations and relatively long slabs uninterrupted by columns, and heavy-timber construction above. The neighborhood was enthusiastic enough about this project to allow a height variance that permitted an extra story, and for the floor-to-floor height to be 11', so that daylight could penetrate far into the units. The wide mix of residents, including professionals, a retired couple and a family with two children – augurs well for the idea that such buildings might represent a popular solution to questions of housing in the city.[14]

Belmont Street is similar to others, where commercial zones allow for the continuing presence of dwelling units including new mixed-use projects. Since the construction of these two projects, numerous similar projects have been built on other streets, providing models for how redevelopment may happen at a small scale (Figs. 11.14 and 11.15).

Indeed, many opportunities for reintroducing shop/houses lie in older mixed-use buildings, which fell out of use as the centers of American cities declined. In some cases the buildings maintained marginal or partial uses, in which the upstairs was abandoned or used for storage, while the retail space brought in only minimal rent. The historic preservation movement, along with the economic revival of many downtowns, made these buildings appealing again. Since construction volume in existing buildings is rising relative to that in new construction, the rehabilitation of existing buildings is critical.

[14] Conversation with John Holmes, Holst Architecture, April 26, 2007.

11.13 Belmont Lofts, designed by Holst Architecture.
Photograph by author.

However, the rehabilitation of these buildings, which are often modest two- and three-story buildings that occupied only a small portion of a block, was often prevented by building codes that required so much additional work relative to the rehabilitation that the project became economically unfeasible, and/or destroyed the building's historic character. This often required that the entire building be brought up to current codes for new construction, even if the work to be done was modest or did not concern certain aspects of the code.

The state of New Jersey implemented a new rehabilitation subcode in 1998, which does not require that work be done beyond that which is necessary for the renovation, as long as the work done for the renovation meets the safety requirements of the code. The code eliminates unnecessary work and helps make the total cost of projects commensurate with the actual work necessary for the renovation or rehabilitation. Implementation of this code increased the amount of rehabilitation work in the state, and the code has since been adopted by Maryland, Rhode Island and other states.[15]

An exemplary example of building rehabilitation is in New York, where the Front Street Redevelopment, near the Brooklyn Bridge, involves seventeen existing buildings dating from the first half of the nineteenth century. Peck Slip, on the east of the site, was once a slip for sailing ships (Figs. 11.16 and 11.17; Plate 60).

Determined to maintain the small scale of the buildings and to sign local New York businesses as retail tenants, the developers rejected advances that would have made the development an extension of the adjacent South Street Seaport. Despite its location in Lower Manhattan, the site is somewhat out of the way – so it took persistence and synergies among the various tenants to make the project work.[16]

[15] See Gabarine, "New State Code," New Jersey's Rehabilitation Subcode, accessed July 4, 2011, www.nj.gov/dca/codes/rehab/rehabguide.shtml.
[16] The developers were Zuberry LLC. Thanks to Dick Berry, a principal of the firm, for this information.

11.14 **"Box & One," view from street.**
Photograph by author.

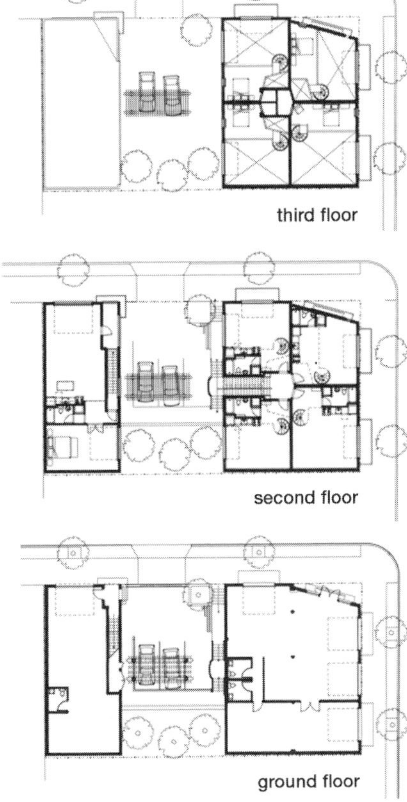

11.15 **Kevin Cavenaugh acted as designer, developer and client for this two-building project, "Box & One," in a Portland residential/commercial neighborhood. The corner building consists of a café-bakery and four residential rental lofts of 600–700 square feet each. The second building was designed as a shop with residential unit above. Mr. Cavenaugh attributes the project's success to the neighborhood location as a "village" within the city, the small size of the project that allows for flexibility in the development process and the ongoing process of rental, and the simple construction and detailing.**
Kevin Cavenaugh.

11.16 Front Street Redevelopment, designed by Cook+Fox Architects. Site plan with ground-floor plans.
© Cook+Fox.

11.17 13 Front Street/ 24 Peck Slip.
© Seong Kwan for Cook+Fox.

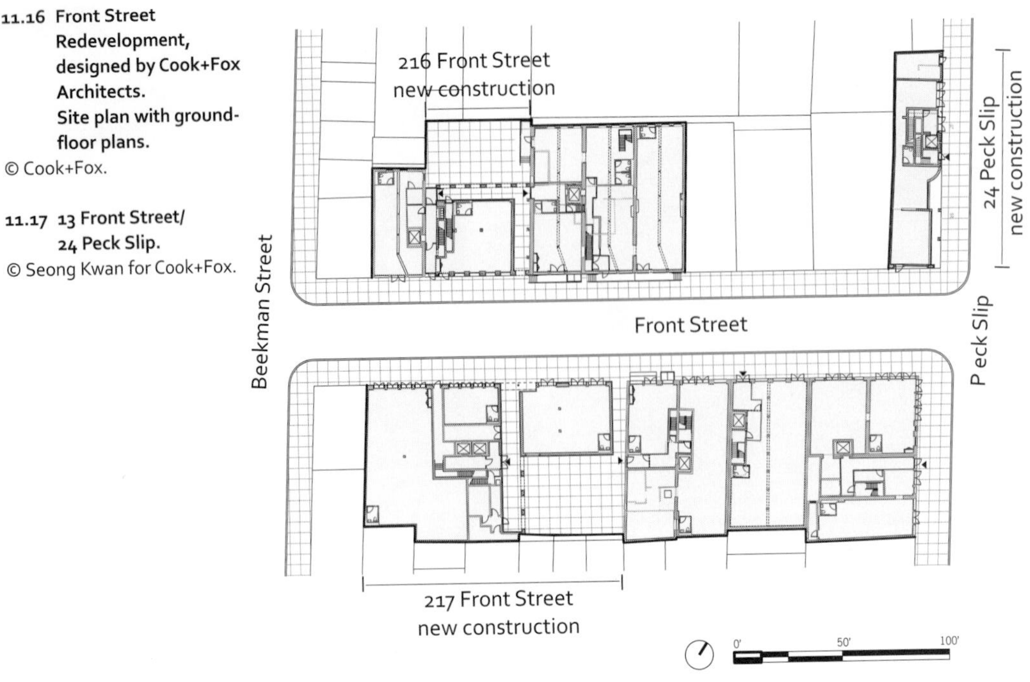

The material quality of the old buildings was maintained, while advanced techniques such as geothermal heating were introduced. The new building presents a modern façade to Peck Slip, but has wooden screening devices and tension canopy supports that evoke the wood and rigging of the old ships. Maximum commercial frontage is maintained by putting the residential entrances into inner courtyards. This is consistent with the old buildings, which had openings to the street across the length of their façades.

The project has almost full occupancy, healthy rent levels, a sense of community – and many children for whom a local pre-school was organized.

Changing the rules: financing, zoning and building codes

Emergence of the shop/house as a common urban idea depends on a building culture in which zoning and building codes, and rules about financing, are not inhibiting.

Financing and the initiation of projects

Until now, the financing of moderate- or small-sized urban shop/houses has been hindered by several things:

1 an emphasis on lending for larger projects;
2 an emphasis on lending for suburban rather than urban projects;
3 an emphasis on lending for projects on clear, "greenfield' sites rather than sites that may have existing buildings;
4 an emphasis on lending for new buildings rather than renovations that may be particularly suited to shop/houses;[17] and finally
5 a fragmentation of the lending industry that separates developers and lenders that concentrate on commercial projects from those that concentrate on residential projects; and an emphasis within each of those groups on known types such as tract development, three-story suburban apartment buildings, and one-story retail development.

Since lending decisions are largely based on appraisals of recently built projects, these emphases result in a vicious cycle of lending and development. New projects tend to be the same, from a financial point of view, as others that were most recently built. Appraisers have to be conservative – but as a result of the way they do this, they reinforce the status quo.

However, mixed-use projects are in demand by some municipalities, and many perform well financially once built. In fact, when infrastructure costs are factored in, they may be more cost effective than projects at a lower density.[18] But financial models that only recognize short-term returns result in cheaper construction costs and lower quality. And this mitigates against buildings that are more complex, and/or which may take more time to produce a suitable return on the investment. However, there are investors who would agree to see their financial return over a longer term, if such financial models were available.[19] Christopher Leinberger argues that different groups of borrowers and lenders, each of which might be interested in different rates of return, should be matched to develop a wider variety of projects.

The value of building for the long term is starting to become clear again, and municipalities are realizing the potential of an increased tax base from quality mixed-use buildings, and the advantages to infrastructure costs of urban infill.

[17] See for example Leinberger and Kozloff, "Financing Mixed-Use."
[18] Leinberger, *Option of Urbanism*, 79.
[19] Leinberger and Kozlof, "Financing Mixed-Use."

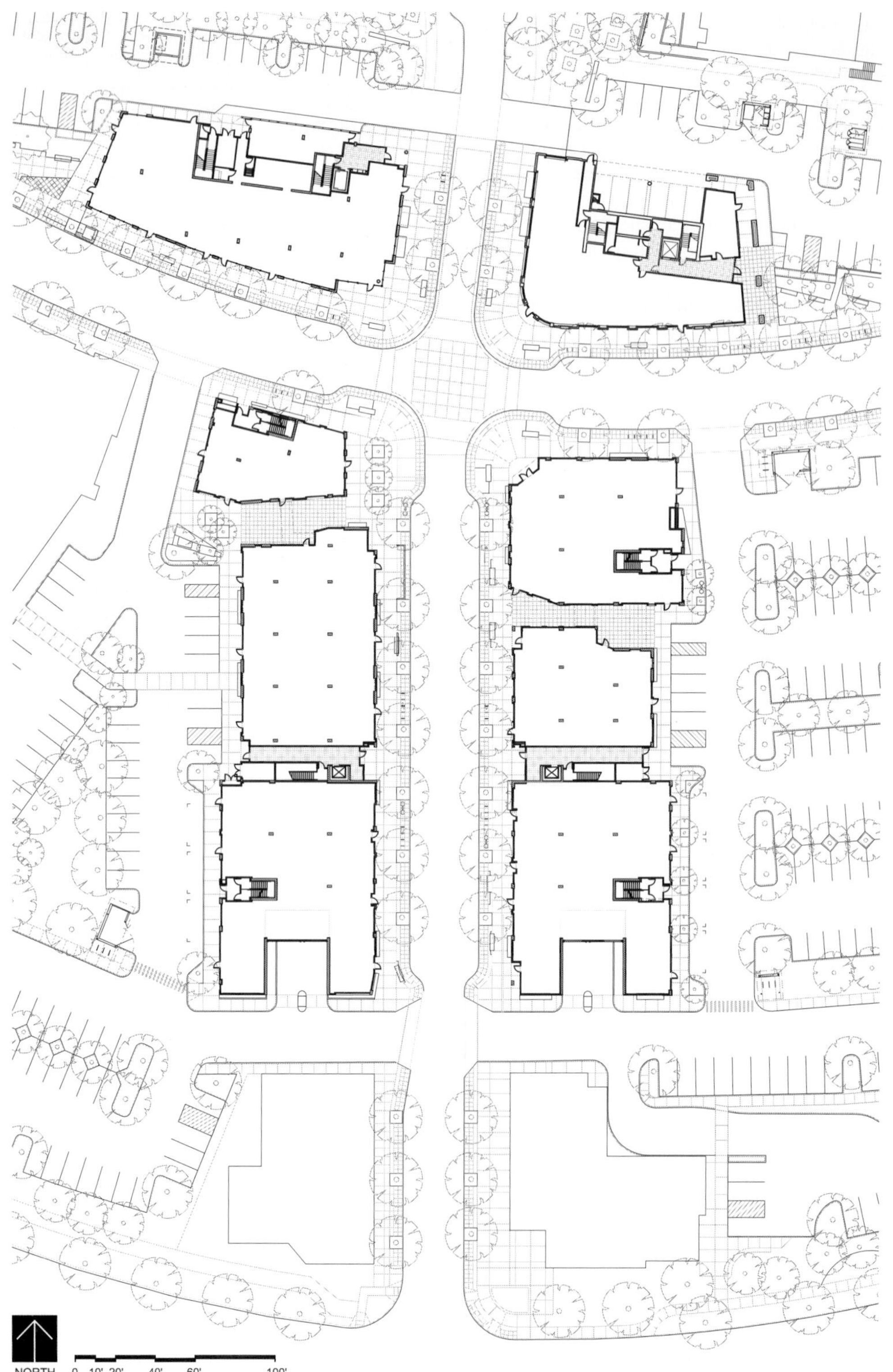
NORTH
0 10' 20' 40' 60' 100'

11.18 (previous page) Site plan of Crescent Village, designed by Rowell Brokaw Architects, showing paths leading to main street from parking and specificity of building footprints. Courtesy Rowell Brokaw Architects.

11.19 Rendering of main street of project. Courtesy Rowell Brokaw Architects.

These changing attitudes will help induce developers' banks to change their investment policies in ways that promote the reinvigoration of the city with mixed-use development.

A willingness to assume a slightly higher level of risk than usual may also be needed.[20] Like all investors, developers operate differently from each other. Within this variety, there are developers who are willing to combine a different vision of the city with what may be, at least initially, a slighter riskier venture. If the projects are successful, they will provide examples for more conservative investors who will realize that such investments are not as risky as they originally thought.

The first phase of Crescent Village in Eugene, Oregon, designed by Rowell Brokaw Architects, includes two mixed-use buildings with 31,424 square feet of commercial space and 102 residential units, detached town houses, semi-detached row houses, a cluster of office buildings, two commercial buildings without dwellings and a supermarket. Because the main buildings are only four stories tall, the commercial rents represent a substantial part of the potential income, and having businesses with higher rents on the ground floor allows for higher rents in the apartments above, since residential tenants are attracted to places that have high-quality retail services nearby.

The developers are a small and agile organization, wanting to use local banks, contractors and architects, and willing to take risks in a city with little precedent for this kind of project.[21] But financing was not straightforward. Since lenders had no nearby comparables, they based appraisals on single-use buildings such as garden apartments and strip retail – buildings for which appraisals

[20] Besides Leinberger's work, see also Schwanke, *Mixed-Use Development Handbook*, 33.

[21] The quality of flexibility, and not having to "answer to numerous sources and levels of command," is important for the success of mixed-use projects. See Schwanke, *Mixed-Use Development Handbook*, 33.

were low. Financing was eventually secured and the project is successful. In the first phase, apartments commanded higher rents than originally projected, and some of the commercial space rented before completion.[22]

Crescent Village is an upscale project on a greenfield site, but similar projects in existing neighborhoods are associated with gentrification and displacement of lower-income residents. Christopher Leinberger, although a strong advocate for reform in the way projects that will have a positive impact on the city are financed, also argues that "you cannot and should not avoid gentrification; it is the market at work."[23] While this may be true in large segments of today's market economy, the larger question is, of course, how can substantial long-term investment be made on mixed-use projects, including shop/houses, that will give good rates of return to investors of different kinds, while not expelling people of lower incomes from neighborhoods and cities?

Michael Pyatok has spoken strongly against the idea that neighborhoods should be improved by development that is part of a market-based paradigm. He argues that contemporary mixed-use development within the New Urbanist model is based too much on the image of place rather than on the real human and economic interactions that actually make authentic place, and that such projects force out people who made the neighborhood what it is in the first place, whose livelihoods depend on their ability to maintain their location, and their rent.[24]

He therefore sees it the other way around: "These enlightened developers [those who build affordable housing] see well-managed affordable workforce housing by the non-profit developers as the necessary first step to prove to the higher-end buying public that a neighborhood is worth moving into."[25]

Pyatok's projects, which often include the capability for people to operate businesses out of their homes, are often developed so people with less than median incomes can afford them. He involves himself strongly in the development/financing phases of projects, recognizing that low-income communities often need a kind of expertise that is not otherwise available to them. Projects may involve multiple funding sources and Pyatok's experience with such projects positions him to help organize them. Although he is a skilled architect, he sees design as part of an activity that includes forming the project itself (working closely with client groups, non-profit organizations and funders) and building the project (working closely with contractors) (Figs. 11.03 and 11.04).

Instead of making a choice between the two ideas, it seems more important to *provide a choice*, by recognizing the importance of both kinds of investment. From ancient Rome to eighteenth-century London to early twentieth-century American inner suburbs to today, urban growth has always been driven from the ground up as well as by developers building for sale or rental. The balance is different in different places – and contemporary cities are polarized between the two modes of development. This polarization can be seen most clearly in cities such as Mumbai or Bangkok, where large internationally financed developments are built adjacent to informal settlements. In the United States and western Europe, there is no doubt that large-scale development has made grassroots efforts difficult. But a local developer who wants to build a small project, with apartments and shops for rent, cannot automatically be faulted. Property development and speculation are not by definition problematic, but may become problematic when their scale overwhelms existing neighborhoods, when they force neighboring land values up too quickly, or when their

22 Conversation with Mark Miksis, May 4, 2007.
23 Leinberger, "Developer's Viewpoint," 4.
24 See, for example, Pyatok, "New Urbanism."
25 Pyatok, "Tale of Two Cities."

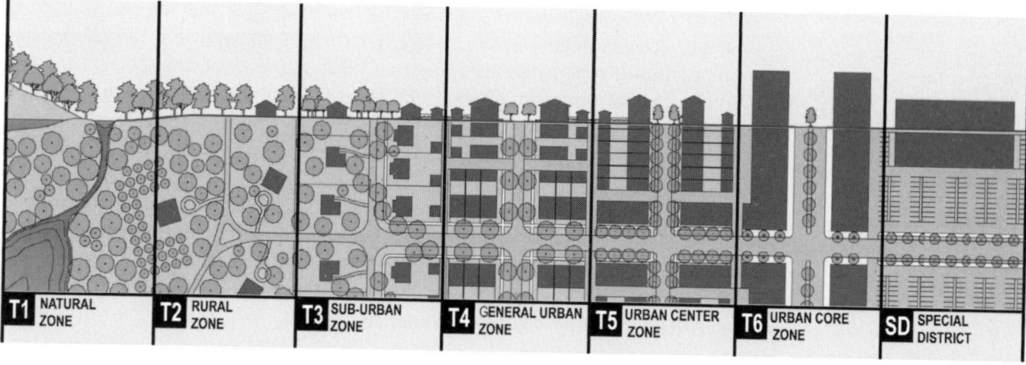

11.20 Rural-to-urban transect.
Courtesy Center for Applied Transect Studies/Duany Plater Zyberg and Company.

financing mechanisms trump the ability to build something of quality. Both grassroots efforts and developers' efforts may be useful to the city and its economic life.[26]

Zoning

Although zoning is a means to restrict the location, use or design of buildings to prevent unwanted effects of development, or to preserve the character and economic value of neighborhoods, some new zoning initiatives are less restrictive than previous codes. In this way, a new provision in a zoning ordinance may act as an incentive, allowing for a use that was not previously allowed in that zone.

In some new codes, sometimes called *form-based* codes, building types, densities, building form, and placement on lots, rather than building uses, are the guiding principles in zoning. This is sometimes (but not necessarily) associated with the *transect*, which defines a series of zones by their distance from the city center, each of which has buildings that meet certain attributes of form and placement (Fig. 11.20). The transect accords well with detailed studies of the phases of outward city development carried out by urban geographers,[27] and with the work of Christopher Alexander, that lays out an approach to coherent environments that is based on the existence of strongly formed centers, such as city centers, that focus other strongly formed centers, such as neighborhoods, toward them.[28]

In the transect, and in applications of form-based codes that do not rely on the transect, use separations are de-emphasized or eliminated, so mixed-use buildings have more of a chance. Within each zone, standards do not disallow either residential or retail functions, nor prevent such functions from co-existing in the same building. They do specify the amount of a particular function that might be present in the zone. In one version of such a code, commercial space in a particular zone must be "in the first story of buildings at corner locations, not more than one per block . . ." – and limiting the use to a "neighborhood store [that may or may not have a dwelling over it], or food service seating no more than 40"– part of a quite clearly expressed vision for a residential neighborhood.[29]

Although such codes may be written in a place-specific way, as now formulated they do not strongly enough reflect the dynamic nature of neighborhoods.

[26] Zukin, *Naked City*, 245–246. In the conclusion to *Naked City*, a book that criticizes the way the notion of "authenticity" has been co-opted by large developers and the municipalities that support them, Sharon Zukin writes about the need for this co-existence: "If mom-and-pop stores are more 'authentic' than big-box chains, the state should mandate their inclusion in every new building project and in every shopping block. If the social life of the streets is truly important, the state should make sure that all the men and women who use the streets have affordable rents so they can continue to live in their neighborhood."

[27] The classic study is Conzen, *Alnwick, Northumberland*. Conzen's work led to many subsequent studies, by Conzen, Whitehand and others.

[28] See Alexander's, *Nature of Order*, Book 1.

[29] For a brief discussion of form-based codes, see Talen, *Design for Diversity*, 117–122. A book on the subject is Parolek, *Form-Based Codes*. See also Duany and Talen, "Making the Good Easy," 1445–1468.

What if two people want to open a small home business on the same block, or what happens when density naturally increases, or what are the procedures for rezoning when density increases? But these criticisms should lead to increasing refinements of the code itself, rather than an outright rejection of the idea.[30] The shared vision implicit in a form-based code can be one of diversity that is dynamic over time.[31]

Form-based codes are not the only available tool. The economic flexibility and consequent physical informality that the shop/house represents – rooms added onto the fronts of houses; the makeshift conversions of shops, warehouses and the ground floors of houses; new, small projects – may also be fostered by a loosened, standard zoning ordinance.

As they did in the early days of zoning, model ordinances provide a framework for cities to develop standards for mixed-use zones. The American Planning Association has published both a "Model Mixed-Use Zoning District Ordinance" and a "Model Live-Work Ordinance."[32] These ordinances lay out a range of permitted uses, including commercial and residential uses, in particular zones, and are offered with the idea that individual municipalities will modify them according to local conditions.

The Portland (Oregon) 2040 Plan, a framework that sets agendas for individual municipalities within the metropolitan area, offers three options for creating mixed-use zones – updating existing zones, creating new districts, and creating overlay zones over existing districts. It argues for financial incentives to encourage mixed-use development, and stresses the need for flexibility by recommending both performance-based standards and a variety of explicit exceptions to specific rules. Portland's zoning ordinance already allows – with a conditional-use permit – commercial facilities in some multi-family districts, as well as residential uses in commercial districts, and many new mixed-use projects are being built on commercial streets.

New mixed-use zones often simply recognize what is already happening in peoples' basements, garages and spare bedrooms. One simple change is to simplify existing zoning ordinances through more flexibility of uses, by grouping uses according to their real impacts evaluated with the use of performance standards, and looking carefully at the size of the proposed activity.[33] Another is to create more mixed-use zones, allowing for "predictable flexibility" in uses.[34]

Austin, Texas, has considered standards that encourage "vertical mixed use," with different uses in the building, stacked vertically, and the requirement for at least one floor of residential use. In Washington State, the Spokane County mixed-use zone lays out allowed and conditional uses, permitting residential uses of all densities along with a variety of retail and commercial uses. Allowable floor-area ratios are different for different combinations of residential and non-residential uses, and there are bonuses if public amenities are included. The residential floor-area ratio (FAR) is combined with the non-residential FAR, allowing for a mixed-use building that is the sum of the two – effectively giving a density bonus for a mixed-use building. (Table 11.1)

In Berkeley, California, a mixed-use residential zone exists in a working-class residential area adjacent to an industrial zone. In this district, small businesses have sprouted that are run from converted spaces in houses, often at the ground floors, or from new buildings on the same properties (Fig. 11.21). In a

[30] The legal authority for regulating the number of businesses in a particular neighborhood is dealt with in McElyea, "Playing the Numbers."
[31] See Talen, "New Urbanism" for a discussion of the need for clearly articulated principles in the analysis of new planning processes such as those contained in "new urbanism."
[32] Morris M., *Smart Codes*.
[33] Elliott, *Better Way to Zone*, 140–141.
[34] Elliott, *Better Way to Zone*, 153.

Table 11.1 Allowed floor-area ratios in Spokane County's mixed-use zone

Basic allowable floor-area ratio by use			Maximum floor-area ratio by use with public amenities		
Non-residential	Residential	Combined residential and non-residential	Non-residential	Residential	Combined residential and non-residential
0.2	0.5	0.7	0.8	1.5	2.3

Source: Spokane County Zoning Code, Table 608-2.

quick walk around a two-block area of this district, the following businesses-combined-with-small-homes were found, many of which would not be allowed in an ordinary residential zone:[35] accountant, junkman/recycler, boatbuilder-turned-metalworker, chiropractor, business to convert spent vegetable oil from restaurants into biofuel for diesel engines, organic food business, cabinetmaker, glass artist, fine-art painter (2), electrical contractor, electrician who works on movie sets, notary, insurance sales, printer.

In adjacent Oakland, the architect Tom Dolan has advocated live/work through the development of new codes and projects. His policy work deals with such issues as neighborhood compatibility, parking, and how to deal with employees and walk-in customers – all potential issues of contention when work uses enter residential neighborhoods.[36] (There are also issues when residential uses enter industrial neighborhoods. In cities with a large housing demand, live-work projects may revert to all-residential uses, and commercial and industrial owners feel threatened when new residents complain about industrial uses that have actually been there all along.)

Revising zoning regulations may work in concert with other strategies. The public sector can also provide incentives for mixed-use development through

[35] Thanks to Seth Wachtel for pointing out this district to me, and for taking me on the walk in 2009.

[36] Thomas Dolan's website is www.live-work.com. He discussed these issues with me and showed me his projects in about 2004.

11.21 Houses in front and businesses in rear in Berkeley's mixed-use residential zone.
Photograph by author.

[37] Schwanke, *Mixed-Use Development Handbook*, 142.
[38] White, K., "Housing Above Retail."
[39] Martin, A., "Miles of Aisles." In the U.K. as well, major supermarket chains have built many such small markets.
[40] Cohen, "Making Grocers More Appetizing."
[41] Conversation with David Baker, San Francisco, March 11, 2009.
[42] This section was prompted by a conversation with Donald Corner.
[43] Seattle Mayor's Economic Opportunity Task Force, "Lowering the Cost," 23–24.

streamlining the permit approval process, subsidizing the cost of land, making land available, financing public buildings within a project and developing plans and then seeking developers.[37]

A 2004 San Francisco report claims that there are 100 acres of under-utilized retail sites in the city which, if developed as mixed-use projects with housing above retail at an average density of 45 units per acre, could yield 4,500 additional units of housing.[38] The report recognizes that "Most developers are either experts at housing or at retail," that "Very few know how to do both," and that retailers themselves may offer the most resistance to such projects, since risks are not as known, and because they see ease of parking as being compromised with certain new projects in which parking might be less visible.

Ideas for zoning incentives would increase building bulk and perceived density over what is now allowed, but they also include means to mitigate the effects of such increases. Suggestions include:

1. Allow up to ten additional feet of height in 20-foot-height-limit areas if needed to accommodate a ground floor with high ceilings with three floors of housing above.
2. Use height and bulk controls to shape the building envelope instead of restricting the number of units.
3. Allow more parking as-of-right for large stores.
4. Allow the project to move forward without the need for conditional-use authorization if the project is a grocery store or if no individual retailer other than a grocery store is more than 6,000 square feet and is not a fast-food restaurant.

The report includes a detailed description of a proposed "large retail mixed-use zoning overlay," and is aimed at sites that have large retail stores that are mostly one-story tall. Portland and Seattle both have projects in which supermarkets have been combined with housing above them.

At the same time, the idea that retail spaces have to be large is being questioned. The average size of new supermarkets has been shrinking, and there is a movement toward markets that are larger than convenience stores but smaller than supermarkets.[39] New York City has begun an incentive program to lure grocery stores to underserved neighborhoods, mostly in poor minority areas, by giving density bonuses to residential developers to include small supermarkets, without parking, in their projects.[40] Even more striking is a view that there is a rental market for retail shops that are as small as just 150 square feet, in places where pedestrian density is high.[41] These trends can lead to the easier design of commercial/residential buildings, as the required building footprint of commercial spaces decreases.

Minimum building height and lot coverage requirements[42] and requirements for inclusion of commercial space

When zoning ordinances originated in the first quarter of the twentieth century, they were written with the assumption that the less density, the less height and the less mixture of uses, the better. They specify maximum building heights, maximum lot coverage, and severely restrict the mixture of uses within a district. Now, to some extent, density, height and mixture of uses represent the solution rather than the problem. The environmental imperative may also help justify specifying minimum buildings heights and/or lot coverage – which would have the effect of requiring shop/houses in neighborhood commercial districts, for example, where now the vast majority of building is one-story. Such ordinances have been instituted or are being considered in various cities, including Burlington, Vermont, Madison, New Jersey and Hillsboro, Oregon.

In Seattle, ordinances required the inclusion of commercial space in otherwise all-residential buildings in commercial districts. This requirement came about because the high demand for housing was prompting the construction of residential buildings that had little life at the street. But in some cases, such buildings had to be built where there was little market for commercial space – and the commercial space went unleased. One report recommends that the commercial requirement be reviewed for its feasibility, and that flexibility be allowed in the use of ground-floor spaces until retail use becomes viable.[43]

A similar requirement for provision of ground-floor commercial space in certain zoning districts applied in Vancouver, British Columbia. In some places that space went unrented for several years after it was built. But since the original cost calculation for the project took the vacancies into account, the projects as a whole remained viable. There was enough flexibility to allow at least some of the commercial space to be rented at considerably lower rents than the developer originally wanted, until rents could increase.

Requiring commercial space in projects, or setting minimum building heights, may be seen as disincentives. The critical balance between regulations like this, that are seeking to further an environmental "common good", and regulations that loosen regulations to directly encourage the initiation of individual projects, is a matter for a particular city to decide for itself. Any act of building must come to terms with that balance, as it contributes to the larger good at the same time that it satisfies individual needs.

Cooperation between planners and architects

Regulations are most effective when people have common intentions, and new hybrids may require a new level of collaboration. Almost since the founding of Vancouver, B.C., in the late nineteenth century, the shop/house was an important feature of neighborhood commercial districts (Fig. 11.22). Such buildings were built all through the twentieth century, even during the decades when U.S. urban renewal was wiping out neighborhoods with these buildings. During the sixties, when there was not yet much pressure for the construction of new housing, ordinances that mandated the inclusion of ground-floor commercial space remained on the books. (Jane Jacobs was highly respected and her book had a major effect on planning policy in Canada.[44])

A high level of cooperation between planners and architects has helped shape one of the Vancouver mixed-use districts. The C-2 zone, formed after groups of commercial/residential buildings had already been established on thoroughfares at the edge of mostly residential neighborhoods, provides for mixed-use buildings up to four stories. Over the last fifteen years, the regulations for the C-2 zone have evolved through a process that entails simulations, design, construction and use. Architects contracted by the planning department have done design simulations that helped refine the regulations themselves; the experiences of built projects have helped provide criticism of the regulations that have then been changed with the use of new design simulations (Fig. 11.23).

[44] Conversation with Trish French, Vancouver Planning Department, July 2003. Jane Jacobs moved to Canada in about 1968 and took up residence in Toronto.

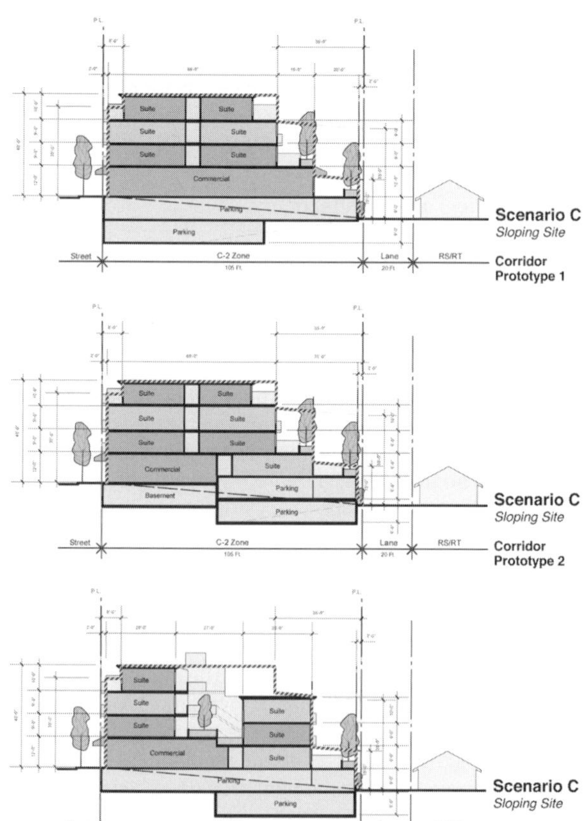

11.22 Shop/houses in Vancouver.
Photograph by Stephen Duff.

11.23 Three prototypes from zoning study for Vancouver's C-2 district. All are intended to bring down the scale of mixed-use buildings adjacent to residential districts.
Courtesy Neale Staniszkis Doll Adams Architects, Vancouver.

Building construction and codes

In the American West, many multi-story, mixed-use buildings are built of a hybrid concrete-and-wood system. The wooden structure sits on a post-tensioned slab, providing the required fire separation between uses. The slab transfers vertical loads to widely spaced columns, allowing freedom of planning of the apartments and flexibility in layout of the commercial space, and provides good acoustic separation between dwellings and commercial space. Except for the location of fire stairs, each use can be planned separately from the other.[45]

Contemporary building codes are changing, making it easier to build mixed-use buildings. These changes include:

- *More height*. The city of Seattle has allowed for the measurement of height for a wooden structure to start at the concrete podium, rather than the ground, allowing for an extra story of dwelling units above retail. This height differential may make the difference between a viable and a non-viable project.
- *Longer common path to the fire exit*. In the International Building Code (IBC), the maximum path from the door to a dwelling unit to a fire stair has been increased from 75′ to 125′, when fire sprinklers are used. This allows for more flexibility in layout, and may permit larger unobstructed retail spaces, since fire stairs may be further apart.
- *Other allowances when the building is sprinklered*. Previous codes, for example, allowed for either fewer vertical fire separations in the retail space or a larger number of stories, when the building was sprinklered. Now, having fire sprinklers in the building permits both of these.

The transformation of the twentieth-century built landscape

Suburbs all over the world are changing their economic and social characteristics. In the United States, the roles of suburbs and central cities have reversed, with formerly immigrant areas of cities now being repopulated by a new, upper-middle class, and the suburbs, which were once aspired to by the middle class, now being repopulated by immigrants and low-income people.[46] The same is true in European cities such as Amsterdam, where post-war housing estates of apartment buildings set among large green spaces have been populated by immigrants from North Africa and the Middle East. These housing estates have been the sites of social unrest, which was exacerbated by the physical environment. Doug Saunders calls many of these places, from South Central Los Angeles to Amsterdam South to Kreuzberg, Berlin, "arrival cities." He argues that they are the crucible of opportunity for people who are upwardly mobile, with the potential to strongly contribute to the urban economy.[47]

But these places were built for different populations than now occupy them, and this results in social problems. The modernist suburbs of European cities are often not well connected to places of employment, and do not have a vibrant street life or opportunity for grassroots economic development. American suburbs, at a lower density, have similar problems. Zoning rules for residential areas – originally developed to maintain a certain density and the ability for a particular economic class to feel secure – hamper people's ability to live in ways that are consistent with their own cultural roots, and their ability to use their buildings as vehicles to enter the formal economy.[48] Many shopping

[45] Thanks to Greg Brokaw, Elaine Lawson and Mark Young of Rowell Brokaw Architects in Eugene, and John Holmes of Holst Architecture in Portland, for conversations about the application of building codes to mixed-use buildings.
[46] See, for example, Singer, "The Rise of New Immigrant Gateways," and Press, "The New Suburban Poverty."
[47] Saunders, *Arrival City*.
[48] See Fahim, "Housing Crackdown."

malls and big-box stores have been abandoned, are underperforming or incorporate under-utilized land or air space. As the metropolitan model that was based on the illusion of cheap transportation begins to change, there is the chance to restructure large areas of cities in ways that better serve changing economic needs and ways of life.

This restructuring is beginning to happen. In Amsterdam, the reconstruction of mid-twentieth century housing areas is introducing a finer mix of commercial and residential buildings, including places for start-up businesses.[49] Many North American suburbs are considering changing zoning rules to allow unrelated occupants in houses, and accepting changing ethnic populations. And numerous projects are renovating or rebuilding shopping malls built in the twentieth century, making them denser, connecting them to nearby streets and introducing a mix of different multi-story housing types to areas once characterized by one-story commercial space and acres of parking.

In Lakewood, Colorado, Belmar is a new town center on the site of a once-successful shopping mall that failed. The project includes a new street grid and a mix of building types including civic and commercial buildings, housing and mixed-use buildings that have housing over commercial space. The intention is not simply a replacement with new buildings, but a place that can evolve over time.[50] Other suburbs have grassroots transformations that spur policy changes, such as in Montgomery County, Maryland, where new zoning rules and direct efforts worked to help Vietnamese and Latino immigrants find an economic foothold in the community.[51] In San Francisco, there are plans to redevelop Park Merced, which was originally developed in the 1940s as a suburban-like development with large areas of green space (designed partly by the modernist landscape architect Thomas Church). The redevelopment will include denser housing mixed with corner stores.[52] The suburbs will persist, but there is also a growing interest in transforming them to accommodate contemporary, mixed-function lives.

These transformations are only beginning, and need to be seen as tentative first steps within a building culture that is still overwhelmingly characterized by the production of Leinberger's "standard real estate types," within planning protocols that mandate the separation of those types from each other. It will be market acceptance that ultimately determines the success of these new efforts. As the economy continues to be restructured, as the increasing price of oil results in more efficient land-use patterns, and as more people retreat from overly-consumptive lifestyles, choices that include mixed-use districts with shop/houses of different types will become increasingly popular.

Indeed, we should not be looking for the immediate and wholesale transformation of our cities – that could not happen in any case, since the physical fabric of cities persist a lot longer than the ideas that make cities persist. Instead, the initiation of pragmatic policies and prototypes that increase choice, and that do not mandate the continued production of mono-functional buildings within mono-functional districts, should be the ongoing goal of clients, designers and policy makers. Such increased choice will put people into a position where they can decide for themselves how they want to live, and that opportunity will result in a built environment that is better able to respond to social and economic change.

* * *

[49] Saunders, *Arrival City*, 292–293.
[50] Dunham-Jones and Williamson, *Retrofitting Suburbia*, 154–166. This book provides a comprehensive account of transformations of American shopping malls. Dunham-Jones argued, at a lecture at the University of Oregon in February 2011, that such rapid redevelopment is consistent with the speed of building such places as Morningside Heights on the Upper West Side of Manhattan, much of which was built within a time span of a couple of decades, and which remains robust in its value and usefulness.
[51] Saunders, *Arrival City*, 98–99.
[52] Kane, "Park Merced," A1.

Slowly and haltingly, the building culture is changing to once again help buildings contribute in a robust way to a resilient city. The cultural change is happening within different professions and among many different players, and sometimes as the result of different motivations. It is striking that an idea about building that has so many individual manifestations, all over the world, seems to be such a shared goal. This may be due to the fact that at its root, the shop/house, in whatever guise, is the result of an attitude to daily life that makes ordinary human sense.

CONCL.01 Lower Manhattan from the High Line elevated walkway.
Photograph by author.

CONCL.02 Street on the Upper West Side of Manhattan.
Photograph by author.

CONCLUSION

Hybrid urban practice

City processes in real life are too complex to be routine, too particularized for application as abstractions.[1]

(Jane Jacobs, *The Death and Life of Great American Cities*)

In the end, this book is very much about how architecture has respected ordinary daily life over the centuries, and needs to do so again. Architects and others who are responsible for making the built world need to be open to its human realities, and in a position to see value in approaches that may at first glance seem at odds with each other. This is a hybridity of practice, within a framework of shared intentions.

It may seem unusual, for example, to be writing favorably about projects that are largely financial investments, and favorably about initiatives that recognize the struggle that small family businesses have to survive, often in the face of large investors.

But both are needed in the world, because they both do useful things. The family shop/house has clear value and a long history. But speculative development has also existed since ancient Rome, and rental space – even with its attendant evils – has always served to help people gain a foothold in the city's economy. London was built through a unique model of development with nested leaseholds, and people making money at every level.[2] The American city was built through speculative development of plats that later became neighborhoods. What differed in the auto-dominated, post-World War II suburb was not the speculative idea itself but the location of new developments, the subsidies that were made available to them and the principles that guided their design.

So although it might well be argued that public policy should only be used to support the efforts of individual owners to survive – because their struggle is so difficult – there can also be value to what developers do. They bring resources and expertise; they deal with urban form at a larger scale than the individual entrepreneur; they may set frameworks for future development. As with many complex processes, this is not a black-and-white issue – and we are not in a position to reject institutions that in fact are the ones that have built cities.

In the long run, we are after urban growth that gives the individual voice, power and opportunity; in which wealth is returned to the community; that exhibits beauty at different scales; that respects place and cultural memory. The complexity that characterizes a city, and the enormously diverse histories that cities have had, mitigates against precluding any one mode of production.

1 Jacobs, *Death and Life*, 441.
2 Olsen, *Town Planning in London*, 99–103.

[3] Talen, *New Urbanism and American Planning*, 19.
[4] Kelbaugh, "Preface,", 8.

Emily Talen identifies "four urbanist cultures" into which different approaches to urban planning fit. These are:

1 *Incrementalism* – small-scale actions that begin with, and respect, the existing city, exemplified by the work of Camillo Sitte, William Whyte, Jane Jacobs and Christopher Alexander;
2 *Urban plan-making* – the development of large-scale plans that also begin with the existing city, exemplified by the City Beautiful Movement, and the work of Daniel Burnham, John Nolen, Thomas Adams and Robert Moses;
3 *Planned communities* – "utopian and quasi-utopian ideas about the proper place of cities in the region, the correct functioning of society within urban areas, and the formation of new towns, villages or neighbourhoods . . ." exemplified by Ebenezer Howard, Raymond Unwin and Barry Parker, John Nolen, Clarence Stein, and Henry Wright; and
4 *Regionalism* – an emphasis on settlement in its "natural, regional context," exemplified by Patrick Geddes, Lewis Mumford, Frederick Law Olmsted and Ian McHarg.[3]

Similarly, Douglas Kelbaugh writes that following modernist city planning, and in addition to the "conventional urbanism" that now characterizes the production of the American city, there are three "intentional . . . self-conscious urbanisms being practiced, theorized and written about:"

1 *Everyday urbanism*, an emphasis on the small and contingent, not necessarily the result of formal design;
2 *New urbanism*, connected to the movement of the same name; and
3 *Post urbanism*, exemplified by the work of architects such as Rem Koolhaas and Frank Gehry,[4] in which traditional notions of context are challenged.

So here are seven different ways of urban practice, in addition to "conventional urbanism," the familiar practices characterized by Euclidean zoning and developers. And certainly at first blush they are incompatible – the differences of philosophy and practice between Jane Jacobs and Robert Moses, or Rem Koolhaas and Andres Duany, are well known. The different intellectual discourses also tend to happen within different economic/political frameworks – urban plan-making is often associated with large-scale infusions of public money; new urbanism is often associated with private speculators and developers; incrementalism is often associated with grassroots activity and disdain for the large developer. We tend to assume that these different approaches have nothing to do with each other.

But the pragmatics of practice are not as ideologically neat. Consider the Seattle recommendation described in Chapter 11, "that the commercial requirement be reviewed for its feasibility, and that flexibility be allowed in the use of ground-floor spaces until retail use becomes viable." This is, at once:

- within the paradigm of zoning, modernism's most successful tool to control urban form;
- within the paradigm of new urbanism, as the original regulation comes out of new urbanism's concern for life at the street level of buildings;
- within the paradigms of incrementalism and everyday urbanism, as the proposed exception seeks to recognize that, even within a particular zone, small changes may happen over time and need to be accommodated.

Or, consider the Peck Slip project in New York, also in Chapter 11. This project is, at once:

- within the paradigm of conventional urbanism and zoning, done within a zoning district that allowed this mixture of uses by right;
- within the paradigm of incrementalism, at the developer's insistence on the inclusion of small local businesses instead of national chains;
- within the paradigm of everyday urbanism, paying as much respect as possible to the existing old buildings, that in the hands of a different development team might very well have been destroyed.

Similar overlaps of theory characterize many of the initiatives in this book. The ideological differences that may exist between them need to be set aside in favor of a detailed examination of the content of each. This might lead to understandings of how one initiative might be connected to others, and of the potential usefulness of a hybrid, pragmatic approach. In fact, theory is lagging behind practice in the same way that real buildings do not reflect hybrid types – and it would be helpful for theory to see hybrid, pragmatic practice as significant as any "ism" in its ability to make a better city.

In the end, we come back to everyday hybridity: the idea that everyday life is not easily classifiable into clear functional zones or standard architectural types. The daily life of a household, street or neighborhood is characterized by interactions among the functions that make it up that are so powerful that they render a reductive analysis much too simplistic. In support of this complex daily life, the shop/house is a "model hybrid." It connects people and functions inside it; it is symbiotically connected to the neighborhood outside it; it changes cyclically over time in its use and is malleable in its architectural form.

For much of the history of cities, hybridity was lived and not discussed as an intellectual idea. Until recent times, the economic life of cities was at least partly dependent on local transactions between producers and distributors, between distributors and retailers, between retailers and consumers. In many cases these roles were combined in one person or family, but even when they were not, connections were strong and local, and they transcended economic interactions to include the social and even the religious.

The fragmentation that modern institutions have inflicted on daily life will only be partly repaired by our emerging globalized and digitized culture. This culture is opening up great possibilities for innovation, for art, for the sharing of knowledge, for cultural solidarity, for trade, for the kinds of human associations that would not have been possible a generation ago. It is reforming political institutions and changing the nature of design, production and consumption.

This new culture is sometimes interpreted as eliminating the need for localism, which is often seen as anti-modern and a throwback to a past world. But less visible than the internet and the increasing pervasiveness of global media is a new sense of the importance of place, of local production, of a recognition that the environmental imperative has implications in the way people will live, and of the need for buildings that are not bound to ways of life and work that are becoming outmoded. What we have is not a fight between the local and the global, with one to reign supreme, but a necessary accommodation of one to the other.

Many people want the ability to live local lives in a global world and have the means to do so with their lifestyle and employment. Other people in the West, caught in the pits and cracks of unstable economies, want to be able to free themselves from dependence on uncertain employment. And yet other people, in still-"developing" countries, are doing what they have always done, seeing enterprise-at-home as a natural part of their lives.

Instead of seeing these people as altogether different from each other – the "creative professionals," the "low-income service worker", the "Third World slum dweller" – we might see them as having a shared desire for self-determination regarding their own economic lives, to be able to live in ways that are anchored to their physical places in the world.

It is tempting to say that the neighborhoods of the next few decades, in which such self-determination will be harbored, and perhaps in which shop/houses may gain a foothold, may not be outwardly like such neighborhoods of the past, and that the shop/houses themselves will be different, perhaps not recognizable.

Undoubtedly such new forms will emerge – perhaps as the dysfunctional low-rise suburbs of American cities or the high-rise suburbs of European cities are transformed. But at the same time, the very block of Hudson Street where Jane Jacobs lived and wrote in the 1950s exists today in much the same form as then, with shops and bars and children walking to school, and people living over the store. In many countries, such places where they still exist are among the most desirable to live. The emerging urban fabric that harbors shop/houses will itself be a hybrid of the new and the old, and incorporating neighborhoods with people of all economic means.

* * *

The shop/house is ordinary, up until now neglected in architectural writing, and largely unrealized in recent practice. It is, however, in many places the ultimate "fabric building," the background against which other buildings of the city can express their own uniqueness, and the anchor for a fine-grained neighborhood economic life. Its ordinariness has its own story, straddling the boundaries between architecture and the contexts within which architecture exists.

BIBLIOGRAPHY

Abbott, Carl. "The Neighborhoods of New York, 1760–1775." *New York History* 60, no. 1 (1974): 35–54.

Abeyasekere, Susan. *Jakarta: A History*. Singapore: Oxford University Press, 1987.

Adams, Daniel, Allyson Coyne, Mason Kirby, Luigi Lucaccini, Fernando Marti, Rose McNulty, Eugene Muscat, Seth Wachtel and Meredith Walters. *Enterprise Housing for San Francisco: The Future of Home-Based Family Businesses*. San Francisco: Asian Neighborhood Design and School of Business and Management, University of San Francisco, 2007.

Ahrentzen, Sherry. "Housing Home Businesses in Urban Neighborhoods: Implications for the City of Milwaukee." Center for Urban Initiatives and Research, Department of Architecture, University of Wisconsin–Milwaukee, vol. 14, no. 1 (Winter 2001).

Ajmar-Wollheim, Marta and Flora Dennis, eds. *At Home in Renaissance Italy*. London: V & A Publications, 2006.

The "Albany," New York. *American Architect and Building News* 1 (December 23, 1876): two plates before p. 413.

Alexander, Christopher, "A City is Not a Tree." *Architectural Forum* (April–May 1965): 58–62.

—— "The City as a Mechanism for Sustaining Human Contact." In *Environment for Man: The Next Fifty Years*, edited by W. Ewald, 60–109. Indiana: American Institute of Planners Conference, Indiana University Press, 1967.

—— *The Timeless Way of Building*. New York: Oxford University Press, 1979.

—— *The Nature of Order: An Essay on the Art of Building and the Nature of the Universe*. Books 1–4. Berkeley: Center for Environmental Structure Publishing, 2001.

Alexander, Christopher, Sanford Hirshen, Sara Ishikawa, Christie Coffin and Shlomo Angel. *Houses Generated by Patterns*. Berkeley: Center for Environmental Structure Publishing, 1970.

Alexander, Christopher, Sara Ishikawa and Murray Silverstein with Max Jacobson, Ingrid Fiksdahl-King and Shlomo Angel. *A Pattern Language*. New York: Oxford University Press, 1977.

Alexander, David. *Retailing in England during the Industrial Revolution*. London: Athlone Press, 1970.

Alonso, William. "The Economics of Consumption, Daily Life, and Urban Form." Working Paper No. 139, Institute of Urban & Regional Development, University of California, Berkeley, December 1970.

Ambler Realty Co. vs. Village of Euclid, Ohio, et al. District Court, N.D. Ohio, Eastern Division. 297 F. 307.

Aries, Phillipe. *Centuries of Childhood*. New York: Vintage, 1962.

Arreola, Daniel. "Mexican–American Housescapes." *Geographical Review* 78, no. 3 (1988): 299–315.

Aston, James and Michael Bond. *The Landscape of Towns*. London: J.M. Dent & Sons, 1976.

Auer, Gerhard, B. Kolver and Niels Gutschow. "Domestic Architecture of Nepal." *Art and Archeology Research Papers* 12, (1977): 64–69.

Bailey, Barbara Ruth. *Main Street Northeastern Oregon: The Founding and Development of Small Towns*. Portland: Oregon Historical Society, 1982.

Banfield, Frank. *The Great Landlords of London*. London: S. Blankett, 1890.

Bascià, Luciana, Paolo Carlotti and Gian Luigi Maffei. *La Casa Romana nella Storia della Città all'Ottocento*. Firenze: Alinea, 2000.

Beasley, Ellen. *The Corner Store*. Washington D.C.: National Building Museum, 1999.

Belfoure, Charles and Mary Ellen Hayward. *The Baltimore Rowhouse*. New York: Princeton Architectural Press, 2001.

Ben-Joseph, Eran and Terry S. Szold. *Regulating Place: Standards and the Shaping of Urban America*. New York: Routledge, 2005.

Benjamin, Walter. *The Arcades Project*. Cambridge and London: Harvard University Press, 1999.

Bernheimer, Charles, ed. *The Russian Jew in the United States*. Philadelphia: Jewish Publication Society, 1905.

Berry, Brian J.L. *Geography of Market Centers and Retail Distribution*. Englewood Cliffs: Prentice-Hall, 1967.

Blau, Eve. *The Architecture of Red Vienna 1919–1934*. Cambridge: M.I.T. Press, 1999.

Blumin, Stuart M. *The Emergence of the Middle Class: Social Experience in the American City, 1760–1900*. Cambridge and New York: Cambridge University Press, 1989.

Boethius, Axel. *The Golden House of Nero: Some Aspects of Roman Architecture*. Ann Arbor: University of Michigan Press, 1960.

Borsay, Peter. "The English Urban Renaissance: The Development of Provincial Urban Culture c1680 –c1760." In *The Eighteenth-Century Town 1688–1820: A Reader in English Urban History*, edited by Peter Borsay, 159–187. London: Longman, 1990.

Botan. *Letters from Thailand*. Thailand: Silkworm Books, 2002.

Brand, Stewart. *How Buildings Learn*. New York: Penguin Books, 1995.

Bridenbaugh, Carl. *The Colonial Craftsman*. Chicago: University of Chicago Press, 1950.

Brown, Frank E. "Continuity and Change in the Urban House: Developments in Domestic Space Organization in Seventeenth-Century London." *Comparative Studies in Society and History* 28, no. 1 (1986): 558–590.

Brown, Jonathan and Sadie Ward. *The Village Shop*. London: Cameron Books and Rural Development Commission, 1990.

Brunskill, Ronald. *Illustrated Handbook of Vernacular Architecture*. London: Faber and Faber, 1978.

Burdett, Ricky and Deyan Sudjic, eds. *The Endless City: The Urban Age Project by the London School of Economics and Deutsche Bank's Alfred Herrhausen Society*. London: Phaidon Press, 2007.

Burnett, John. *A Social History of Housing 1815–1985*. London and New York: Routledge, 1986.

Büttner, Horst, and Günter Meissner. *Town Houses of Europe*. New York: St. Martin's Press, 1982.

Calliat, Victor. *Parallèle des maisons de Paris construites depuis 1830 jusqu'à nos jours*. Paris: Bance, 1857.

Candee, Richard M., ed. *Building Portsmouth: The Neighborhoods & Architecture of New Hampshire's Oldest City*. Portsmouth, N.H.: Portsmouth Advocates, Inc., 1992.

Cappel, Andrew J. "A Walk Along Willow: Patterns of Land Use Coordination in Pre-Zoning New Haven." *Yale Law Journal* 101, no. 3 (1991): 617–642.

Casault, André, Denise Piché, and Myriam Blais. *The Habitat of Ha Noi*. Québec: Presses de l'Université Laval, 2006.

Certeau, Michel de. *The Practice of Everyday Life*. Berkeley: University of California Press, 1988.

Chaichongrak, Ruethai, Somchai Nil-athi, Ornsiri Panin and Saowalak Posayanonda. *The Thai House*. Bangkok: Asia Books, 2002.

Chapelot, Jean and Robert Fossier. *The Village and House in the Middle Ages*. Berkeley and Los Angeles: University of California Press, 1985.

Chase, John, Margaret Crawford and John Kaliski. *Everyday Urbanism*. New York: Monacelli Press, 2008.

City of Aurora vs. Burns, 319 Ill. 84 (1925).

City of St. Louis vs. Morris Evraiff et al., 301 Mo. 231 (1923).

Clarke, Linda. *Building Capitalism*. London: Routledge, 1992.

Clowney, Stephen. "A Walk Along Willard: A Revised Look at Land Use Coordination in Pre-Zoning New Haven." *Yale Law Journal* 115, no. 1 (2005): 116–184.

Cohen, Nevin. "Making Grocers More Appetizing to Developers." *Planetizen*, May 25, 2009. www.planetizen.com/node/38890.

Condon, Patrick. "Growing a Greater Vancouver Region: Population Scenarios for a Region of 4 Million People." *Foundation Research Bulletin*. Design Centre for Sustainability, University of British Columbia, 2006.

Conzen, Kathleen Neils. "Patterns of Residence in Early Milwaukee". In *The New Urban History: Quantitative Explorations by American Historians*, edited by L.F. Schnore, 145–183. Princeton: Princeton University Press, 1975.

Conzen, Michael P. and Kathleen Neils Conzen. "Geographical Structure in Nineteenth-Century Urban Retailing: Milwaukee, 1836–90." *Journal of Historical Geography* 5, no. 1 (1979): 45–66.

Conzen, M.R.G. *Alnwick, Northumberland: A Study in Town-Plan Analysis.* London: The Institute of British Geographers, publication no. 27, London: George Philip & Son, 1960.

Cooper, Lee E. "Post-War Housing Includes No Stores; 13 New Projects Planned by City Authority to Consist of Apartments Only; Agency Sidesteps Trade; Shopping Facilities Near Large Developments to be Left to Private Enterprise." *New York Times*, October 7, 1944, amusement section, page 15.

Correa, Charles. *Housing and Urbanization*. London: Thames and Hudson, 2000.

Cox, Nancy. *The Complete Tradesman: A Study of Retailing, 1550–1820*. Aldershot: Ashgate, 2000.

Cromley, Elizabeth Collins. *Alone Together: A History of New York's Early Apartments*. Ithaca: Cornell University Press, 1990.

—— *The Food Axis: Cooking, Eating and the Architecture of American Houses.* Charlottesville and London: University of Virginia Press, 2010.

Cruickshank, Dan and Peter Wyld, *London: The Art of Georgian Building*. London: Architectural Press, 1975.

Daunton, M.J. *House and Home in the Victorian City: Working-Class Housing 1850–1914*. London: Edward Arnold, 1983.

Davis, Howard. *The Culture of Building*. New York: Oxford University Press, 1999.

—— "The Commercial-Residential Building and Local Urban Form." *Urban Morphology* 13, no.2 (2009): 89–104.

Davis, Mike. *Magical Urbanism*. London and New York: Verso Books, 2000.

—— *Planet of Slums*. London and New York: Verso Books, 2006.

DeForest, Robert W. and Lawrence Veiller, eds. *The Tenement House Problem, Including the Report of the New York State Tenement House Commission of 1900*. New York: Macmillan Company, 1903.

Derry, T.K. "The Repeal of the Apprenticeship Clauses of the Statute of Apprentices." *The Economic History Review* 3, no. 1 (1931): 67–87.

Deutsch, Sarah. *Women and the City: Gender, Space and Power in Boston, 1870–1940*. New York: Oxford University Press, 2000.

Dow, George F. *Every Day Life in the Massachusetts Bay Colony*. Boston: Society for the Preservation of New England Antiquities, 1935.

Duany, Andres, Elizabeth Plater-Zyberk and Jeff Speck. *Suburban Nation: The Rise of Suburban Sprawl and the Decline of the American Dream*. New York: North Point Press, 2000.

Duany, Andres and Emily Talen. "Making the Good Easy: The Smart Code Alternative." *Fordham Urban Law Journal* XXIX, no. 4 (2002): 1445–1468.

Duffy, Frank. *Work and the City*. London: Black Dog Publishing, 2008.

Dunham-Jones, Ellen and June Williamson. *Retrofitting Suburbia: Urban Design Solutions for Redesigning Suburbs*. Hoboken, New Jersey: John Wiley & Sons, 2009.

Durand, J.N.L. *Précis des leçons d'architecture données a l'École Polytechnique*. Paris: l'Auteur, 1802–05. Translated by David Britt as *Précis of the Lectures in Architecture*. Los Angeles: Getty Research Institute, 2000.

Dyos, H.J. *Victorian Suburb: A Study of the Growth of Camberwell*. Leicester: Leicester University Press, 1961.

Echanove, Matias and Rahul Srivastava, "Taking the Slum Out of 'Slumdog'." *New York Times*, February 21, 2009. Accessed July 4, 2011, www.nytimes.com/2009/02/21/opinion/21srivastava.html?scp=1&sq=slum%20slumdog&st=cse.

Eckstein, Nicholas. "Neighborhood as a Microcosm." In *Renaissance Florence: A Social History*, edited by Roger J. Crum and John T. Paoletti, 219–239. New York: Cambridge University Press, 2006.

Edwards, Norman. *The Singapore House and Residential Life 1819–1939*. Singapore: Oxford University Press, 1990.

Eleb, Monique and Anne Debarre. *Architectures de la vie privée*. Paris: Hazan, 1999.

Elisséeff, Nikita. "Damas à la lumière des théories de Jean Sauvaget." In *The Islamic City: A Colloquium, Papers in Islamic History I*, edited by A.H. Hourani and S.M. Stern, 157–177. Oxford: Bruno Cassirer, 1970.

Ellin, Nan. *Integral Urbanism*. New York and London: Routledge, 2006.

Elliott, Donald. *A Better Way to Zone: Ten Principles to Create More Livable Cities*. Washington D.C., Covelo and London: Island Press, 2008.

Euclid vs. Ambler. 272 U.S.365 (1926).

Evans, Robin. *Translations from Drawing to Building and Other Essays*. Cambridge: M.I.T. Press, 1997.

Everitt, Alan. "Country, County and Town: Patterns of Regional Evolution in England." In *The Eighteenth Century Town 1688–1820: A Reader in English Urban History*, edited by P. Borsay, 83–115. London: Longman, 1990.

Fahim, Kareem. "Housing Crackdown Hits Indian Immigrants." *New York Times*, August 6, 2007. http://www.nytimes.com/2007/08/06/nyregion/06crowd.html.

Falke, Jacob von. *Greece and Rome: Their Life and Art*. New York: Henry Holt and Company, 1886.

Fanelli, Doris D. "William Polk's General Store in Saint George's, Delaware." *Delaware History* 19, no. 4 (1981): 212–228.

Fenton, Joseph. *Hybrid Buildings, Pamphlet Architecture No. 11*. New York and San Francisco: Pamphlet Architecture and William Stout Architectural Books, 1985.

Flint, Anthony. *Wrestling With Moses: How Jane Jacobs Took On New York's Master Builder and Transformed the American City*. New York: Random House, 2009.

Florida, Richard. *The Rise of the Creative Class*. New York: Basic Books, 2002.

Ford, George B. *Building Height, Bulk and Form: How Zoning Can be Used as a Protection Against Uneconomic Types of Buildings on High-Cost Land*. Cambridge: Harvard University Press, 1931

Freitag, Joseph Kendall. *Fire Prevention and Fire Protection: A Handbook of Theory and Practice*. New York: John Wiley & Sons, 1912.

Friedlaender, Susan. "New Urbanism: Innovative Concepts in Mixed-Use Development: The Zoning Perspective." March 14, 2002. Institute of Continuing Legal Education. Accessed July 8, 2011, www.michbar.org/realproperty/pdfs/20022B7196.pdf

Friedman, Avi. *The Grow Home*. Montreal: McGill-Queen's University Press, 2001.

Frug, Gerald. *City Making: Building Communities Without Building Walls*. Princeton: Princeton University Press, 1999.

Gabarine, Rachelle. "New State Code to Ease Rehabilitation-Project Costs." *New York Times*, January 18, 1998. Accessed July 7, 2011, www.nytimes.com/1998/01/18/realestate/in-the-region-new-jersey-new-state-code-to-ease-rehabilitation-project-costs.html.

Garbee, Jenn. *Secret Suppers: Rogue Chefs & Underground Restaurants in Warehouses, Townhouses, Open Fields & Everywhere in Between*. Seattle: Sasquatch Books, 2008.

Garnett, Nicole Stelle. "On Castles and Commerce: Zoning Law and the Home–Business Dilemma." *William and Mary Law Review* 42, no. 1191 (April 2001): 1191.

—— "Ordering and Order in the City." *Stanford Law Review* 57, no. 1 (2004): 1–58.

Geretsegger, Heinz and Max Peintner, *Otto Wagner 1841–1918: The Expanding City, The Beginning of Modern Architecture*. New York: Praeger, 1970.

Gladwell, Malcolm. *Outliers: The Story of Success*. New York: Little Brown, 2008.

Glassie, Henry. "Eighteenth-Century Cultural Process in Delaware Valley Folk Building." In *Common Places: Readings in American Vernacular Architecture*, edited by Dell Upton and John Michael Vlach, 394–425. Athens and London: University of Georgia Press, 1986.

Goy, Richard. *Venetian Vernacular Architecture: Traditional Housing in the Venetian Lagoon*. Cambridge: Cambridge University Press, 1989.

Guillery, Peter. *The Small English House of the Eighteenth Century*. New Haven: Yale University Press, 2004.

Gutschow, Niels, Bernhard Kolver and Ishwaranand Shresthacarya. *Newar Towns and Buildings: An Illustrated Dictionary Newari–English*. Sankt Augustin: VGH Wissenschaftsverlag, 1987.

Habraken, N.J. *Variations: The Systematic Design of Supports*. Cambridge: Laboratory of Architecture and Planning at M.I.T., 1976.

Hakim, Besim. *Arabic–Islamic Cities: Building and Planning Principles*. New York: Kegan Paul International, 1986.

Hamlin, Talbot. *Forms and Functions of Twentieth-Century Architecture*. New York: Columbia University Press, 1952.

Hanchett, Thomas W. *Sorting Out the New South City: Race, Class and Urban Development in Charlotte, 1875–1975*. Chapel Hill and London: University of North Carolina Press, 1998.

Hareven, Tamara K. *The Silk Weavers of Kyoto: Family and Work in a Changing Traditional Industry*. Berkeley: University of California Press, 2002.

Harrington, Virginia. *The New York Merchant on the Eve of the Revolution*. New York: Columbia University Press, 1935.

Hayden, Dolores. *Building Suburbia: Green Fields and Urban Growth, 1820–2000*. New York: Vintage, 2004.

Hayward, Mary Ellen and Charles Belfoure. *The Baltimore Rowhouse*. New York: Princeton Architectural Press, 2001.

Hermansen, Gustav. *Ostia: Aspects of Roman City Life*. Edmonton: University of Alberta Press, 1981.

Hesselgren, G.C., Publishing Co. *Apartment Houses of the Metropolis*. New York: G.C. Hesselgren Publishing Co., 1908.

Heynen, Hilde. *Architecture and Modernity: A Critique*. Cambridge: M.I.T. Press, 1999.

Hillier, Bill and Julienne Hanson. *The Social Logic of Space*. Cambridge: Cambridge University Press, 1984.

Hirschhorn, Joel. *Sprawl Kills: How Blandburbs Steal your Time, Health and Money*. New York: Sterling and Ross, 2005.

Hofstra, Warren. *The Planting of New Virginia*. Baltimore and London: Johns Hopkins University Press, 2004.

Holliss, Frances. "The Workhome . . . a New Building Type?" Ph.D. dissertation, London Metropolitan University, 2007.

Horn, Pamela. *Behind the Counter: Shop Lives from Market Stall to Supermarket*. Stroud: Sutton Publishing, 2006.

Hower, Ralph M. *History of Macy's of New York, 1858–1919: Chapters in the Evolution of the Department Store*. Cambridge: Harvard University Press, 1943.

Hoyt, Homer. "One Hundred Years of Land Values in Chicago: The Relationship of the Growth of Chicago to the Rise of Its Land Values, 1830–1933." Ph.D. thesis, University of Chicago, 1933.

Hubka, Thomas. *Big House, Little House, Back House, Barn*. Hanover and London: University Press of New England, 1984.

Innes, Billy G. *The "Lower Sort:" Philadelphia's Laboring People, 1750–1800*. Ithaca: Cornell University Press, 1990.

International Council on Shopping Centers website. Accessed July 4, 2011, www.icsc.org/srch/faq_category.php?cat_type=research&cat_id=3.

Jackson, Kenneth T. *Crabgrass Frontier: The Suburbanization of the United States*. New York: Oxford University Press, 1987.

Jackson, Richard J. "The Impact of the Built Environment on Health." *American Journal of Public Health* 93, no. 9 (2003): 1382–1383.

Jacobs, Allan, Elizabeth MacDonald and Yodan Rofé. *The Boulevard Book: History, Evolution, Design of Multiway Boulevards*. Cambridge: M.I.T. Press, 2002.

Jacobs, Jane. *The Death and Life of Great American Cities.* New York: Vintage, 1961.

—— *The Economy of Cities*. New York: Vintage, 1969.

—— *The Nature of Economies*. New York: The Modern Library, 2000.

John R. Spann vs. City of Dallas et al., 111 Tex 350.

Johns, Michael. *Moment of Grace: The American City in the 1950s*. Berkeley: University of California Press, 2003.

Johnson, Matthew. *Housing Culture: Traditional Architecture in an English Landscape*. London: U.C.L. Press, 1993.

Johnson, Steven. *Emergence: The Connected Lives of Ants, Brains, Cities and Software*. New York: Scribner, 2002.

Joshi, Kiran. *Documenting Chandigarh: The Indian Architecture of Pierre Jeanneret, Edwin Maxwell Fry, Jane Beverly Drew*. Middleton, N.J.: Grantha Corporation, 1999.

Kaijima, Momoyo, Junzo Kuroda and Yoshiharu Tsuramoto. *Made in Tokyo*. Tokyo: Kajima, 2001.

Kalman, H. "The Architecture of Mercantilism: Commercial Buildings by George Dance the Younger." In *The Triumph of Culture: Eighteenth Century Perspectives*, edited by Paul Fritz and David Williams, 69–96. Toronto: University of Toronto Press, 1972.

Kane, Will. "Park Merced: Lofty Plan Would Revamp Neighborhood." *San Francisco Chronicle*, February 2, 2011.

Kawashima, Chuji. *Minka: Traditional Houses of Rural Japan*. Tokyo: Kodansha, 1986.

Kazin, Alfred. *A Walker in the City*. New York: Harcourt Brace and Company, 1951.

Kelbaugh, Douglas. "Preface." In *Everyday Urbanism: Margaret Crawford vs. Michael Speaks*, edited by R. Mehrotra, 8–10. Ann Arbor: University of Michigan Press, 2005.

Kellett, P. "Voices from the Barrio: Oral Testimony and Informal Housing Process." *Third World Planning Review* 22, no. 2 (2000): 189–205.

—— "Exploring Space: Researching the Use of Domestic Space for Income Generation in Developing Cities." E.N.H.R., I.A.P.S. and K.T.H. International Conference, *Methodologies in Housing Research*, September 2003.

Kellett, P. and W. Bishop. "Work and Home: Spatial Implications of Income Generation in the Domestic Setting." In *Places, People and Sustainability*, edited by G. Moser, E. Pol, Y. Bernard, M. Bonnes, J. Corraliza and V. Giuliani, 196–208. Gottingen: Hogrefe and Huber, 2000.

Kellett, P. and A.G. Tipple. "The Home as Workplace: A Study of Income-Generating Activities within the Domestic Setting." *Environment and Urbanization* 12, no. 1 (2000): 203–213.

Kelly's Directories, London, Kelly's *Post Office London Directory*, numerous editions.

Kershen, Anne J. *Strangers, Aliens and Asians: Huguenots, Jews and Bangladeshis in Spitalfields 1660–2000*. Farmington Hill, M.I.: Gale Group, 2005.

King, Anthony. *The Bungalow: The Production of a Global Culture*. London: Routledge and Kegan Paul, 1984.

Knapp, Ronald, ed. *Asia's Old Dwellings: Tradition, Resilience and Change*. Oxford: Oxford University Press, 2003.

—— *Chinese Houses of Southeast Asia: The Eclectic Architecture of Sojourners and Settlers*. North Clarendon: Tuttle Publishing, 2010.

Kniffen, Fred B. "Folk Housing: Key to Diffusion." *Annals of the Association of American Geographers* 55, no. 4 (1965): 549–77.

Kohl, D.G. *Chinese Architecture in the Straits Settlements and Western Malaya: Temples, Kongsis and Houses*. Kuala Lumpur: Heinemann Asia, 1984.

Komossa, Susanne, Han Meyer, Max Risselada, Sabien Thomaes, and Nynke Jutten, eds. *Atlas of the Dutch Urban Block*. Bussum: Thoth Uitgeverij, 2005.

Kunstler, James Howard. *Home from Nowhere: Remaking Our Everyday World for the 21st Century*. Beaverton, O.R.: Touchstone Press, 1998.

Lavin, Sylvia. *Quatremere de Quincy and the Invention of a Modern Language of Architecture*. Cambridge: M.I.T. Press, 1992.

Le Corbusier (Charles Edouard Jeanneret). *Oeuvre Complète*. Basel: Birkhauser, 1999.

Lee, Ho Yin. "The Singapore Shophouse: An Anglo-Chinese Urban Vernacular." In *Asia's Old Dwellings: Tradition, Resilience and Change*, edited by R. Knapp, 115–134. New York: Oxford University Press, 2003.

Lees, Martha A. "Preserving Property Values? Preserving Proper Homes? Preserving Privilege?: The Pre-Euclid Debate Over Zoning for Exclusively Private Residential Areas, 1916–1926." *University of Pittsburgh Law Review* 56 (1994–95): 367.

Lefebvre, Henri. *Everyday Life in the Modern World*. New York: Harper & Row, 1971.

—— *The Production of Space*. Translated by Donald Nicholson-Smith. Oxford: Blackwell, 1991.

—— *The Urban Revolution*. Minneapolis: University of Minnesota Press, 2003.

Leinberger, Christopher. "Developer's Viewpoint: Urban Markets Strengthen, But Standard Real Estate Products Are Not Suited for Mixed-Use Urban Development Communities." accessed October 23, 2007, www.philadelphiafed.org/cca/winter05.html.

—— *The Option of Urbanism: Investing in a New American Dream*. Washington D.C.: Island Press, 2008.

Leinberger, Christopher B. and Howard Kozloff. "Financing Mixed-Use." *Multifamily Trends* 6, no. 4 (2003).

Lepik, Andres. *Small Scale, Big Change: New Architectures of Social Engagement*. New York: The Museum of Modern Art, 2010.

Letarouilly, Paul. *Edifices de Rome Moderne, Reprint of original edition published by Bance, Paris, 1860.* New York: Princeton Architectural Press, 1982.

Lewis, Paul, Marc Tsurumaki and David J. Lewis. *Lewis. Tsurumaki. Lewis: Opportunistic Architecture.* New York: Princeton Architectural Press, 2008.

Liang, Samuel. "Where the Courtyard Meets the Street: Spatial Culture of the Li Neighborhoods, Shanghai, 1870–1900." *Journal of the Society of Architectural Historians* 67, no. 4 (2008): 482–503.

Ligtelijn, Vincent. *Aldo van Eyck, Werken*. Basel: Birkhäuser, 1999.

Lim, Jon S.H. "The Shophouse 'Rafflesia': An Outline of its Malaysian Pedigree and its Subsequent Diffusion in Asia." *Journal of the Royal Asiatic Society* LXXI, part 2 (1993): 122.

Lipton, M. "Family, Fungibility and Formality: Rural Advantages of Informal Non-Farm Enterprise Versus the Urban–Formal State." In *Human Resources, Employment and Development, Vol. 5, Developing Countries*, edited by S. Amin, 184–242. London: Macmillan, 1980.

Lockwood, Charles. *Bricks and Brownstone: The New York Row House 1783–1929*. New York: Abbeville Press, 1972.

Lofgren, Karin. *Machiya: Architecture and History of the Kyoto Town House*. Stockholm: K.T.H. Royal Institute of Technology, 2003.

Longstreth, Richard. "Wieboldt's, Goldblatt's and the Creation of Department Store Chains in Chicago." *Building & Landscapes: Journal of the Vernacular Architecture Forum* 14, (Fall 2007): 13–49.

Loyer, Francois. *Paris Nineteenth Century: Architecture and Urbanism*. New York: Abbeville Press, 1988.

Lukez, Paul. *Suburban Transformations*. New York: Princeton Architectural Press, 2007.

Mallgrave, Harry Francis. Introduction to *Modern Architecture: A Guidebook for His Students to This Field of Art*. Otto Wagner. Translation by Harry Francis Mallgrave. Santa Monica: Getty Center for the History of Art and the Humanities, 1988.

Mann, Thomas. *Buddenbrooks: The Decline of a Family*. New York: Vintage, 1994.

Marcuse, Peter and Ronald van Kempen, eds. *Of States and Cities: The Partitioning of Urban Space*. New York: Oxford University Press, 1994.

Markus, Thomas. *Buildings and Power: Freedom and Control in the Origin of Modern Building Types*. London and New York: Routledge, 1993.

Martin, Andrew. "Miles of Aisles for Milk? Not Here." *New York Times*, 2008. Accessed July 4, 2011, www.nytimes.com/2008/09/10/business/10grocery.html.

Martin, Ann Smart. "Commercial Space as Consumption Arena: Retail Stores in Early Virginia." In *People, Power, Places: Perspectives in Vernacular Architecture VIII*, edited by Sally McMurry and Annmarie Adams, 201–218. Knoxville: The University of Tennessee Press, 2000.

Mayo, James M. *The American Grocery Store: The Business Evolution of an Architectural Space*. Westport, C.T.: Greenwood Press, 1993.

McDonald, John F. and Daniel P. McMillen. "Land Values, Land Use, and The First Chicago Zoning Ordinance." *Journal of Real Estate Finance and Economics* 16, no. 2 (1998): 135–150.

McElyea, William D. "Playing the Numbers: Local Government Authority to Apply Use Quotas in Neighborhood Commercial Districts." *Ecology Law Quarterly* 14, (1987): 325.

McKibben, Bill. *Deep Economy: The Wealth of Communities and the Durable Future*. New York: Times Books/Henry Holt and Company, 2007.

Meiggs, Russell. *Roman Ostia*. Oxford: Oxford University Press, 1973.

Meischke, R., H.J. Zantkuijl, W. Raue and P.T.E.E. Rosenberg. *Huizen in Nederland: Amsterdam.* Zwolle: Wanders Uitgevers and Vereniging Hendrick de Keyser, 1995.

Mitchell, Stacy. *Big Box Swindle: The True of Cost of Mega-Retailers and the Fight for America's Independent Businesses*. Boston: Beacon Press, 2006.

Modan, Akbar Nazim, "Study of the Systems of Construction in the Traditional Ahmedabad Houses: Query in Earthquake Resistance." Undergraduate thesis, C.E.P.T. University, Ahmedabad, India, 2005.

Moore, Deborah Dash. *At Home in America: Second Generation New York Jews*. New York: Columbia University Press, 1981.

Morris, Douglas. *It's a Sprawl World After All: The Human Cost of Unplanned Growth – and Visions of a Better Future*. Gabriola, B.C.: New Society Publishers, 2005.

Morris, Marya. *Smart Codes: Model Land-Development Regulations*. Chicago: American Planning Assocation, 2009.

Mui, Hoh-Cheung and Lorna H. Mui. *Shops and Shopkeeping in Eighteenth-Century England*. Montreal: McGill-Queens University Press, 1989.

Muthesius, Stefan. *The English Terraced House*. New Haven and London: Yale University Press, 1982.

Nakagawa, Takeshi. *The Japanese House: In Space, Memory and Language*. Tokyo: I-House Press, 2005.

Nasaw, David. *Children of the City: At Work and at Play*. Garden City, N.Y.: Anchor Press/Doubleday, 1985.

Nasser, Haya El. "'New Urbanism' Embraces Latinos" *USA Today*, February 16, 2005. Accessed August 27, 2007, www.usatoday.com/news/nation/2005-02-15-latinos-usat_x.htm.

National Board of Fire Underwriters. *National Building Code Recommended by the National Board of Fire Underwriters.* New York: James Kempster Printing Company, 1909.

Nevola, Fabrizio. *Siena: Constructing the Renaissance City*. New Haven and London: Yale University Press, 2007.

—— "Palaces, Shops and Clientage Clustering in Early Modern Siena." *Città e Storia* II, (2007): 365–379.

New Jersey, Rehabilitation Subcode. Accessed July 4, 2011, www.nj.gov/dca/codes/rehab/rehabguide.shtml.

New York City Housing Authority. First Houses (pamphlet), 1986.

New York City Housing Authority website. Accessed July 4, 2011, www.nyc.gov/html/nycha/html/home/home.shtml.

New York City Zoning Resolution, 1916.

Oliver, Paul. *Dwellings: The House Across the World*. Austin: University of Texas Press, 1990.

Oliver, Paul, ed. *Encyclopedia of Vernacular Architecture of the World*. Cambridge: Cambridge University Press, 1998.

Oliver, Paul and Marcel Vellinga. *Illustrated Atlas of Vernacular Architecture*. London: Routledge, 2008.

Olsen, Donald. *Town Planning in London, Second Edition*. New Haven and London: Yale University Press, 1982.

Ongsavanchai, Nawit and Shuji Funo. "Spatial Organization and Transformation Process of Shophouse in Ratanakosin Area, Bangkok: A Comparative Study of Shophouses from Three Different Landowners." *Journal of Architecture and Planning (Transactions of the Architectural Institute of Japan)* 586 (2004): 1–8.

Ortiz, Francesca. "Biodiversity, The City, and Sprawl." *Boston University Law Review* 82 (2002): 145.

Orum-Nielsen, Jorn. *Dwelling: At Home, In Community, On Earth*. Copenhagen: Danish Architectural Press, 1996.

Owen, David. "Green Manhattan." *The New Yorker*, October 18, 2004: 111–123.

Packer, James E. *The Insulae of Imperial Ostia. Memoirs of the American Academy in Rome, XXXI.* Rome: American Academy in Rome, 1971.

Pader, Ellen-J. "Sociospatial Relations of Change." In *Women and the Environment*, edited by Irwin Altman and Arza Churchman, 73–103. New York: Plenum Press, 1994.

Page, Max. *The Creative Destruction of Manhattan 1900–1940*. Chicago and London: University of Chicago Press, 1999.

Panin, Ornsiri. "Thai-Mon Vernacular Houses." *Silpakorn University International Journal* 2, no. 1 (2002): 27–46.

Parolek, Daniel G. *Form-Based Codes: A Guide for Planners, Urban Designers, Municipalities, and Developers*. Hoboken: J. Wiley & Sons, 2008.

Paul, Samuel. *Apartments: Their Design and Development*. New York: Reinhold, 1967.

Peintner, Heinz and Max Geretsegger. *Otto Wagner 1841 –1918: The Expanding City, The Beginning of Modern Architecture*. New York: Praeger, 1970.

Pendery, Steven R. "Merchants and Artisans in Colonial Charlestown, Massachusetts." *Archaeology* 39, no. 3 (1986): 64–77.

Pergament, Danielle. "Their House is Your Trattoria." *New York Times*, sec. 5, July 15, 2007, p. 1.

Pevsner, Nikolaus. *A History of Building Types, Bollingen Series XXXV*. Princeton: Princeton University Press, 1976.

Platt, Colin. *The English Medieval Town*. London: Granada, 1979.

Plunz, Richard. *A History of Housing in New York City*. New York: Columbia University Press, 1990.

Polano, Sergio. *Henrik Petrus Berlage: Complete Works*. New York: Rizzoli, 1988.

Portland, Oregon. *Portland Building Code, 1918, 1919, 1924, 1927, 1956*.

Portman, D. *Exeter Houses, 1400–1700*. Exeter: Exeter University, 1966.

Pounds, N.J.G. *Hearth and Home: A History of Material Culture*. Bloomington and Indianapolis: Indiana University Press, 1993.

—— *The Culture of the English People*. Cambridge: University of Cambridge Press, 1994.

Power, Garrett. "The Unwisdom of Allowing City Growth to Work Out Its Own Destiny." *Maryland Law Review* 47, (1988): 626.

Prakash, Aditya. *Reflections on Chandigarh*. New Delhi: B.N. Prakash, 1983.

Pramar, V.S. *Haveli: Wooden Houses and Mansions of Gujarat*. Middletown: Grantha, 1989.

Pratt, Joanne H. *Homebased Business: The Hidden Economy*. U.S. Small Business Administration, Office of Advocacy, 2000.

Press, Eyal. "The New Suburban Poverty. *The Nation*, April 23, 2007. www.thenation/com/article/new-suburban-poverty.

Pritchard, R.M. *Housing and the Spatial Structure of the City: Residential Mobility and the Housing Market in an English City Since the Industrial Revolution*. Cambridge: Cambridge University Press, 1976.

Pyatok, Michael. "The New Urbanism: To Whom Should We Listen: The Social Policies of Urban Renewal" New Village Journal 2, (2000). Accessed July 7, 2011, www.newvillage.net/Journal/Issue2/2newurbanism.html.

—— "Tale of Two Cities: Dot Comers and the Rest of Us." *Design/Builder Magazine* (2000). Accessed July 7, 2011, www.pyatok.com/writingsarticle3.html.

—— "Design of Affordable Housing: The Return of the Homestead." *Multifamily Trends* (December 2000). Accessed July 7, 2011, www.pyatok.com/writingsArticle4.html.

Rae, Douglas W. *City: Urbanism and its End*. New Haven and London: Yale University Press, 2003.

Rasmussen, Steen Eiler. *London: The Unique City*. New York: Macmillan, 1937.

Rice, Charles. *The Emergence of the Interior: Architecture, Modernity, Domesticity*. London and New York: Routledge, 2007.

Ritzdorf, Marsha. "Zoning Barriers to Housing Innovation." *Journal of Planning Education and Research* 4, no. 3 (1985): 177–184.

—— "Gender and Residential Zoning in the United States." In *Women and the Environment*, edited by I. Altman, Arzah Ts'erts'man, Arza Churchman, 255–280. New York: Plenum Press, 1994.

Roberts, Marion, Tony Lloyd-Jones, Bill Erickson and Stephen Nice. "Place and Space in the Networked City: Conceptualizing the Integrated Metropolis." *Journal of Urban Design* 4, no. 1 (1999): 51–66.

Robertson, D.S. *Greek and Roman Architecture*. London: Cambridge, 1969.

Rock, Howard B. *Artisans of the New Republic: The Tradesmen of New York City in the Age of Jefferson*. New York and London: New York University Press, 1984.

Rosenthal, Elizabeth. "Cement Industry is at Center of Climate Change Debate." *New York Times*, 2007. Accessed July 4, 2011, www.nytimes.com/2007/10/26/business/worldbusiness/26cement.html?scp=1&sq=cement%20industry%20is%20at%20center&st=cse.

Rothschild, Nan A. *New York City Neighborhoods: The Eighteenth Century*. San Diego: Academic Press, 1990.

Royal Commission on the Historical Monuments of England. *Houses of the North York Moors*. London: Her Majesty's Stationery Office, 1987.

Ruskin, John. *The Stones of Venice, 1 and 2*. New York: John Wiley & Sons, 1885.

Saga, Junichi. *Memories of Silk and Straw: A Self-Portrait of Small-Town Japan*. Tokyo: Kodansha, 1987.

Salzman, L.F. *Building in England Down to 1540*. Oxford: Oxford University Press, 1967.

Sarti, Raffaella. *Europe at Home: Family and Material Culture 1500–1800*. New Haven: Yale University Press, 2002.

Sassen, Saskia. "The Informal Economy: Between New Developments and Old Regulations." *Yale Law Journal* 103, no. 2 (1994): 289–304.

Saunders, Doug. *Arrival City: The Final Migration and Our Next World*. Toronto: Alfred A. Knopf Canada, 2010.

Sawtelle, Gayle Elizabeth. "The Commercial Landscape of Boston in 1800: Documentary and Archaeological Perspectives on the Geography of Retail Shopkeeping," Ph.D. dissertation, Boston University, 1999.

Scheftel, Michael. *Gange, Buden und Wohnkeller in Lübeck*. Neumünster: Karl Wachholtz Verlage, 1988.

Schneider, Tatjana and Jeremy Till. *Flexible Housing*. Oxford: Architectural Press, 2007.

Schnore, Leo. *The New Urban History: Quantitative Explorations by American Historians*. Princeton: Princeton University Press, 1975.

Schwanke, Dean. *Mixed-Use Development Handbook*. Washington D.C.: Urban Land Institute, 2003.

Schwarz, L.D. "Social Class and Social Geography: The Middle Classes in London at the End of the Eighteenth Century." In *The Eighteenth Century Town: A Reader in English Urban History 1688–1820*, edited by P. Borsay, 315–337. London and New York: Longman, 1990.

Scott, James C. *Seeing Like a State: How Certain Schemes to Improve the Human Condition Have Failed*. New Haven and London: Yale University Press, 1998.

Seattle Mayor's Economic Opportunity Task Force. "Lowering the Cost of Building Housing in Seattle." *Open for Business* (July 2002): 23–24.

Sennett, Richard. "The Open City." In *The Endless City*, edited by Ricky Burdett and Deyan Sudjic, 290–297. London: Phaidon, 2007.

Shammas, Carole. "The Domestic Environment in Early Modern England and America." *Journal of Social History* 14, (1980): 1–24.

Sharma, Kalpana. *Rediscovering Dharavi: Stories from Asia's Largest Slum*. New Delhi: Penguin Books, 2000.

Shaw, Diane. *City Building on the Eastern Frontier: Sorting the Nineteenth-Century City*. Baltimore and London: Johns Hopkins University Press, 2004.

Shuman, Michael. *The Small-Mart Revolution: How Local Businesses are Beating the Global Competition.* San Francisco: Berrett-Koehler, 2006.

Singer, Audrey. "The Rise of New Immigrant Gateways." Washington, D.C.: The Brookings Institution, Center on Urban and Metropolitan Policy, February 2004.

Slusser, Mary. *Nepal Mandala: A Cultural Case Study of the Kathmandu Valley*. Princeton: Princeton University Press, 1982.

Smith, William. *A Dictionary of Greek and Roman Antiquities*. London: John Murray, 1878.

Solnit, Rebecca. "Nonconforming Uses: Teddy Cruz On Both Sides of the Border." In *Storming the Gates of Paradise: Landscapes for Politics*, by Rebecca Solnit, 97–111. Berkeley: University of California Press, 2007.

Song, Miri. "Between 'The Front' and 'The Back': Chinese Women's Work in Family Businesses." *Women's Studies International Forum* 18, no. 3 (1995): 285.

—— "Chinese Children's Work Roles in Immigrant Adaptation." In *Hidden Hands: International Perspectives on Children's Work and Labour*, edited by Phillip Mizen, Christopher Pole, and Angela Bolton, 55–69. London: Routledge, 2001.

Stansell, Christine. *City of Women: Sex and Class in New York, 1789–1860*. Urbana and Chicago: University of Illinois Press, 1987.

Stanton, Gary. "'Alarmed by the Cry of Fire.' How Fire Changed Fredericksburg, Virginia." In *Perspectives in Vernacular Architecture VI* edited by Carter L. Hudgins and Elizabeth Collins Cromley, 122–134. Knoxville: University of Tennessee Press, 1997.

State vs. City of New Orleans, 97 So. 444, quoted in Euclid v. Ambler, 272 U.S.365 (1926).

Stilgoe, John R. *Borderland: Origins of the American Suburb, 1820–1939*. New Haven: Yale University Press, 1990.

Stobart, J. "Accommodating the Shop: The Commercial use of Domestic Space in English Provincial Towns, c. 1660–1740." *Citta e Storia* II, no. 2 (July–December 2007): 351–364.

Stolberg, Sheryl Gay. "From the Top, White House Loosens its Buttoned-Up Style." *New York Times*, January 28, 2009, www.nytimes.com/2009/01/29/world/americas/29iht29whitehouse.19767783.html.

Strobel, Richard. *Das Bürgerhaus in Regensburg*. Tubingen: Ernst Wasmuth, 1976.

Summerson, John. *Georgian London*. New York: C. Scribner's Sons, 1946.

Sutherland, Daniel E. *The Expansion of Everyday Life 1860–1876*. New York: Harper & Row, 1989.

Talen, Emily "New Urbanism and the Culture of Criticism." *Urban Geography* 21, no. 4 (2000): 318–341.

—— *New Urbanism and American Planning: The Conflict of Cultures*. New York and London: Routledge, 2005.

—— *Design for Diversity: Exploring Socially Mixed Neighborhoods*. Oxford: Architectural Press/Elsevier, 2008.

Thomas Dolan Architects, 2009. Accessed July 4, 2011, www.live-work.com.

Tindall, Gillian. *City of Gold: The Biography of Bombay*. New Delhi: Penguin Books, 1982.

—— *The Fields Beneath*. London: Weidenfeld and Nicolson, 2002.

—— *Footprints in Paris: A Few Streets, a Few Lives*. London: Pimlico, 2010.

Tipple, Graham. "Shelter as Workplace: A Review of Home-Based Enterprises in Developing Countries." *International Labour Review* 132, no. 4 (1993): 521–539.

—— *Extending Themselves: User-Initiated Transformations of Government-Built Housing in Developing Countries*. Liverpool: Liverpool University Press, 2000.

Tjoa-Bonatz, Mai-Lin. "Ordering of Housing and the Urbanization Process: Shophouses in Colonial Penang." *Journal of the Royal Asiatic Society* LXXI, part 2 (1998): 122.

Trincanato, Egle R. *Venezia Minore*. Milano: Edizione del Milione, 1948.

United States Bureau of Labor Statistics, Department of Labor. "Work at Home in 2004." Report U.S.D.L. 05–1768, September 22, 2005.

United States. Department of Commerce. Building Code Committee. "Recommended Minimum Requirements for Fire Resistance in Buildings." *Bureau of Standards. Building and Housing*, no. 14 (1931).

Upton, Dell. *Another City: Urban Life and Urban Spaces in the New American Republic*. New Haven and London: Yale University Press, 2008.

Upton, Dell and Vlach, John Michael. *Common Places: Readings in American Vernacular Architecture*. Athens and London: University of Georgia Press, 1986.

Vance, James E., Jr. "Housing the Worker: Determinative and Contingent Ties in Nineteenth Century Birmingham." *Economic Geography* 43, no. 2 (1967): 95–127.

Venturi, Robert. *Complexity and Contradiction in Architecture*. New York: Museum of Modern Art, 1966.

Village of Euclid vs. Ambler Realty Co., 272 U.S. 365 (1926).

Villari, Sergio. *J.N.L. Durand (1760–1834): Art and Science of Architecture*. Translated by Eli Gottlieb. New York: Rizzoli, 1990.

Waddy, Patricia. *Seventeenth-Century Roman Palaces: Use and the Art of the Plan*. Cambridge: M.I.T. Press, 1990.

Wagner, Otto. *Modern Architecture: A Guidebook for His Students to This Field of Art*. Introduction and translation by Harry Francis Mallgrave. Santa Monica: Getty Center for the History of Art and the Humanities, 1988.

Wallace-Hadrill, Andrew. *Houses and Society in Pompeii and Herculaneum*. Princeton: Princeton University Press, 1994.

Wallenstein, Hermann. *Stadt, Wald, Hochgebirge, Bauernhof*. Giessen: Emil Roth, 1902.

Ward, Jonathan, and Sadie Brown. *The Village Shop*. Moffat, U.K.: Cameron and Hollis Books, 1990.

Warner, Sam Bass. *Streetcar Suburbs*. Cambridge: Harvard University Press, 1978.

Warnes, A.M. "Early Separation of Homes from Workplaces and the Urban Structure of Chorley, 1780 to 1850." *Transactions of the Historic Society of Lancaster and Cheshire* 122, (1970): 105–135.

Weisman, Leslie Kanes. *Discrimination by Design: A Feminist Critique of the Man-Made Environment*. Urbana and Chicago: University of Illinois Press, 1994.

Welch, Evelyn. *Shopping in the Renaissance: Consumer Cultures in Italy 1400–1600*. New Haven and London: Yale University Press, 2005.

Welty, Eudora. "The Little Store." In *Eudora Welty, Stories, Essays & Memoir*, by Eudora Welty, 819–826. New York: Library of America, 1998. Story originally published in *Esquire*, December 1975.

Wermiel, Sara. *The Fireproof Building*. Baltimore: Johns Hopkins University Press, 2000.

—— "No Exit: The Rise and Demise of the Outside Fire Escape." *Technology and Culture* 44, (2003): 258–284.

White, Jerry. *Rothschild Buildings: Life in an East End Tenement Block 1887–1920*. London: Routledge and Kegan Paul, 1980.

White, Kate. "Housing Above Retail: Creating Incentives for the Replacement of Single-Story Retail Sites With Mixed-Use Projects: A S.P.U.R. Report." *S.P.U.R. Newsletter Calendar Report* 427, (May 2004): 1, 3–5.

Whitehand, J.W.R. "The Study of Variations in the Building Fabric of Town Centres: Procedural Problems and Preliminary Findings in Southern Scotland." *Transactions of the Institute of British Geographers* 4, no. 4 (1979): 559–575.

Wood. *The New England Village*. Baltimore: Johns Hopkins University Press, 1997.

Xu, Yinong. *The Chinese City in Space and Time: The Development of Urban Form in Suzhou.* Hawaii: University of Hawaii Press, 2000.

Zukin, Sharon. *Naked City*. New York: Oxford University Press, 2009.

INDEX